Madison's Music

ALSO BY BURT NEUBORNE

Building a Better Democracy: Reflections on Money, Politics and Free Speech: A Collection of Writings by Burt Neuborne

El papel de los juristas y del imperio de la ley en sociedad Americana (The Role of Judges and the Rule of Law in American Society)

Free Speech, Free Markets, Free Choice: An Essay on Commercial Speech

Emerson, Haber, and Dorsen's Political and Civil Rights in the United States, volume 1 (with Paul Bender and Norman Dorsen) and volume 2 (with Paul Bender, Norman Dorsen, and Sylvia Law)

The Rights of Candidates and Voters (with Arthur Eisenberg)

Unquestioning Obedience to the President: The Constitutional Case Against the Vietnam War (with Leon Friedman)

Madison's Music

On Reading the First Amendment

Burt Neuborne

NEW YORK
LONDON

Published in the United States by The New Press, New York, 2015
Distributed by Perseus Distribution

LIBRARY OF CONGRESS CATALOGING-IN-PUBLICATION DATA

Neuborne, Burt, 1941– author.
Madison's music : on reading the First Amendment / Burt Neuborne.
pages cm
Includes bibliographical references and index.
ISBN 978-1-62097-041-6 (hardback)—ISBN 978-1-62097-053-9 (e-book)
1. United States. Constitution. 1st Amendment. 2. Civil rights—United States—History. 3. Constitutional history—United States. I. Title.
KF45581st .N48 2015
342.7308'5—dc23 2014026735

The New Press publishes books that promote and enrich public discussion and understanding of the issues vital to our democracy and to a more equitable world. These books are made possible by the enthusiasm of our readers; the support of a committed group of donors, large and small; the collaboration of our many partners in the independent media and the not-for-profit sector; booksellers, who often hand-sell New Press books; librarians; and above all by our authors.

www.thenewpress.com

Composition by dix!
This book was set in Electra

Printed in the United States of America

2 4 6 8 10 9 7 5 3 1

Odysseus the Tailor

Odysseus the Tailor's real name was Sam. A gentle, unassuming man who stood all of five five, my father was one of a dozen U.S. Navy frogmen dropped into the English Channel several hours before the Normandy invasion in 1944, with instructions to attach explosives to a wall of underwater steel spikes designed to tear the bottoms out of Allied landing craft. Once the explosives were in place, Pop and his buddies swam to the beach and crouched in the surf until the invasion boats neared the French coast. Then they blew a hole in the steel wall, opening a bloody path to the liberation of Europe. After D-Day, Pop was assigned to "Patton's Navy," a small combat unit supporting amphibious crossings of French rivers during the Third Army's push toward Paris. From our kitchen in the Greenpoint section of Brooklyn, my mother and I anxiously plotted Odysseus's progress across Europe. My job was to keep Pop up-to-date on his beloved New York Giants. Each letter from me contained baseball box scores laboriously clipped from the *Brooklyn Eagle*. Pop's heavily censored replies promised a glorious future when we would see a baseball game together at the Polo Grounds.

When Odysseus the Tailor finally came home in the summer of 1946, I oiled my baseball glove and waited for the great day. July passed into August—but no baseball. Pop reopened his tailor shop, and we sat comfortably in the warm sunlight while silver needles danced in his thimbled fingers—but no baseball. School began after Labor Day—but no baseball. Finally, in mid-September, I broke down at dinner. "What have I done," I wailed, "that we can't go to a Giants game." My father, who had forgotten his wartime promise, was stricken. He hugged me. "I love you, Butchie," he whispered. "But we can't go to a Giants game yet. . . . They still don't let black people play, and we just don't support things like that."

Instead, we took the ferry across the Hudson River to see the world champion Newark Eagles play a Negro League game at Ruppert Stadium. I don't remember much about the game, other than the beautifully dressed, multiracial crowd, the noise, the sunlight, and the joy of being my father's son.

Farewell, Odysseus of the silver needles. This book is for you.

CONTENTS

Madison's Music

1

Reading the First Amendment as a Poem

This is not a work of history. I claim no special expertise about James Madison's interior life. Nor do I claim to be describing his subjective purpose. I don't even claim that Madison himself was wholly responsible for his music. As we'll see, Madison's arranger, Roger Sherman, deserves some credit. Rather, it is an effort to read the First Amendment's forty-five words—all of them—as a coherent whole in order to recapture what I call Madison's music.

I rest this book on the phrasing, rhythm, order, and placement of the forty-five words themselves. When we read a great poem, we do not ask whether the poet intended to achieve a particular emotional, aesthetic, or intellectual response. It is enough that the choreography of words triggers a responsive chord in a careful reader. The thesis of this book, dear reader, is that a careful study of the order, placement, meaning, and structure of the forty-five words in Madison's First Amendment will trigger a responsive poetic chord in you that will enable us to recapture the music of democracy in our most important political text.

Today we hear only broken fragments of Madison's music. Instead of seeking harmony and coherence in the First Amendment, we read the First Amendment (indeed, the entire Bill of Rights) as a set of isolated, self-contained commands, as if the Founders had thrown a pot of ink at the wall and allowed the order, placement, and structure of each provision in the Bill of Rights to be randomly determined by the splatter. The result is an arbitrary constitutional jurisprudence that has left us with a dysfunctional, judge-built "democracy" that is owned lock, stock, and barrel by five thousand wealthy oligarchs, a pseudodemocracy in which district lines have been carefully gerrymandered to rig the outcomes of most legislative elections, only half the population bothers to vote, and cynics erect barriers designed to disenfranchise the weak and the poor.

It doesn't have to be that way. A poetic vision of the interplay between democracy and individual freedom is hiding in plain sight in the brilliantly ordered text and structure of the Bill of Rights, but we have forgotten how to look for it. Recovering our ability to hear Madison's music would pave the way to a democracy-friendly First Amendment aimed at reinforcing Lincoln's hope that "government of the people, by the people, and for the people shall not perish from the earth."

We honor James Madison as the driving force behind the Bill of Rights. We recognize him as Thomas Jefferson's indispensable political lieutenant. We applaud him as the nation's fourth president. But we'll never do Madison full justice until we revere him as a great poet—not a literary poet like Wallace Stevens, but a political poet like Abraham Lincoln or Ronald Reagan. Madison's poetic genius was structural—a mastery of the contrapuntal interplay between the collective practice of democracy and individual liberty. His poetic voice speaks to us in the harmony of the 462 words, thirty-one ideas, and ten amendments—each in its perfectly chosen place and all interacting to form a coherent whole—that constitute the magnificent poem to democracy and individual freedom called the Bill of Rights.

When we read a great literary poem like "The House Was Quiet and the World Was Calm," Wallace Stevens's celebration of the miracle of reading, we concentrate deeply on each word and pay particular attention to the rhythmic cadence of the language and stanzas, and to the imagery they spin.

The house was quiet and the world was calm.
The reader became the book; and summer night

Was like the conscious being of the book.
The house was quiet and the world was calm.

The words were spoken as if there was no book,
Except that the reader leaned above the page,

Wanted to lean, wanted much most to be
The scholar to whom his book is true, to whom

The summer night is like a perfection of thought.
The house was quiet because it had to be.

The quiet was part of the meaning, part of the mind:
The access of perfection to the page.

And the world was calm. The truth in a calm world,
In which there is no other meaning, itself

Is calm, itself is summer and night, itself
Is the reader leaning late and reading there.

The magical quality of "The House Was Quiet" is not merely in its 141 words and its elegant phrases. Wallace Stevens achieves great poetry in the interplay between and among his words, and in the capacity of their order, rhythm, cadence, and imagery to generate meaning and mood that enriches and ennobles the plain text, imbuing it with a kind of music. Every great poem has an internal music that hides in plain sight with not a word out of place or an image wasted. What if we were to read Madison's Bill of Rights—especially his First Amendment—with the same respect and intensity that we lavish on a Wallace Stevens poem, paying close attention, not only to the individual words and phrases of the first ten amendments, but also to their interplay, order, cadence, and imagery? Would we find the music of poetry in Madison's handiwork? I have no doubt that the answer is yes.

In Wallace Stevens's words, I invite you to rediscover Madison's music, to be the scholar to whom Madison's Bill of Rights is most true, to be "the reader leaning late and reading there."

2

Why Reading the First Amendment Isn't Easy

Reading the First Amendment isn't easy. Consider the text:

> Congress shall make no law respecting an establishment of religion, or prohibiting the free exercise thereof; or abridging the freedom of speech, or of the press; or the right of the people peaceably to assemble, and to petition the Government for a redress of grievances.

NEITHER THE WORDS NOR THE HISTORY HELPS MUCH

The words themselves aren't much help. Reading the first word, "Congress," literally would leave the president, the military, fifty governors, and your local cops free to ignore our most important set of constitutional protections. Reading the fourth and fifth words, "no law," literally would wind up protecting horrible verbal assaults like threats, fraud, extortion, and blackmail. The three most important words in the First Amendment—"the freedom of"—the words that introduce, modify, and describe the crucial protections of speech, press, and assembly, simply cannot be read literally. The phrase "the freedom of" is a legal concept that has no intrinsic meaning. Someone must decide what should or should not be placed within the protective legal cocoon. Finally, the majestic abstractions in the First Amendment, like "establishment of religion," "free exercise thereof," "peaceful assembly," and "petition for a redress of grievances" do not carry a single literal meaning. In the end, each of the abstractions protects only the behavior we think it should protect.

So much for the literal text.

History (or what's sometimes called originalism these days) is even worse as a firm guide to reading the First Amendment. The truth is that the First Amendment as we know it today didn't exist before Justice William Brennan Jr. and the rest of the Warren Court invented it in the 1960s. In fact, history turns out to be the worst place to look for a robust First Amendment. Thomas Jefferson thought free speech was a pretty good idea, but the ink wasn't dry on the First Amendment before President Adams locked up seventeen of the twenty newspaper editors who opposed his reelection in 1800. One of the jailed editors was Benjamin Franklin's nephew Benjamin Franklin Bache. He died in jail. Despite the newly enacted First Amendment, not only did the federal courts remain silent in the face of Adams's massive exercise in government censorship; they often initiated the prosecutions. Matthew Lyon, Vermont's only Jeffersonian member of Congress, was jailed for four months and fined $1,000 for criticizing the president in his newspaper. Lyon had the last word, though. He was released just in time to cast Vermont's swing vote for Thomas Jefferson when the presidential election of 1800 was thrown into the House, helping to seal Adams's defeat.[1]

The nineteenth and early twentieth centuries were free-speech disasters. Before the Civil War, antislavery newspapers were torched throughout the North. All criticism of slavery was banned in the South. Slaves were even forbidden to learn to read.[2] During the Civil War, President Lincoln held opponents of the war in military custody for speaking out against it. After the Civil War, labor leaders went to jail in droves for picketing and striking for higher wages. Labor unions were treated as unlawful conspiracies.[3] Radical opponents of World War I were sentenced to ten-year prison terms and eventually deported to the Soviet Union—for leafleting.[4] In 1920, Eugene Debs polled more than one million votes for president from his prison cell in the Atlanta federal penitentiary, where he was serving a ten-year jail term for giving a speech in 1917 praising draft resisters. Released in 1921, Debs, his health broken, was banned from voting or running for office; he died in 1926.[5] After World War II, fear of communism translated into jail or deportation for thousands of political radicals guilty of saying the wrong thing or joining the wrong group, culminating in 1951 with the Supreme Court's affirmance of multiyear jail terms for the leadership of the American Communist Party, despite its status as a lawful political party.[6]

So much for history, unless you want to *erase* the First Amendment.

SEARCHING FOR THE FIRST AMENDMENT'S "PURPOSE" HELPS ONLY A LITTLE

If we can't read the First Amendment literally or rely on its checkered history for firm guidance about how to read it today, perhaps we can read each of the forty-five words in light of its underlying purpose. The problem, of course, is agreeing on whose purpose counts, figuring out what that purpose is, and deciding how best to advance it. When he finally awakened to the need for a robust First Amendment, the great justice Oliver Wendell Holmes Jr. told us that its real purpose is to ensure a "free market in ideas," so that the best ideas will triumph in the long run through free competition.[7] That, of course, is the mantra of free-market capitalism—to say nothing of Darwinism—trusting that free competition will lead us to the best of all possible worlds: political, economic, social, and biological. We know from bitter experience that the extreme version of the free-market mantra can be wrong in the economic sphere. History teaches that completely unregulated economic markets can lead to disaster. Witness the stock market collapse of 1929 and the economic collapse of 2008. The key is knowing when and how to regulate the economic market and when to let it alone. The same goes for the idea market. The vast bulk of the time, a free market in political ideas works fine, but history teaches that occasionally false (or at least horrendous) ideas triumph with disastrous social consequences—witness the broad popular acceptance of Nazism in pre–World War II Germany, the stubborn persistence of racial prejudice everywhere, the perennial lure of anti-Semitism, the unending worldwide oppression of women, widespread support for slavery in the old South and in much of the world today, and the modern embrace of jihadist terror.

Moreover, neither the economic market nor the idea market is ever really free. We know that powerful economic entities can stifle competition and foist inferior products on consumers at excessive cost. That's why we have antitrust laws and bans on false advertising. But the idea market is also far from free. Given the high cost of mass speech, only the rich and powerful can afford to engage in effective mass political communication. The poor suffer the speech they must.

Thus, while Holmes's notion of a free market in ideas is both a useful metaphor and a helpful guide, it is not a fail-safe key to reading the First Amendment, especially in settings such as campaign finance reform or access to the mass media, where vast private concentrations of power and huge resource imbalances systematically distort the market.

Justice Louis Brandeis, who joined with Holmes in pioneering the modern First Amendment, tells us that the real purpose of the First Amendment is to enhance human dignity by protecting individual self-expression and autonomous choice. According to Brandeis, respect for the inherent dignity of the speaker as a human being requires us to tolerate efforts at self-expression, even when they do not help our choice-dependent institutions to work better.[8] Brandeis's recognition of the close link between speech and human dignity infuses the First Amendment with a deep moral purpose worth fighting for. But is it an automatic trump that invalidates all speech regulation? What about speech that mocks human dignity? It's hard to find much human dignity in virulent hate speech, pornography about brutalizing women, cigarette ads linking sex and smoking, violent video games aimed at children, libel, or unlimited corporate electioneering. And what happens when the speaker's dignitary interest in self-expression runs headlong into the hearer's dignitary interest in self-worth, or a speech target's dignitary interest in privacy or accuracy? Should the speaker's dignity always outweigh everyone else's?

Finally, many modern free-speech theorists argue that the real purpose of the First Amendment is prophylactic, designed to keep government out of the business of regulating communication because governments inevitably seek to manipulate the minds of ordinary citizens in order to stay in power.[9] There is good reason to distrust government as a censor. Has there ever been a dictatorship that did not use censorship to keep itself in power? But two factors complicate the effort to explain and apply the First Amendment as an unyielding prophylactic ban on government efforts to regulate speech.

First, the most egregious historical examples of abusive government censorship have taken place in totalitarian or authoritarian regimes. While democracies engage in their fair share of abusive censorship, it's much harder to censor in a democracy when everyone is watching. After all, democracies have successfully operated vast public education programs for more than a century, with all the capacity for ideological brainwashing that such an enterprise entails, without slipping into First Amendment hell. In fact, the public schools' record on toleration and openness, while far from perfect, is a good deal better than that of private schools, most of which function as ideological Xerox machines.

Second, removing government from the equation doesn't mean that speech becomes free. When an unyieldingly prophylactic First Amendment takes government out of the speech regulation game entirely, it creates a regulatory vacuum that will quickly be filled by powerful private entities such as Amazon with the capacity to influence what gets seen and heard by the population. What should frighten us more? A democratically elected government tweaking the speech market to protect the weak or a wholly unregulated speech market dominated by a few massive corporations?

A TALE OF TWO READINGS

Disagreement over the relative importance and persuasiveness of the three usual candidates for the First Amendment's underlying purpose—preserving free markets in ideas, respecting human dignity, and avoiding government censorship—has split the current Supreme Court into two First Amendment wings: "deregulatory" and "aspirational." The five current Republican justices, intuitively drawn to unregulated markets, supportive of the rhetoric (if not always the reality) of personal autonomy, and intensely suspicious of government regulation in any setting, tend to read the First Amendment as an iron deregulatory command. Once the five Republican justices have taken the government out of the speech-regulation game, they don't worry much about what goes on in the vacated space, as long as it doesn't interfere with their parallel commitment to stable hierarchies. Speakers at the bottom of hierarchies, such as public employees, prisoners, soldiers, and high school students, don't get much free-speech protection from the five Republican justices, but corporations, wealthy ideologues, and big media receive intense deregulatory protection.

The four Democratic justices, suspicious of wholly unregulated markets and intuitively drawn to a more egalitarian vision of human dignity, are more tolerant of government efforts to level the speech playing field. They read the First Amendment as an aspirational vision of a tolerant self-governing community. Unlike their deregulatory colleagues, the four aspirational justices are willing to uphold government regulation of the electoral speech of corporations and wealthy individuals aimed at protecting political equality and are more sympathetic to speakers at the bottom of a hierarchy.

Much of the time, the Court's deregulatory and aspirational

wings beat in harmony. Because deregulation of the speech process usually coincides with aspirational concerns about respect for human dignity, the two wings have combined in recent years to forge the strongest First Amendment Supreme Court in our history. It's no coincidence that the iconic Supreme Court decisions in 1989 and 1990 holding flag burning to be protected by the First Amendment turned on the votes of three aspirational and two deregulatory justices.[10] But the wings do not always agree. In settings where the deregulatory First Amendment allows the speech process to be dominated by the strong to the detriment of the weak, the Court often splits 5–4 over the constitutionality of efforts to restrain overly powerful speakers, enhance weak ones, and protect vulnerable hearers.[11]

Until now, believers in an aspirational First Amendment have been hampered by the diffuse nature of their goals. Apart from an ill-defined romantic link to Justice Brandeis's idea of human dignity and a formulaic invocation of Justice Holmes's free-market metaphor, there hasn't been much discussion of exactly what the aspirational First Amendment aspires to. Justice Breyer has begun to root his aspirational reading of the Constitution in respect for democratic governance.[12] I hope to build on his intuition by providing an aspirational footing based on the forty-five words that make up the First Amendment, especially their remarkably disciplined order and structure.

Don't get me wrong. I'm not an expert on Madison's psyche. I don't insist that he or his colleagues sat down and composed the First Amendment with democracy in mind—although I strongly suspect that they did just that. It is enough that what finally came out of Madison's quill pen in the summer of 1789 was a precisely organized textual blueprint for a robust democracy. Madison's First Amendment text brings together six ideas—no establishment of religion, free exercise of religion, free speech, free press, free assembly, and the right to petition for redress of grievances—in a rights-bearing document for the first time in human history and deploys the six ideas in a rigorous chronological narrative of free citizens governing themselves in an ideal democracy. What matters today is not holding midnight séances with long-dead rich white men in a search for some fictive authorial purpose, but the enduring reality of the text—the order, placement, and meaning of the forty-five words themselves.

3

Madison's Music: Lost and Found

Again please consider Madison's remarkable First Amendment as a whole:

> Congress shall make no law respecting an establishment of religion, or prohibiting the free exercise thereof; or abridging the freedom of speech, or of the press; or the right of the people peaceably to assemble, and to petition the Government for a redress of grievances.

Now consider its fate.

MADISON'S MUSIC LOST

The current Supreme Court takes the ten words of the Free Speech Clause—"Congress shall make no law . . . abridging the freedom of speech"—tears them from the First Amendment's full text, and treats the artificially isolated phrase as the source and full definition of our most important set of constitutional protections. Worse, in practice, the Court uses only seven of the ten words, omitting "the freedom of" and reading the clause as if Madison had written "Congress shall make no law abridging speech." By ignoring the inconvenient three words "the freedom of," the Supreme Court dumbs down the Free Speech Clause from a challenge to decide what a man-made legal abstraction called "the freedom of speech" should include to a simplistic command to deregulate the process of communication.

Moreover, in reading the truncated seven-word Free Speech Clause, the justices do not ask why the ten amendments constituting the Bill of Rights open with the protections listed in the First Amendment[1] or why the forty-five words and six ideas in its text are ordered as they are. Why did Madison and his friends put the First Amendment first, and why does it begin with two religion clauses? Within the religion clauses, why does the prohibition on government "establishment of religion" come before protection of "free exercise of religion"? Why do the three immensely important freedoms of speech, press, and assembly follow the two religious freedom clauses in that particular order, and why does the right to petition for a redress of grievances bring up the textual rear?

We don't even try to understand how freedom of association, a seventh First Amendment right, which is not mentioned in the First Amendment's text, relates to the six textual protections in the amendment itself or ask whether similar nontextual First Amendment rights, like the rights to vote, run for office, and enjoy fair political representation, are also hiding in plain sight in Madison's text.

Nor do we ask why the remaining nine amendments in the Bill of Rights are placed in their particular order or why each unfolds as it does. Why, for example, does the intensely controversial Second Amendment—

> A well-regulated Militia, being necessary to the security of a free State, the right of the people to keep and bear Arms, shall not be infringed—

have pride of place immediately after the iconic First? And how should the Second Amendment's "well-regulated Militia" clause interact with the "keep and bear Arms" clause in a world where the Revolutionary-era citizens' militia has evolved into a full-time citizens' army and eighteenth-century muskets have been beaten not into ploughshares but into assault rifles.

We do not ask why the protections of the Fourth, Fifth, Sixth, Seventh, and Eighth Amendments follow the Second and Third and why they are ordered as they are, horizontally within each amendment and vertically from amendment to amendment.[2] Why, for example, does the Fourth Amendment's ban on "unreasonable searches and seizures" come before the Fifth Amendment's ban on compulsory self-incrimination? Why does the Fifth Amendment open with the Grand Jury Clause and close with the Due Process and Takings clauses? Why do the protections of the Fourth and Fifth Amendments precede the Sixth Amendment's guaranty of a jury trial, and why does the Eighth Amendment's ban on "cruel and unusual punishment" follow it?

Finally, we do not ask why Madison elected to close the Bill of Rights with the Ninth Amendment's tantalizing reminder that

> The enumeration in the Constitution, of certain rights, shall not be construed to deny or disparage others retained by the people

and the Tenth Amendment's austere admonition that

> The powers not delegated to the United States by the Constitution, nor prohibited by it to the States, are reserved to the States respectively, or to the people.

In short, we close our eyes—and our ears—to the possibility of a deep structure in the Bill of Rights worthy of a great poem. Instead of a poem, we read our most revered political text as a series of unconnected verbal commands, each clause—indeed, each word of each clause—existing in splendid isolation. In twenty-first-century America, we have lost the ability to hear Madison's music.

MADISON'S MUSIC FOUND

It would be easy to dress the Bill of Rights up to look like a poem. I could probably publish the phone book in blank verse. But is there a deep structure in the Bill of Rights worthy of being called poetic? My answer is an emphatic yes. The poetic structure can be found both vertically, in the order of the first ten amendments, and horizontally, in the substantive structure of each amendment. Vertically, the Bill of Rights is organized as thirty-one ideas gathered into ten amendments ordered from one to ten with remarkable coherence and discipline. Horizontally, each amendment is carefully structured to tell a story of individual freedom and democratic order. Not an idea or word is out of place. In short, Madison's poem to individual freedom and democratic self-government is as carefully wrought as a Wallace Stevens poem. We owe its reading the same respect.

4

The First Amendment as a Narrative of Democracy

The Bill of Rights opens with a blueprint for an ideal "city on a hill"[1]—a place of respect for individual conscience, robust political discussion, and democratic self-government. The First Amendment is a crucial milestone in the evolution of political thought, marking the first (and thus far the only) time in human history that six foundational ideas—freedom from religion (establishment), freedom of religion (free exercise), freedom of speech, freedom of the press, freedom of assembly, and freedom to petition for a redress of grievances—have been united in a single rights-bearing text. It's not that any of the six ideas were new in 1789 or even particularly original. Each had appeared, albeit fragmentarily and in random order, in many of the important rights-bearing documents that had preceded the Bill of Rights. By my count, Madison had the benefit of forty-two important rights-bearing documents when he set out to catalog our basic rights in the summer of 1789.[2] Each of the six textual rights codified in Madison's First Amendment had appeared and reappeared in many of the precursors, but it took Madison's genius (with a little help from his friends)[3] to unite and deploy the six freedoms in a single text as the chronologically organized evolution of a democratic idea.

Madison deploys the foundational concepts in his First Amendment on a disciplined inside-to-outside axis, beginning in the two religion clauses with freedom of thought, progressing through three ascending levels of individual interaction with the community—free expression of an idea by an individual, mass dissemination of the idea by a free press, and collective action in support of the idea by the people—and culminating in the petition clause with the introduction of the idea into the formal process of democratic lawmaking. In short, a chronological description of the arc of a democratic idea—from conception to codification. No document in the history of self-government prefigures such a carefully drawn, chronologically organized blueprint of democracy in action.

Madison's poem begins where any poem celebrating individual freedom and self-government must begin—in the interior precincts of the human spirit—with protection of religious (and eventually secular) conscience. Madison, deeply affected by enlightenment philosophers such as Immanuel Kant and John Locke, who argued that human beings are naturally endowed with freedom to shape their own personalities and beliefs, understood that the success of any democratic "city on a hill" rests on the shoulders of a free people, who must be at peace with themselves individually before they can hope to govern others. Since Madison knew in 1789, as George Orwell would tell us in *1984*, that nothing crushes the human spirit like being forced to act affirmatively to betray a cherished belief, Madison begins his poem with the Establishment Clause, a ban on forcing a free citizen to support or endorse religious beliefs she does not hold. The First Amendment's narrative then moves naturally to the Free Exercise Clause's ban on government interference with religiously motivated behavior. The careful inside-to-outside order of the two religion clauses reflects Madison's remarkably prescient assessment of the relative harm to individual dignity caused by government-coerced *affirmative* betrayals of conscience as opposed to government-imposed *negative* prohibitions on conduct reflective of conscience.

Madison understood that protection of freedom of conscience as the starting point of democratic life cannot stop with religious conscience. His original version of what became the First Amendment explicitly protected both religious and secular conscience.[4] Although the House of Representatives adopted Madison's secular conscience clause, the Senate deleted it in a secret session before sending the Bill of Rights to the states for ratification. We'll never know why. But as we shall see, the modern Supreme Court has restored the opening lines of Madison's great poem to their original comprehensive form by providing comparable First Amendment protection to deeply felt beliefs: both religious and secular.[5] With freedom of thought secure as the necessary starting point of democratic life, the First Amendment's narrative turns to "the freedom of speech" as the next logical step in the evolution of a democratic idea. As with the two religion clauses, the Free Speech Clause looks both inward, protecting the internal secular thought processes of a free citizen, and outward, preserving the freedom to convey information and ideas to others.

Because Madison understood that a single free voice, no matter how earnest and intellectually compelling, can reach only a relatively small audience, his First Amendment narrative turns chronologically and logically to a fourth component of robust democracy—freedom of the press, designed to ensure a free speaker the ability to reach a mass audience.

Once a democratic idea has been freely conceived, freely expressed, and widely disseminated, Madison's poem turns naturally to the fifth chronological foundational component of democracy—collective action in support of an idea. In 1789, Madison called it freedom of assembly, protecting the ability of a free people to act collectively in furtherance of a democratic idea. Freedom of assembly ensures that the streets really do belong to the people. Every great political movement in American history has been born and has thrived in the safe haven of Madison's remarkable understanding that democratic governance rests on forms of collective action, such as body rhetoric, that are available to all, not just the privileged few. In 1958, Justice John Marshall Harlan, writing for a unanimous Supreme Court, recognized that the careful order of the First Amendment's six textual ideas implied the existence of a seventh, nontextual right to engage in collective action short of physical assembly. Justice Harlan called the new implied

First Amendment right "freedom of association," and deployed it to shield the membership lists of the NAACP from hostile scrutiny by Alabama officials.

Madison's First Amendment poem culminates in the Petition Clause, assuring citizens the formal right to seek a redress of grievances from their government, completing the evolution of a democratic idea from its genesis in the interior recesses of a free citizen's conscience (non-establishment and free exercise), through three levels of communicative interaction with the community—public expression (freedom of speech), mass dissemination (freedom of the press), and collective advancement (freedoms of association and assembly)—to the right of petition in an effort to transform the idea into law. No document in the eight hundred years of our rights-bearing heritage comes close to telling such a disciplined story of democracy in action.

It's possible, of course, that Revolutionary-era monkeys on a typewriter (or mice with quill pens) would have randomly stumbled upon such a fine-tuned democratic chronology. But even if the disciplined order of the six textual ideas is merely the result of random good fortune, the full First Amendment, as Madison and his friends wrote it, should be democracy's best friend. It's tragic that the current Supreme Court majority, utterly ignoring Madison's music, has turned the isolated, artificially truncated seven-word Free Speech Clause into democracy's bad parent.

DEMOCRACY'S BAD PARENT— SUFFOCATING ONE DAY, ABSENT THE NEXT

Congress enacted a campaign finance law limiting the massively unequal electoral power of the rich. The suffocatingly strict Supreme Court said no, ruling that the Free Speech Clause guaranties the rich uncontrollable power to dominate the democratic process.[6]

Arizona tried to help underfunded candidates compete with rich ones by providing campaign subsidies designed to match the spending of the rich, privately funded candidate. The suffocatingly strict Supreme Court said no, ruling that matching campaign subsidies unconstitutionally "penalize" the free-speech rights of rich candidates.[7]

Congress, following the advice of Teddy Roosevelt, sought to wall off the vast trove of corporate wealth from our elections. The suffocatingly strict Supreme Court said no, ruling that unlimited corporate electioneering is protected by the Free Speech Clause because, according to five justices, an unlimited diet of corporate propaganda is actually good for us.[8]

California sought to broaden the two major parties' nominating processes by allowing all voters to participate in the nomination of both Republican and Democratic candidates in a convenient format, the "blanket primary." The suffocatingly strict Supreme Court said no, insisting that opening up the major party nominating process to all voters unconstitutionally dilutes the associational rights of party members.[9]

North Carolina drew legislative lines to help racial minorities recover from centuries of political exclusion. The suffocatingly strict Supreme Court scolded the state officials and said no, insisting that drawing electoral lines in an effort to help racial minorities secure fair political representation is a dangerous form of racism.[10]

In 1965, Congress overwhelmingly adopted a Voting Rights Act aimed at protecting minority voters in the states of the old Confederacy, requiring the Justice Department to sign off on proposed election law changes to make sure that they did not adversely affect black and Latino voters. Congress overwhelmingly reenacted the provision, called "pre-clearance," in 1982, and again in 2006. The suffocatingly strict Supreme Court said no, informing both houses of Congress that minority voters don't really need special protection anymore.[11]

However, when cynical politicians set up hurdles to prevent poor people from voting, including requiring photo identification cards or proof of citizenship, the inexplicably absent Supreme Court can't find a constitutional violation.[12]

When powerful incumbent legislators rig district lines to ensure their permanent reelection, the inexplicably absent Supreme Court looks the other way.[13]

When political bosses of both parties draw partisan district lines to ensure the election of their party's candidates, the inexplicably absent Supreme Court says it's just politics as usual.[14]

In the dysfunctional democracy the justices have built, at least one half of the electorate doesn't vote,[15] the Supreme Court gets to pick a president,[16] the extreme wings of each major party dominate the nominating process, minor parties are rendered powerless, rich ideological outliers control the political agenda, voting can be an ordeal, lobbyists treat elected officials as wholly owned subsidiaries, and rivers of money flowing from secret sources have turned our elections into silent auctions.

Madison would weep.

The sad truth is that for the last half century the Supreme Court, as a bad parent, has decided dozens and dozens of constitutional cases that have shaped the contours of American democracy without paying attention to the quality of the democracy it was building. If an architect designed an expensive house with fancy windows, elegant doors, sweeping staircases, and graceful walls but didn't worry about how they all fit together, no one would want to live in her accidental house. That's just what the Supreme Court has done with American democracy. A narrow majority of the justices has built an accidental, dysfunctional democracy that no one except the superrich and the politically powerful wants to live in.[17]

Can Madison's democracy-friendly First Amendment help us to think our way out of our current democratic malaise? I'm sure that the answer is yes, but only if we recover the ability to read Madison's entire First Amendment as a meticulously organized road map of a well-functioning egalitarian democracy. I'll return to what a democracy-friendly First Amendment might look like in the next chapter, but first we should take a quick look at the rest of Madison's great poem, for Madison's music doesn't stop with the First Amendment. The Founders understood that ideal cities perched on imaginary hills are notoriously fragile. They knew that practical defenses rooted in realpolitik had to be put in place to reinforce the First Amendment's "parchment barriers." The Second through Eighth Amendments deploy those defenses in a precisely organized catalog of risks to the First Amendment's ideal democratic polity, organized by category and order of magnitude. No similarly ordered catalog of democratic risks and remedies exists in the eight hundred years of our rights-bearing heritage.

MADISON'S SURPRISINGLY EGALITARIAN SECOND AMENDMENT

The Second (and Third)[18] Amendments reflect the Founders' fearful (but all too accurate) understanding that subversion or overthrow by force of arms is the fate of most democracies. Placement of the Second Amendment immediately after the iconic First telegraphs their concern that, despite the protections built into the 1787 Constitution,[19] the risk of armed subversion by the military remained the greatest threat to their democratic handiwork. Madison's characteristically pragmatic antidote was to insert checks and balances into the organizational structure of the new nation's military forces. On one hand, he envisioned a typical eighteenth-century mercenary standing army, nominally commanded by the president but having little kinship with or loyalty to the people it supposedly served. On the other, he envisioned a reserve standby army consisting of the entire white male population in arms in the form of a "well-regulated" citizens' militia. Madison hoped that the very existence of such a militia would check the mercenary standing army.

The challenge today is to give meaning to the Second Amendment in a world where the eighteenth-century mercenary standing army has evolved into a modern citizens' army that looks just like the people it serves, organized citizens' militias no longer exist, and the prospect of an ad hoc group of armed citizens deterring a military takeover is a teenage fantasy that makes a good movie, nothing more. Unfortunately, in a classic example of what happens when a piece of the constitutional text is torn from its roots and viewed in isolation, a majority of the current Supreme Court ignores the structural relationship between the First and Second Amendments. Instead of reading the Second Amendment as a structural protection of First Amendment democracy against military overthrow, five members of the current Court tear the "keep and bear arms" clause from the full text, completely ignore the "well-regulated militia" clause, and insist on reading a fragment of the Second Amendment as creating a freestanding constitutional right to own guns for self-defense and sport, unconnected to the defense of democracy.[20]

The current "individual self-defense" reading of the Keep and Bear Arms Clause ignores Madison's prescient understanding that a standing army that doesn't look like the population it purports to serve poses a unique threat to democratic governance. Madison predicted—and history teaches—that such an unrepresentative military is a good bet to turn on the polity, especially the excluded segments of the population. The ugly example of England's religious civil wars, when Catholics and Protestants took turns excluding each other from the nation's armed forces as the first step toward massacring each other, was obviously very much on Madison's mind. As the eighteenth-century mercenary-based military painfully evolved during the nineteenth and twentieth centuries into an institution that resembled the society it served, Madison's democratic "city on a hill" no longer needed a "well-regulated" citizens' militia to counter the threat from an unrepresentative standing army. Not surprisingly, the very idea of a well-regulated citizens' militia disintegrated. The disappearance of the citizens' militia does not mean, however, that the Second Amendment has no role in twenty-first-century America. Reducing the Second Amendment to a historical anachronism would be unfaithful to a genuine commitment to reading the Bill of Rights—the *entire* Bill of Rights—as a coherent poem. Efforts by the Supreme Court's liberal minority to consign the Second Amendment to the dustbin of history fail to respect its central place in Madison's poem. Indeed, if forced to choose between an individual-self-defense reading that gives the Second Amendment substantial but erroneous contemporary meaning and a dismissive reading, I would choose the individual rights reading.

But those aren't the only choices. The modern reading of Madison's Second Amendment closest to his original structure is a guaranty that all qualified persons, including gays, women, and people of color, enjoy an equal "right to keep and bear arms" in defense of American democracy as members of a well-regulated military that, thanks to James Madison, will always look just like the people it serves.

MADISON AS INSPECTOR POIRÔT: AMENDMENTS IV–VIII

With the risk of forcible military overthrow dealt with in the Second and Third Amendments (the Third Amendment prohibits troops from commandeering private houses; fortunately, we have had no need to invoke it), Madison's poem turns logically to the next most feared source of armed subversion of democracy—abuse of the civilian law enforcement power. The disciplined order and placement of the Fourth, Fifth, Sixth, Seventh, and Eighth Amendments chronologically replicates the six phases of the criminal law enforcement process:

investigation—Fourth Amendment,
arrest—Fourth Amendment,
formal accusation—Fifth Amendment,
custodial interrogation—Fifth Amendment,
adjudication—Sixth and Seventh Amendments, and
punishment—Eighth Amendment.

At each step of the chronologically organized process, Madison and his friends carefully inserted structural protections against abuse of the law enforcement power.

The Fourth Amendment regulates investigation and arrest by strictly limiting the power of law enforcement agencies to search, seize, and arrest suspected wrongdoers. As with the checks and balances in Madison's Second Amendment, the structural core of the Fourth Amendment is the division of law enforcement powers between the police and the courts. Under the Fourth Amendment's Warrant Clause, the police may not carry out a search, seizure, or arrest unless they persuade a neutral judge that "probable cause" exists to believe that evidence of a crime will be uncovered or a criminal wrongdoer apprehended. In 1961, the Warren Court reinforced Madison's original textual structural protection by construing the Fourth Amendment as requiring the exclusion at criminal trial of evidence wrongfully obtained through an unlawful search, seizure, or arrest.[21] As with Justice Harlan's discovery of implied freedom of association in the First Amendment, the Fourth Amendment "exclusionary rule" is an example of the power of American judges to find implied constitutional rights in the interstices of the constitutional text. We'll explore that process further when we consider Madison's Ninth Amendment.

Once a Fourth Amendment investigation has identified and placed a suspected wrongdoer under arrest, Madison's poem moves logically to the formal charging and interrogation phases governed by the Fifth Amendment, which opens by empowering a group of ordinary citizens sitting as a grand jury to decide whether enough evidence of guilt exists to justify a formal accusation (indictment). Madison's Fifth Amendment then turns logically to custodial interrogation, limiting the power of the police to force a defendant to incriminate himself. As with the Fourth Amendment's exclusionary rule, the modern Supreme Court forbids the introduction at trial of involuntary custodial statements. Of course, statements given under torture are barred. But so are custodial statements taken without informing the accused of the right to remain silent and the right to a free lawyer. That's where so-called Miranda warnings come from.[22]

The Fifth Amendment closes with a prohibition on the

"deprivation of life, liberty, or property without due process of law," and a ban on "taking" private property for public use without just compensation. The Due Process and Takings clauses are placed between the Fifth and Sixth Amendments to keep the police, once they get their hands on the person they believe to be guilty, from being tempted to impose summary punishment without waiting for the adjudicatory formalities described in the Sixth and Seventh Amendments. As such, they are perfectly positioned as the crucial textual bridge to the Sixth Amendment from the Fourth and Fifth.

Once an accused has been properly investigated, arrested, charged, and interrogated under the Fourth and Fifth Amendments, Madison's poem moves logically to the criminal adjudication phase in the Sixth Amendment, which ensures fair notice of criminal charges, the right of a criminal defendant to confront and cross-examine hostile witnesses, the right to summon friendly witnesses, the right to counsel, and the right to a public jury trial in the place where the alleged crime took place. As with the Fourth and Fifth Amendment exclusionary rules, the modern Supreme Court has added nontextual rights to the Sixth Amendment adjudication process, finding an implied requirement that a criminal jury must find guilt beyond a reasonable doubt as to each element of a criminal offense, and that the government provide free counsel in cases threatening loss of liberty.[23]

If a Sixth Amendment criminal jury trial (or a Seventh Amendment jury trial in a noncriminal setting) results in a guilty verdict, the Eighth Amendment's ban on cruel and unusual punishment or excessive fines limits the severity of punishment. No excessive bail at the beginning of the process, for such unfair incarceration is itself a punishment without trial. No death penalty for offenses not resulting in death. No death penalty for juvenile offenders. No death penalty for mentally deficient defendants. Perhaps no death penalty at all. No jail sentence that is grossly disproportionate to the gravity of the crime. No massive punitive damage awards in civil cases that bear little relationship to the actual damages caused by a defendant's unlawful behavior.

As with the careful order of democracy-enhancing ideas in the First Amendment and the military-curbing ideas in the Second and Third Amendments, no other similarly organized catalog of risks and safeguards associated with the civilian law enforcement process exists in our rights-bearing heritage. Yet I know of no modern case that asks why the criminal procedure amendments are ordered as they are or seeks to construe the criminal procedure amendments as a structural whole.[24] To the contrary, since the 1980s, the Court's characteristic approach to criminal procedure is to view each clause of each amendment in splendid isolation, leaving white spaces between them that become loopholes for law enforcement abuse. For example, the widespread use of undercover agents to infiltrate Muslim institutions in the United States is not usually deemed a search, so it escapes the Fourth Amendment. Nor is it deemed custodial interrogation, so it escapes the Fifth Amendment, leaving police free to abuse the technique with no judicial oversight. Similarly, massive data-gathering programs carried out in secret are defended as constitutional because they do not fall within a narrow interpretation of *search* and *seizure* or because we've watered down the warrant clause to virtually nothing.

Madison would be appalled.

A MADISONIAN READING LESSON: RECOVERING THE POETRY IN AMENDMENTS IX AND X

Madison saved the best for last. The key to reading the Bill of Rights as a poem is found in the two closing amendments. Madison understood that without careful instructions about how to read the text, the Bill of Rights risked being mired in semantic chaos. As usual, he was right.

James Madison was a consummate lawyer. He knew that words are slippery things. He knew that from the very beginnings of written language, limits of text and imagination have complicated efforts to use written words to convey important messages to friends and neighbors, to say nothing of conveying complex political instructions to future generations. Witness the current massive disagreement and confusion over how judges should read the Bill of Rights, ranging from Justice Thomas's strict literalism, through various versions of "originalism" favored by Justice Scalia, to Justice Brennan's embrace of the "living constitution," Justice Souter's thoughtful explorations of how best to advance the Founders' basic purposes, and Justice Breyer's invocation of egalitarian democracy as a textual tiebreaker.

Madison also recognized that the Founders, being human, might leave an important right out of the literal text because they forgot it, overlooked it, or erroneously rejected it. As we'll see, that's just what happened when the Senate rejected Madison's secular conscience clause and his clause applying portions of the Bill of Rights to the states. Madison's antidote was to close his poem with careful directions in the Ninth and Tenth Amendments about how to read the constitutional text. The Ninth Amendment, acknowledging the possibility of additional rights "retained by the people," empowers future generations to cope with ambiguous drafting, inadvertent omission, or outright mistakes by: (1) reading the rights-bearing text generously and (2) invoking analogy and structural need, through a process known to the Founders' generation as "the equity of the statute," to imply the existence of nontextual rights.[25] Conversely, the Tenth Amendment instructs future generations to read the power-granting text narrowly and to refrain from implying new powers through analogy and structural need. Madison rooted his constitutional reading lesson in two venerable British parliamentary approaches to construing text, which guide us more than two hundred years later in reading the Constitution and statutes today. One technique—summarized by the Latin phrase *inclusio unis est exclusio alterium*, "inclusion of one thing is exclusion of the other"—instructed British judges to read parliamentary statutes in a narrow, literal way. If something was not actually mentioned in the literal text, *inclusio unis* forbade a British judge from extending the text's coverage to closely analogous settings. For example, if the British Parliament enacted legislation regulating "betting establishments," British bookies were free to ignore the regulations as long as the bet was made at the track and not at the "betting establishment."

The competing statutory construction technique was the "equity of the statute," authorizing British judges to expand laws beyond their literal wording to closely related, analogous settings, but only when such expanded coverage was broadly consistent with the text and was deemed necessary to carry out Parliament's intentions more effectively. For example, if Parliament made it a hanging offense for "a servant to strike *his* master," applying the equity of the statute to the male pronoun *he* would by analogy extend it to a female pronoun, *she*, permitting the death sentence to be imposed on both male and female servants.

That is exactly what Justice Harlan did in 1958 when he used analogy and implication to uncover the right of free association latent in the First Amendment's text.[26] It is also what the Court did when it found extratextual exclusionary rules in the Fourth and Fifth Amendments,[27] when it inserted an extratextual requirement of proof beyond a reasonable doubt into the Fifth and Sixth Amendments,[28] and when it interpreted the Sixth Amendment to include an extratextual right to appointed counsel.[29] Finally, Justice Harlan used the same technique to bridge the constitutional gap between religious and secular conscience created by the Founders' failure in 1789 to accept Madison's original freedom of conscience clause.[30] A close look at the history of the Ninth and Tenth Amendments explains why Justice Harlan was right.

The immediate historical origins of the Ninth and Tenth Amendments are easy enough to trace. During the debates over the 1787 Constitution, critics argued first that listing our basic rights in a single document would be a dangerous mistake because the Founders might leave something important out of the catalog of rights. It was not a frivolous objection. The Founders made at least two serious mistakes when the Senate deleted Madison's freedom of secular conscience clause and his proposed clause applying portions of the Bill of Rights to the states. It's heartbreaking to speculate about what might have been if Southern antislavery forces had been able to invoke the First Amendment in the years leading up to the Civil War. Opposition to slavery among whites existed in most of the slave states. In 1832, for example, there was a major debate over abolition in the Virginia legislature. Once iron censorship laws had silenced antislavery voices throughout the South, however, local opposition disintegrated, intensifying sectional polarization and depriving the nation of the possibility of a political solution to slavery. Similarly, failure to include Madison's secular conscience clause in the 1791 Bill of Rights permitted the imprisonment of supporters of the Underground Railway, engaged in aiding escaped slaves to reach safety in Canada, and the jailing of pacifist opponents to World War I. It took 150 years—and a dose of Ninth Amendment Madisonian poetry—for the Supreme Court to correct both mistakes, by: (1) recognizing an implied First Amendment protection of secular conscience; and (2) applying the Bill of Rights to the states through the word magic of the Fourteenth Amendment's Due Process Clause.

Today when someone invokes a constitutional right of privacy—such as the right to use birth control, to choose whether to bear a child, or to terminate a life of pain and suffering with dignity—many constitutional experts, including many thoughtful judges, answer that if the Founders had wished to protect privacy in the Constitution, they would have explicitly included the protection in the text of the Bill of Rights. They argue that because the right can't be found in the original text it doesn't exist. That's just what opponents of the Bill of Rights were worried about in 1787 when they blocked a Bill of Rights for the original constitution. The Ninth Amendment was Madison's antidote.

Opponents of a Bill of Rights also feared that singling out a right might imply the existence of a correlative government power. Ironically, in 1798, supporters of the now infamous Alien and Sedition Acts, which censored the press, argued that if regulatory power over the press didn't exist, why did the Founders need to insert a Free Press Clause limiting it? Similarly, the Fifth Amendment closes with a clause forbidding the United States from taking private property for public use without paying just compensation. The Founders' decision to insert such an explicit right in the Bill of Rights has given rise to an argument that they must have intended the national government (as opposed to the states) to possess implied power to take private property for public use through eminent domain, even though no such power is mentioned in the constitutional text. The Tenth Amendment was Madison's antidote to such government power creep.

Unfortunately, current readings of both the Ninth and Tenth Amendments ignore Madison's music. Justice Douglas read the Ninth Amendment as authorizing a kind of judicially enforceable "natural law." Natural law is a magnificent philosophical abstraction that seeks to identify and catalog rights that are (or should be) enjoyed in the very nature of things by all human beings. The idea of natural law as a protector of human dignity has been a glorious banner behind which millions have marched in the struggle against oppression. Natural law was Thomas Jefferson's inspiration when he wrote, "We hold these truths to be *self-evident*, that all men are created equal, that they are endowed by their Creator with certain *unalienable* rights, that among these are Life, Liberty and the pursuit of Happiness." Natural law forbidding slavery was the banner under which Union troops fought and died during the Civil War. Respect for dignitary values rooted in natural law was the banner that the United States carried throughout the twentieth century in its successful struggles against Nazism and Communism. It was the guiding principle of the Nuremberg trials. It is the hope that we hold out today to the Arab Spring (or what's left of it), Chinese dissidents, and the emerging democracies of Asia, Africa, and South America.

However, because it is hopelessly subjective, the idea of natural law has not proved a useful concept in actually governing a tolerably fair democracy. For example, a reasonably developed theory of natural law can protect a woman's right to choose whether to bear a child, but it can also protect a fetus's right to life. It can protect a right to health, housing, and nutrition, but it can also insist on economic markets inherently free from government regulation. Appeal to natural law can protect the inherent sanctity of gay marriage, but it can also condemn gays to opprobrium and discrimination. In short, the idea of natural law is often an empty vessel into which we pour our most cherished personal values. In a truly democratic society, unelected judges should not be empowered to force citizens to embrace a set of personal values simply because the judge, in the process of reading the Ninth Amendment, labels them as flowing logically from respect for human dignity. But the alternative modern reading of the Ninth Amendment is even worse. When Robert Bork was asked about the meaning of the Ninth Amendment during his ill-fated Supreme Court confirmation hearings, he dismissed it as an "ink blot" having no judicially enforceable effect.

Current Supreme Court efforts to read the Tenth Amendment are also stuck at the extremes, only this time the political positions are reversed. Many conservatives read the Tenth Amendment as an open-ended invitation to codify and enforce their subjective vision of American federalism by protecting *inherent* attributes of state sovereignty (natural law, anyone?) against usurpation by Congress or the president. The problem is that there is no consensus about what counts as an inherent attribute of sovereignty, leaving the Tenth Amendment hostage to whatever political theory about federalism a majority of the justices happen to embrace at any given time. But the alternative modern reading of the Tenth Amendment is also untenable. Liberals, echoing Robert Bork's "ink blot" approach to the Ninth, argue that the Tenth is simply a political truism, too amorphous to be given effective judicial content. According to them, Madison was just blowing symbolic smoke when he drafted the Tenth Amendment.

Predictably, neither liberals nor conservatives acknowledge the deeply inconsistent nature of their respective cross-readings of the closing amendments. If, however, we respect the structural reasons for placing the Ninth and Tenth Amendments at the close of the document, we see that Madison was neither adopting natural law, inviting judge-made theories of federalism, nor creating meaningless ink blots. Rather, faced with the political need to say something about omitted rights and implied powers, Madison turned the two closing amendments into a brilliant reading lesson. The Ninth Amendment tells us that when omitted individual rights are at issue, we should not be afraid to expand the literal text in favor of freedom, using the disciplined technique of equity of the statute. The Tenth Amendment tells us that when implied government power is at stake, we should do exactly the opposite, limiting the literal grant of powers by invoking *inclusio unis*.

Once we understand Madison's poetic Ninth Amendment as authorizing American judges to read the rights-bearing provisions of the constitutional text against the disciplined background of the equity of the statute, it becomes possible for us to recover the rest of Madison's music embedded in the text of the First through Eighth Amendments—especially Madison's democracy-friendly First Amendment.

inclusio unis [est exclusio alterium]; See bottom of pg. 29

5

Madison's Music Restored

Recovering Madison's Democracy-Friendly First Amendment

Democracy has always been beset by an internal contradiction. While the ethos of democracy calls for equal exercise of political power by all the governed, the practice of democracy has tended to exclude the weak and reinforce the strong. The ancient Greeks invented democracy, but the Athenian Constitution parceled out the vote to a fraction of the potential electorate, excluding women, slaves, aliens, and the poor. The Italian and Swiss city-states popularized democracy in the seventeenth and early eighteenth centuries, but the Florentine, Venetian, and Genevois versions of democracy were really government by merchant princes. The British proved that mass democracy could work but did not formally embrace "universal" suffrage until 1884 and even then denied the vote to women until 1918. France didn't enfranchise women until 1946.

AMERICA'S THREE-TIER DEMOCRACY

Not surprisingly, American democracy began its life in the late eighteenth century by formally denying the vote to the weakest segments of society—women, blacks, Native Americans, and the poor. Most efforts at democratic reform in the United States have concentrated on expanding a narrow formal definition of the franchise. In 1870, the Fifteenth Amendment sought to end racial obstacles to the ballot. In 1920, the Nineteenth Amendment guaranteed the vote to women. In 1964, the Twenty-Fourth Amendment protected the poor by banning poll taxes in federal elections. In 1971, the Twenty-Sixth Amendment extended the vote to eighteen-year-olds in federal elections. Beginning in the early 1960s, a blizzard of Supreme Court opinions wiped out property qualifications and durational residence requirements for voting, and invalidated malapportioned legislative districts favoring rural voters at the expense of urban interests. Only the constitutionally malapportioned Senate, where rural states with about 21 percent of the population can control fifty-one senators, survives. In 1975, Congress barred literacy tests for voting nationwide, overturning a 1959 Supreme Court decision that had unanimously upheld the practice. Enactment and vigorous enforcement of the Voting Rights Act of 1965, as amended in 1982—especially the preclearance requirement of Section 5—finally ended the shameful de facto exclusion of racial minorities from the electorates of the states of the old Confederacy. Let's hope there is no backsliding now that the Supreme Court has ruled that preclearance is no longer necessary because it has worked so well.

By 2000, therefore, with the important exceptions of ex-felons in a few states, notably Florida and Virginia, and the perennial dilemma of how to provide political representation for long-term resident aliens and children, the formal American electorate finally embraced all of the governed (with the exception of the residents of the District of Columbia, Puerto Rico, and American Samoa), with virtually no legally mandated exclusions.

And yet the age-old contradiction between inclusionary aspiration and its exclusionary reality continues to plague American democracy in the twenty-first century. The rosy formal picture of a universal American electorate masks a darker political reality that resembles the exclusionary electorates of the past. American democracy is currently divided into three tiers of citizens—I call them supercitizens, ordinary citizens, and spectator citizens.

An economically elite top tier of supercitizens, consisting of the wealthiest 1 to 2 percent of the population, wields enormously disproportionate political power. Supercitizens of both parties set the national political agenda, select the candidates, bankroll the campaigns (virtually all campaign contributions and expenditures come from the top 2 percent of the economic ladder), and enjoy privileged postelection access to government officials (whose telephone call does a busy senator take?). Membership in the supercitizen tier is neither defined by law nor confined to the wealthy. It is possible to become a supercitizen on the basis of talent, fame, good looks, family status, inheritance, or sheer persistence. But money gets you in with no questions asked. Likewise, membership in the top tier is not formally confined to white men. Women and people of color occasionally crack the ceiling. But having substantial disposable income for politics is still overwhelmingly a white male prerogative in American society.

A second tier of ordinary citizens consists of the 40 percent to 60 percent of the formally eligible electorate who actually vote. Ordinary citizens navigate among the choices made available to them by supercitizens. After supercitizens have set the table by deciding what issues are worth debating, what campaign speeches are worth funding, and what candidates are worthy of running, ordinary citizens—like jurors in a lawsuit or judges in a beauty pageant—choose among the issues and candidates that have been put before them. Ordinary citizens often wield real power. Choosing between the (usually two) alternatives offered by supercitizens can be important, as long as the alternatives provide a real choice. Often, though, the range of available alternatives is constrained by the relatively homogeneous, economically privileged supercitizen slice of the electorate that formulates them. Moreover, the potential electoral power wielded by ordinary citizens is diluted by widespread political gerrymandering, rendering the outcome of most legislative elections a foregone conclusion.

A third tier, I call them spectator citizens, is made up of the 40 percent to 60 percent of the eligible electorate that does not vote, resulting in an American political reality in which a small economic elite of supercitizens interacts with a second tier of relatively well-off ordinary citizens to produce a form of popular governance that exalts the rich and virtually excludes the poor from political power. Even if the huge mass of nonvoting spectator citizens were a random slice of the population, the existence of such a potentially volatile pool of alienated nonparticipants would pose a threat to American democracy, constituting a proverbial loose cannon just waiting for a demagogue to fire it off. The problem is far worse in the United States than elsewhere, though, because the nonparticipating third tier is not a random slice of the population. Spectator citizens are disproportionately poor, badly educated, and nonwhite.

The unpleasant reality is an American electorate skewed in favor of the powerful, once directly imposed by law but now reproduced indirectly by less obvious means. A century ago, political participation was legally rationed by formal denial of the vote to women, the poor, and newcomers, as well as by de facto prohibitions that prevented blacks and Latinos from voting. Today participation in the democratic process is rationed by the operation of our system of voter registration, election administration, legislative apportionment, and campaign finance, with its capacity to skew available information in favor of the rich. The political rationing system may be less visible to the naked eye, but the effect on the poor and less educated is almost as effective.

The persistence of a disproportionately poor and undereducated third tier of spectator citizens poses an immense moral challenge to American democracy. Most obviously, the consent of the governed is a far less compelling concept when that consent is granted by an electorate that does not reflect the will of the poorest and weakest segments of the society. Less obviously, the feedback interaction between supercitizens and ordinary citizens is robbed of much of its legitimacy when the feedback is generated by an artificially truncated slice of ordinary citizens that does not reflect the needs and concerns of the weak and the poor. Thus, while formal mechanisms of exclusion have been dismantled, we continue to operate a democracy that significantly overrepresents the rich and underrepresents the poor and the weak.

Defenders of the three-tier system tell us that it is the natural result of a series of free choices reflecting individual preferences, abilities, and relative political sophistication. But a three-tier democracy is neither a natural inevitability nor a constitutional given. The first and third tiers are legal constructs, the predictable consequences of ignoring Madison's music in deciding how to structure American democracy. The economically elite first tier of supercitizens exists only because we have decided to treat the necessary costs of operating a complex democracy as an off-the-books expense to be borne by rich volunteers. By allowing the rich to pay the substantial costs of operating a democracy, we think we are getting something for nothing. In the end, though, we undermine the independence and integrity of the men and women who govern us by turning them into political beggars.

Worse, the Supreme Court has made it virtually impossible to deal effectively with the destructive effects of big money on our electoral system. Ignoring Madison's democracy-friendly First Amendment, we force efforts at democratic reform in campaign financing, operation of primaries, and formation of third parties to run a lethal gauntlet created by seven words in an artificially isolated and truncated Free Speech Clause torn from the rest of the First Amendment and cut off from Madison's democratic poetry.

The nonparticipating third tier of spectator citizens is also a legal construct, the predictable result of the Supreme Court's toleration of cynical obstacles to voting, including obsolete equipment in poorer areas, incompetent and Balkanized election administrators beholden to the two major parties, pre-election voter registration requirements, prevention of weekend voting, and requirements for photo ID and proof of citizenship that disproportionately limit electoral participation by weak and unsophisticated spectator citizens. In fact, the Supreme Court has tolerated or perpetuated virtually every antidemocratic practice that currently burdens American democracy—disenfranchising ex-felons, upholding cynical efforts to suppress the vote, permitting ruthless partisan gerrymandering, and allowing the nominating process to be controlled by political bosses and the campaign process by the superrich.

Neither the surrender of the electoral process to the rich nor the de facto disenfranchisement of the poor would be tolerated by a Supreme Court capable of hearing Madison's music.

HOW WE GOT HERE: JUSTICE BRENNAN'S RARE STRATEGIC BLUNDER

John Marshall and William J. Brennan Jr. were the two most successful judicial politicians ever to serve on the Supreme Court. Each was blessed with a first-rate analytical mind and a capacity to write clearly and with great conviction. Each was blessed, as well, with a gregarious personality and the ability to forge warm personal and intellectual bonds with colleagues that led to stable Supreme Court voting blocs. Marshall's mind and heart infused the early nineteenth-century Court; Brennan's, the late twentieth-century Court. As Justice David Souter noted in his moving eulogy for Justice Brennan, the sheer mass of Brennan's thirty-seven years of Supreme Court opinions exercises a gravitational pull on American law that may be unmatched in our history. One of Brennan's talents was assembling five votes on important cases. He was a genius at forging and holding a winning coalition. Indeed, he occasionally took that talent a little too far by holding rump caucuses in his chambers in which five justices would agree on a common position that would control the next day's formal vote. Brennan rarely made a strategic mistake. But when he made one, it was a whopper.

A half-century ago, in *Baker v. Carr*, the "one person, one vote" case,[1] three iconic Supreme Court justices—Felix Frankfurter, William J. Brennan Jr., and John Marshall Harlan—debated the role of the Supreme Court in shaping American democracy. Justice Frankfurter warned that we would rue the day that unelected Supreme Court justices were given substantial power to set the constitutional ground rules for American democracy.[2] Where, Frankfurter asked, would federal judges, functioning without textual guidance as armchair political scientists, find the "judicially manageable standards" to guide their democracy decisions?

Justice Brennan disagreed. He insisted that judges can—and should—use the Constitution to reinforce and protect American democracy. Brennan could have confronted Frankfurter directly, challenging his view that the First Amendment had nothing to do with protecting the right to participate in the democratic process. He could have invoked Madison's music to recognize an implied First Amendment right to democratic participation. Or he could have tried to take the clause guarantying a Republican form of government to the states out of judicial mothballs, where it had languished since 1846.[3] Instead, ever the canny strategist, Brennan took the safest way to "the rule of five" in a very closely contested case arguing that the Fourteenth Amendment's Equal Protection Clause[4] could act in democracy cases as both a source of judicial power and a textual check on judicial overreaching.

Supported by a comfortable Warren Court majority, Justice Brennan and Justice Thurgood Marshall developed an equality-based constitutional law of democracy. They argued that if one person enjoys the "fundamental right" to vote, everyone else is entitled to an equal right to vote, unless the government demonstrates a very persuasive justification for treating others differently. Brennan and Marshall called their equality-based approach "fundamental rights strict scrutiny."

Justice Harlan, a principled conservative who had discovered freedom of association in 1958 and would champion freedom of secular conscience in 1970, warned that relying on strict equality as a one-size-fits-all judicial formula for building a constitutional law of democracy risks blinding judges to larger concerns about the proper functioning of democracy as a whole.[5] Harlan warned that enforcing a strict rule of equality as the only way to protect democracy could lead to appallingly undemocratic results, such as denying the vote to everyone. Sadly, *Bush v. Gore*, where five justices used an ostensible concern for strict equality to terminate the 2000 presidential election in favor of the Republican candidate, proves Justice Harlan's point that equality and democracy do not always overlap.

Brennan won the argument back in 1962, ushering in our equality-based law of democracy. In its first decade or so—from 1962 to 1972—the equality-based constitutional law of democracy was a huge success. Relying on strict equality, the Supreme Court imposed the "one person, one vote" principle, requiring each election district to have roughly the same number of inhabitants, on the House of Representatives, both houses of a state's legislature, local school boards, county governing bodies, and city councils, sweeping away years of discriminatory underrepresentation of urban constituencies, often with large concentrations of nonwhite voters. With "one person, one vote" in place, the Court then recognized an equality-based right to vote and to run for office that doomed durational residence requirements, poll taxes, property ownership requirements, and virtually every other formal barrier to voting that had plagued American democracy since its founding.

Because fundamental rights strict scrutiny seemed to do the job of protecting democracy so effectively, Brennan made no effort to follow his initial instinct to ground the emerging constitutional law of democracy in Madison's First Amendment or in the long-dormant clause obliging the federal government to guaranty each state "a Republican form of government."[6] That decision marked a fateful strategic blunder tying judicial protection of American democracy not to the coherent poetry of Madison's democracy-friendly First Amendment or even to the idea of what constitutes a "republican form of government," but to the vagaries of an unstable and intensely controversial Fourteenth Amendment equality jurisprudence.

THE LIMITS OF EQUALITY-BASED PROTECTION OF DEMOCRACY: DEFINING THE FORMAL ELECTORATE

Despite its justly celebrated status as the world's most successful continuous charter of democratic governance, the U.S. Constitution is guilty of an embarrassing lapse: the original 1787 text says almost nothing explicit about the right to vote, run for office, or enjoy fair political representation. At the time of the founding, only white men with substantial property could vote. While some of the Founders may have believed that the Republican Form of Government Clause would prevent a state from unduly limiting the franchise, or that the adoption of Madison's First Amendment in 1791 had established a right to participate in the national democratic process, the only explicit guidance we get from the 1787 Constitution about the right to vote and run for office is: (1) a promise in Article VI, section 3 that no religious test will ever be imposed on the right to hold office; (2) a recognition in Article I, section 2 that, initially at least, the right to vote in a federal election would parallel the right to vote for the most populous house of the relevant state legislature; (3) a delegation to the states in Article I, section 4 of the power to set the "time, place or manner" for federal voting, subject to congressional override; and (4) the recognition in Article I, section 5 that "each house shall be the judge of the Elections, Returns and Qualifications of its own Members."

Whatever democratic gaps may have existed in the original 1787 text, the constitutional amendment process has been overwhelmingly preoccupied with building and preserving democracy, most importantly expanding the franchise. Of the seventeen constitutional amendments that have been added since the Bill of Rights, twelve have dealt directly with the functioning of the democratic process. Five amendments—Section 2 of the Fourteenth Amendment and the Fifteenth Amendment, both of which dealt with race; the Nineteenth Amendment, which enfranchised women; the Twenty-Fourth Amendment, which dealt with poverty; and the Twenty-Sixth Amendment, which dealt with age—expanded the franchise to previously disenfranchised groups. Two amendments, the Seventeenth, which established the direct popular election of senators instead of allowing state legislatures to elect them, and the Twenty-Third, which provided residents of the District of Columbia with the right to vote in presidential elections, expanded the scope of electoral participation by already enfranchised voters. Five amendments—the Twelfth, which required separate electoral votes for president and vice president;[7] the Twentieth, limiting lame-duck presidencies and Congresses; the Twenty-Second, which imposed a two-term limit on the president; the Twenty-Fifth, clarifying presidential succession; and the Twenty-Seventh, deferring any congressional pay raise until the next Congress was in session—corrected perceived structural flaws in the original democratic text.

Of the five amendments that have nothing to do with improving the democratic process, three are important—the Eleventh, limiting the power of federal courts over state treasuries; the Thirteenth, ending slavery; and the Sixteenth, authorizing the income tax. The Eighteenth and Twenty-First amendments, imposing and repealing prohibition, just take up space on the page.

Despite (or perhaps because of) the repeated use of the amendment process to protect and expand the franchise, the Supreme Court declined for over 180 years to recognize a federal constitutional right to vote or to run for office.[8] While an occasional case invoked the equality norms of the Fourteenth or Fifteenth Amendments in order to invalidate a particularly blatant refusal to permit blacks to vote,[9] no effort was made by the Court until the 1960s to develop a generally applicable constitutional right to participate in the democratic process. As we've seen, one of Justice Brennan's great triumphs in the 1960s was to persuade the Warren Court majority to cobble together a de facto constitutional right to vote based on the protection of equality in the Fourteenth Amendment. Brennan reasoned that if the government allowed one person to vote, denying such a "fundamental right" to someone else required an extremely powerful justification. Using Brennan's equality lever, the Supreme Court quickly eliminated almost every formal impediment to voting, running for office, and equal representation that had plagued American democracy since the founding. Soldiers originally from out of state who were stationed in Texas were granted the right to register and vote in Texas elections.[10] The poll tax was swept away, signaling the end of property qualifications for voting and holding office.[11] Third-party candidates were granted a constitutional right to appear on the ballot.[12] All residents affected by an election were granted an equal right to vote in it.[13] Finally, the Court ended the practice of using durational residence requirements to disenfranchise newcomers.[14]

Even under the Warren Court, however, equality-based democracy protection had its limits. In 1959, literacy was viewed unanimously by the Warren Court as a constitutionally legitimate basis on which to decide who could vote and who could not.[15] The Supreme Court has not found it necessary to revisit the issue because Congress banned literacy tests in the Voting Rights Acts of 1970 and 1975.

Felon disenfranchisement also survived because, in 1974, the newly established Burger Court majority twisted the language of section 2 of the Fourteenth Amendment. All agree that Section 2 of the Fourteenth Amendment was intended to put pressure on Southern states to permit newly freed slaves to vote. In 1868, when the Fourteenth Amendment was adopted, it was politically impossible to rally support for a constitutional amendment guarantying racial minorities the right to vote. That didn't happen until the adoption of the Fifteenth Amendment in 1870. In the meantime, Section 2 provided that "representatives shall be apportioned among the several States" according to "the whole number of persons in each State," but that apportionment must be reduced for any persons whose right to vote in a federal election was "abridged, except for participation in rebellion, or other crime." Although civil rights leaders never got a chance to use Section 2 to reduce the number of representatives from Southern states because the Fifteenth Amendment was adopted within two years, in 1974, Chief Justice Rehnquist twisted the words "rebellion or other crime" in Section 2 to grant affirmative power to states to disenfranchise convicted felons, even though the prison population is—and was—disproportionately black and Latino as the result of systemic racial discrimination in the criminal justice process.[16] So a constitutional amendment designed to help freed slaves has been hijacked as a device to disenfranchise their descendants. Rehnquist ignored the fact that the phrase "rebellion or other crime" as used in section 2 of the Fourteenth Amendment probably referred to unlawful activities in connection with the recent rebellion. Otherwise the word *rebellion* would have no purpose because rebellion was already a crime. That's how Florida gets the power today to disenfranchise 25 percent of its male black voters. Forty years later, we still have not found an effective way to reenfranchise the more than 4 million Americans who cannot vote because of a past criminal conviction.

Despite the literacy blip and the persistence of felon disenfranchisement, if we focus solely on the formal definition of the franchise, Justice Brennan's equality-based protection of democracy looks pretty good, though.[17] Unfortunately, that's where the good democracy news stops.

SUPPRESSING TURNOUT

Even if all formal restrictions on voting were removed, the real-world impact of a universal right to vote would depend on how courts respond to electoral regulations that operate to suppress turnout. Regulation of elections can suppress turnout in three ways: (1) intentional efforts to disenfranchise certain kinds of voters; (2) inadequate consideration of regulations that unnecessarily impede voting; and (3) inaccurate assumptions about the need for and consequences of regulations limiting electoral participation.

Equality-based protection of democracy works pretty well in preventing intentional efforts to keep otherwise qualified folks from voting, but it provides almost no protection against unnecessary or poorly thought out rules that impede voting. Worse, equality-based protection of voting rights turns out to be vulnerable to cynical efforts to suppress turnout that are disguised as legitimate efforts to regulate the electoral process. Sometimes, an intentional effort at suppressing turnout is so transparent that it jumps out of the cake, such as drawing a twenty-eight-sided legislative district obviously designed to exclude black voters[18] or using a phony "grandfather clause" to exempt voters from literacy tests only if their ancestors were entitled to vote before the Civil War.[19] Much of the time, though, election regulations that suppress voter turnout are carefully disguised as "neutral" efforts to deal with an allegedly legitimate issue. For example, the creation of a large district where everyone casts multiple votes to elect multiple representatives can be used to submerge a pocket of black voters within a larger white majority and is often successfully defended as a "neutral" effort to enrich political representation. Similarly, onerous voter identification requirements that disproportionately exclude the poor, such as requiring official voter ID cards or proof of citizenship, are successfully defended as antifraud, devices, even when there's no hint of fraud. Felon disenfranchisement statutes that disproportionately exclude black male voters are defended as efforts to define a trustworthy electorate.

Occasionally the negative impact of a government regulation on voter turnout, like scheduling elections on a workday or requiring voter registration in advance of the election, isn't intentional at all but simply reflects a lack of knowledge or concern about the effect of a given electoral regulation on the working poor. Sometimes, as in literacy tests, a limitation on democratic participation is the result of a good faith mistake about need for a given regulation or a wrong guess as to its consequences.

Justice Brennan's equality-based law of democracy has turned out to be a tolerably effective way to deal with blatantly intentional efforts to prevent otherwise eligible people from voting but an inadequate means of dealing with anything else.

Actually, it isn't Justice Brennan's fault. In 1976, the Supreme Court ruled, over Brennan's dissent, that while the Fourteenth Amendment's Equal Protection Clause bars intentional racial discrimination, it has little or nothing to say about laws that disproportionately harm minorities, as long as the racially discriminatory effect is not intentional.[20] Brennan argued unsuccessfully that statutes carelessly imposing disproportionate burdens on vulnerable groups should be treated no differently than intentional acts of discrimination. He lost, and equality-based protection of democracy lost with him. After 1976, in order to win an equality-based constitutional challenge to a law that impedes voting, it became necessary to prove that the law was motivated by an impermissible legislative purpose. Proving disproportionate racial, gender, political, or economic impact isn't enough. Given how adept politicians are in coming up with neutral-sounding smoke screens—such as avoiding nonexistent voter fraud—far too many cynical exercises in voter suppression fly under the equality-based judicial radar.

Two vignettes demonstrate the real-world limits of equality-based protection of democracy. In my younger days, one of my more pleasant duties was to participate in the Appellate Judges' Seminar held at NYU Law School each summer for newly minted appeals court judges. One particularly enjoyable summer, I was delighted to see considerably more African American judges than usual in attendance. The judges cheerfully explained to me that they were the first black appellate judges elected in Louisiana since Reconstruction ended in 1877. When I asked how this could be so, they told me the story of the seven-member Supreme Court of Louisiana. Five Louisiana Supreme Court justices were (and still are) elected from fixed judicial districts throughout the state, white voters comfortably outnumbering blacks in each district. Two justices were—and are—elected from the City of New Orleans. If the single-member judicial system used elsewhere in the state had been applied in New Orleans, one of the districts would have been black-controlled and almost certainly would have elected Louisiana's first black supreme court justice. Instead, beginning in 1921, Louisiana has elected two supreme court justices at large from a multimember district covering the entire city, so that the city's white majority would control the election of both justices.

How, you are probably asking, could anyone get away with such blatant electoral racism? The answer lies in the insistence by the Supreme Court that black voters challenging the scheme were required to prove that the legislature's decision to use a multimember judicial district in New Orleans was motivated by an intentional desire to limit the power of black voters.[21] So, savvy Louisiana lawmakers told themselves—and everyone else—that the reason for the New Orleans multimember judicial district was to establish a unified urban judicial constituency. And they got away with it for decades, because it was impossible to disprove the legislators' bedtime story.[22]

Years later, I got my own taste of equality-based protection in action. The presidential election of 2000 turned on the disenfranchisement of almost a quarter of Florida's otherwise eligible black male voting population because of past criminal history. In an effort to slam the barn door after the election, or at least repair the door for future elections, I joined a team of Brennan Center lawyers in challenging the constitutionality of Florida's felon disenfranchisement laws. Florida's original felon disenfranchisement provisions were a product of its 1868 constitution. Like Alabama's of 1900, the 1868 Florida felon disenfranchisement provisions had clearly been enacted to undercut the Fourteenth Amendment's guaranty of equal treatment by indirectly suppressing the black vote.[23] Faced in 1868 with an ultimatum—ratify the Fourteenth Amendment or don't rejoin the Union—Florida came up with the ingeniously evil device of ratifying the Equal Protection Clause and then eroding its effect on voting by enacting broad felon disenfranchisement rules that would disproportionately affect black citizens. While some poor whites were disenfranchised, the defined crimes (for instance, not paying debts), coupled with racially discriminatory prosecution patterns, were tailored to ensnare a hugely disproportionate number of blacks. That's just what happened.

In 1974, Florida adopted a new state constitution that, without public debate or discussion, simply reenacted the 1868 felon disenfranchisement provisions almost word-for-word, continuing the disenfranchisement of about 25 percent of Florida's black males. Suing on behalf of several disenfranchised black voters, the Brennan Center argued that reenacting a state constitutional provision that had initially been adopted in order to suppress the black vote and that would continue to disenfranchise a quarter of the state's black male voters could not launder the law's original unconstitutional taint. At a minimum, we argued that Florida had the burden of demonstrating that it had reenacted the originally racist provisions for a legitimate purpose having nothing to do with disenfranchising its black male population. We got nowhere. The Miami federal judge insisted that his hands were tied by the Supreme Court's ruling that a disenfranchised voter must prove discriminatory purpose before invoking the Fourteenth Amendment. It was, he ruled, the job of the black challengers, not the State of Florida, to demonstrate the true motive for the 1868 felon disenfranchisement provision's literal reenactment in 1974. Since the long-dead white politicians who did the deed had been much too shrewd to say anything about why they were reenacting a provision that wiped out a quarter of the state's black male vote, the black voters lost in Miami, just as they had lost in New Orleans.[24] Despite a heroic effort by Judge Rosemary Barkett to shift the burden of proof on racial motive to Florida where it belonged,[25] the full circuit court affirmed the Miami judge, and the Supreme Court didn't even deem the case worthy of review.[26]

Contrast that approach with the Supreme Court's treatment of cases where the white majority actually tries to help minority voters. For most of New York City's history, political power was exercised by shifting coalitions of white voters, with blacks and Hispanics all but left out of the power equation. In 1960, for example, despite a massive black population, Brooklyn had almost no black representation in Congress. In the 1960s and '70s, the electoral map of Brooklyn was repeatedly tweaked in an effort to increase black representation. Wearing my ACLU hat, I helped defend Brooklyn's benign racial reapportionment against a challenge by Orthodox Jews who claimed that their local voting power had been sacrificed to aid blacks. I hated the idea of pitting two politically weak minorities against each other in a scramble for scraps from the majority's table, but I couldn't think of an alternative way to provide blacks in Brooklyn with fair representation in Congress. The tweaked Brooklyn electoral lines barely scraped by with a fragmented 5–4 Supreme Court victory,[27] but the handwriting was on the wall. A few years later, when the white-controlled North Carolina legislature sought to redraw congressional district lines to maximize the likelihood that more blacks would be elected to Congress after a century of racial exclusion, five members of the Supreme Court ruled that such an intentionally benign use of race was unconstitutional racism.[28]

The North Carolina decision may well be doctrinally defensible as a matter of equal-protection jurisprudence. It unleashes withering judicial scrutiny on a purposeful use of race by the government. Even on a purely doctrinal level, though, I believe that the Court erred in refusing to recognize the good faith effort by the white majority to enhance black congressional representation as a justifiable use of racial criteria to correct for past injustices. Whatever its merits as a pure equality case, though, viewed from the perspective of democracy the decision is indefensible. As a matter of democracy, why shouldn't the white political majority be permitted to help marginalized black voters (who had been the target of exclusionary practices for more than a century after emancipation) obtain fair democratic representation as quickly as possible?

So under current equality-based rules protecting democracy, cynical motives often triumph because they can't be proved, while benign motives are penalized. Under Madison's democracy-friendly First Amendment, the outcomes would be reversed. Laws making voting more difficult would be invalidated under a First Amendment that is concerned with the *effect* of a challenged law on voting, not merely its *purpose*, while a law enacted by a white majority making it easier for historically marginalized groups to obtain fair representation would be welcomed as an effort to enhance democratic fairness.

PARTISAN GERRYMANDERING

Once the electorate has been formally defined and the scope of the political majority's power to suppress turnout has been established, the quality of any democracy is dependent on its mechanics.

Unfortunately, as Justice Harlan warned, a formal equality test fails to provide adequate constitutional underpinning for the mechanics of democracy. It turns out that everything can be equally awful.

Under the Supreme Court's formal equality test, the "one person, one vote" rule is vulnerable to the massive partisan and incumbent gerrymandering that has distorted fair representation, rendered votes substantively unequal, and turned far too many American legislative elections into meaningless charades. The problem begins and ends with Justice Brennan's strategic decision to use the Fourteenth Amendment, not the First, as the vehicle to police fair democratic representation. Under pressure from Justice Frankfurter, who insisted that unelected judges lack the capacity to develop a constitutionally enforceable right of fair democratic representation, Justice Brennan fell back on formal mathematical equality. He asked us to imagine two legislative districts—District A with 10 voters and District B with 100 voters, each electing one representative to a legislative body. In such a radically malapportioned world,[29] each voter in District A has a tenth of a say in who wins, while the District B voters have only a hundredth of a say. After doing the math, Brennan triumphantly announced that malapportioned election districts inevitably result in votes of unequal mathematical value. It was as though voters in the sparsely populated rural district had ten votes each, while those in the densely populated urban district each had only one vote.

The math was fine and the outcome welcome, but the Court's failure to recognize a First Amendment principle of fair representation severely weakened the ability of the Constitution to protect the democratic process. The real problem in most malapportionment cases isn't highly attenuated mathematical voting differentials in different districts. Is there any real-world difference between a congressional vote that counts 1/675,000 and one that counts 1/665,000? The real-world problem is that less than 50 percent of the population can wind up controlling much more than 50 percent of the votes in the legislature. That's not merely unequal, it's undemocratic. But without a theory of what it means to have fair representation in a democracy, judges can't confront the problem directly. The fate of the "one person, one vote" test demonstrates the point.

An unintended effect of the "one person, one vote" cases was to require, beginning in 1962, a full-scale redrawing of all legislative lines every ten years to keep pace with population changes reflected in the constitutionally required decennial census. Politicians lost no time in exploiting such a recurring opportunity for self-protection and partisan advantage. Before you could say "one person, one vote," equally populated election districts were being redrawn everywhere with the lines carefully jiggered to make sure that incumbents always won and to maximize the partisan advantage of the political party in power. Democrats gerrymandered California, Texas, and New Jersey. Republicans made a mockery of fair representation in Pennsylvania, taking a swing state with a roughly fifty-fifty party affiliation and delivering more than two thirds of the state's congressional seats to the Republican Party. When Republicans got control of Texas, they did to the Democrats what the Democrats had done to them, resulting in the spectacle of Democratic legislators unsuccessfully trying to hide out in Oklahoma in the hope of preventing a legislative quorum in Texas. In Colorado and Texas, the pols couldn't wait for the ten-year reapportionment bonanza. They decided to rejigger the lines every five years. In recent years, Republicans made a mockery of fair representation in North Carolina and Ohio, packing huge numbers of black Democratic voters into a few landslide districts, enabling white Republicans to win safely, if more narrowly, elsewhere. Democrats hit back in Maryland and Illinois. The best guess is that about half of the Republicans' current thirty-four-seat majority in the House of Representatives is attributable to carefully gerrymandered districts. The partisan gerrymandering toll in state and local legislative elections is far higher. In New York State, for example, the major parties cut a sweetheart deal just after World War II. Election districts in the lower house (the state assembly) were rigged to ensure control by Democrats, while the district lines in the State Senate races were drawn to ensure control by Republicans. Since New York politicians worship at the Church of Our Lady of Perpetual Reapportionment, the New York lines were constantly redrawn over the years so that in a state that swung periodically from Democratic to Republican control and back, Democrats controlled the Assembly and Republicans controlled the Senate for more than a half century. New York's political establishment reached its epiphany when the incumbent legislative reelection rate in the state approached 100 percent.

As the orgy of gerrymandering unfolded, voters implored the Supreme Court to do something about the virtual elimination of contested legislative elections from American democratic life. From a democracy-centered perspective, the Court's response has been appalling. Initially, six justices voted to condemn excessive political gerrymandering as unconstitutional but required a voter seeking judicial help to show that the gerrymander was so extreme she had been effectively excluded from voting.[30] The politicians loved that test because political gerrymandering is never so extreme that it makes it impossible to vote; it just makes it almost impossible for one side to win. After twelve years of futility in the lower courts, during which only one political gerrymander flunked the Court's impossibly strict test, the Court finally withdrew the test, only to substitute something worse.[31] Four Republican justices now argue that courts are wholly incapable of providing equality-based relief against political gerrymanders because it is impossible for judges to set an objective baseline from which to measure deviations from politically fair representation. Four Democratic justices advance three different theories arguing that excessive partisan gerrymandering violates the Equal Protection Clause because it unfairly enhances the voting power of the political majority. Justice Kennedy plays the tease, holding out the theoretical possibility of doing something someday about gerrymandering, possibly under the First Amendment, but never going all the way. The net result has been judicial paralysis and the virtual disappearance of genuinely contested legislative elections from much of the American landscape.

Can you imagine what Madison would say about a democracy without contested legislative elections? Ironically, Senate elections, once the province of state legislatures, are often the only place where citizens have a real choice about whom to elect—and that's only because the pols haven't figured out yet how to gerrymander state lines.

The Supreme Court's self-imposed paralysis has led to a field day for professional politicians, as technology increasingly allows sophisticated political line drawing that lets party leaders and lobbyists divide the electorate into preordained slices, leaving only a few genuinely contestable elections. In effect, the Supreme Court's refusal to deal with partisan gerrymandering has made our democracy even worse than that of ancient Athens, which often substituted random choice of officials by lot for actual elections. Instead of trusting to luck, we empower political bosses and incumbents to choose our representatives for us. Bring back Athenian democracy!

If an alien dropped down from Mars and was asked how to deal with two sets of players in the democratic process—racial minorities emerging from almost four hundred years of exclusion from political power and incumbents deeply embedded in the power structure—a reasonable Martian might say, "Don't let the law help either. Leave them both alone. Now that you finally have a fairly structured democracy, everything will eventually work out for the best."

Another reasonable Martian might say, "Let the law help both. We need the stability and expertise provided by experienced elected officials, and fairness calls for trying to reconstruct the level of minority representation that would have existed but for past racism."

A truly wise Martian would say, "Let powerful incumbents take care of themselves. It's the racial minority that really needs help to balance the books on past exclusion."

Even a foolish Martian would never say, "Design your democracy to lock the powerful incumbents into office, but don't give any help to the racial minority."

Want to bet on what the current Supreme Court says?

SMOKE-FILLED ROOMS

As the Supreme Court sentenced contested legislative elections to death by gerrymander, hope for robust democracy in districts with one-party dominance (natural or artificial) shifted to the nominating process. Even if the general election is a formality, a modicum of democracy still might break out in the primary, where the one-party colossus chooses its nominee. The early Supreme Court precedent was promising. In the 1940s and 1950s, the Supreme Court recognized that the major-party nominating processes are so integral to the general election that, for the purposes of constitutional review, they should be treated as a part of the election itself. So despite the fact that the two major parties are private associations, the Supreme Court treated every part of their nomination process as an integral part of the election itself, even pre-primary private polls. That meant it was unconstitutional to exclude blacks from full participation in the major-party nominating process, no matter how "private" the preliminary proceedings were dressed up to appear.[32] Years later, in 1986, the Court also ruled that Connecticut could not forbid the state Republican Party from opening its primary to independents.[33] From a democracy standpoint, so far, so good.

When the Republican and Democratic political bosses counterattacked, though, the Supreme Court turned Madison's First Amendment *against* democracy. First, the politicians concentrated on neutralizing closed primaries (those open only to party members), arguing that the parties had a First Amendment associational right to protect themselves from "raiding" by hostile outsiders posing as members. Political leaders in New York and Illinois induced the state legislatures they controlled to impose substantial "ideological" waiting periods before a voter was allowed to vote in a closed primary, making it almost impossible for insurgents to recruit new members in order to contest the party bosses' choice of candidate. In 1972, the Supreme Court upheld a New York State law requiring new party members to wait as long as eleven months before they became eligible to vote in a closed Democratic Party primary.[34]

Because New York City is largely a one-party town, missing the Democratic primary is the equivalent of missing the general election. The Supreme Court majority didn't ask whether the waiting period was good or bad for democracy. The majority justices asked only whether, under an equality-based law of democracy, New York had a plausible justification for treating new party members differently from longtime party members. Five justices answered yes, holding that a professed concern over potential interparty raiding was a legitimate reason for requiring new party members to sign up eleven months in advance of the primary, even when the new voters were registering for the first time. Illinois politicians tried to push the ideological waiting period envelope even further, imposing a twenty-three-month voting delay in Mayor Daley's Chicago. That was too much even for the Supreme Court.[35]

In other words, durational residence requirements cannot be imposed on voting in a meaningless general election, the outcome of which has often been preordained by gerrymandering, because waiting periods discriminate against newcomers, but a long waiting period *can* be imposed on the right to vote in the primary election that is the only democratic game in town. Party leaders then reinforced their stranglehold on the nominating process by persuading the Supreme Court that "sore loser" laws, preventing the loser in a major party primary from mounting a third-party or independent challenge in the general election, are constitutional.[36] Thus in the name of political stability, leaders of the two major parties were granted a constitutional license by armchair political scientists dressed as Supreme Court justices to perpetuate their personal power and their duopoly of the electoral process. Maybe Frankfurter was right, after all.

With closed primaries safely neutralized by long ideological waiting periods and sore-loser laws, party leaders turned to undermining two more adventurous efforts to democratize the major-party nominating process—open primaries, in which all registered voters can vote, and blanket primaries, in which all voters pick the major party candidate they wish to nominate for each office in a single, unified primary election. Despite the fact that California's adoption of blanket primaries had increased voter turnout by 10 percent and tended to favor moderates of both parties, the Supreme Court ruled that blanket primaries violated the First Amendment because they allowed nonparty members too much power over the selection of a party's nominee.[37] The Court pumped a little democratic air back into the nominating process by narrowly upholding Washington State's nonpartisan "top two" primary, in which all candidates for a given office are listed on a single ballot and the top two vote getters advance to the general election.[38] The justices warned, though, that evidence of voter confusion over which candidates actually belonged to what party might invalidate the practice.

The Supreme Court's ban on blanket primaries and its equivocal approach to the top-two primary cast doubt on the constitutionality of open primaries, where any voter, regardless of party affiliation, can choose to vote once in one or the other major party's primary. Several lower courts have suggested that open primaries can survive by treating a voter's decision to participate in a party's primary as an "indicia of affiliation," turning the voter into an instant member of the party. Such formalistic nonsense highlights the absurdity of viewing the two major parties as if they were hermetically sealed private associations when they choose their nominees, especially in areas where securing the nomination is tantamount to election.

The Court's insistence on treating major parties as private associations for the purpose of the nominating process even casts doubt on whether political parties can be forced to nominate through primaries at all, instead of allowing the political bosses to choose the candidate in a "smoke-filled room." The justices make almost no effort to harmonize recent cases, which treat the major-party nominating process as a purely private exercise, with earlier cases that treated it as an adjunct of the election itself. The two inconsistent lines of precedent simply run side-by-side on parallel tracks. Being on the wrong track can be fatal to reform efforts. For example, New York State purportedly elects its judges. But the reality is that they are patronage appointments by local Republican and Democratic leaders, ratified by rigged judicial nominating conventions and uncontested general elections where the two major parties often cross-endorse each other's judicial candidates. The lower federal courts put the case on the older track of precedent where the major-party nominating process is viewed as an adjunct of the general election. Both the district court and the Second Circuit had no difficulty recognizing that New York's boss-controlled judicial nominating system denied challengers a fair chance to contest the bosses' choice for the nomination. The Supreme Court simply switched tracks, insisting that the major-party judicial nominating process was a private affair, immune from constitutional review. To add insult to injury, the Court claimed to be protecting the First Amendment associational rights of the very party members who wanted to challenge the nominating process.[39]

The story of the failed effort to pump democracy into the nominating process closes with Oklahoma's decision to forbid a minor political party from inviting members of the two major parties to vote in its primary. Six justices upheld the ban.[40] When the smoke cleared, only independents were able to join with minor-party members in voting in a minor-party primary. Members of the Republican and Democratic parties were imprisoned in their respective ideological spaces. So major parties have a constitutional right to open their primaries to independents and possibly to defecting members of the other major party. But ideological protest parties, seeking to challenge the electoral status quo, can be forbidden from inviting members of the two major parties to vote in their primaries. From a democracy standpoint, it's hard to imagine anything worse.

If political gerrymandering overpowers democracy in the general election and excessive deference to local party bosses erodes democracy at the nominating stage, the only other democratic game in town is competition from third parties. Once again, the early precedents were hopeful. In the nineteenth century, a vibrant third-party political culture posed constant challenges to the major parties. Abraham Lincoln won a four-party race for president in 1860. In 1968, six justices recognized an equality-based constitutional right to ballot access for third parties.[41] Once again, however, equality-based constitutional protection of democracy failed to follow through on its early promise.

Instead of viewing ideologically driven minor parties as dissenting voices with a First Amendment right to participate in the electoral debate, the justices have insisted on treating them as if they were genuine competitors for electoral success. The resulting constitutional doctrine invalidates "unduly burdensome" third-party ballot access regulations but permits rules requiring a showing of significant electoral support before third parties can gain a ballot listing. It forbids participants in a major-party primary from signing a third-party nominating petition. It encourages the major parties (which control the legislatures) to impose the most onerous statutory requirements possible on ballot access for minor-party challengers without triggering the Supreme Court's amorphous constitutional veto.[42] The restrictions typically force minor parties to secure a significant number of signatures on nominating petitions during a relatively short period of time long in advance of the election from a shrinking pool of eligible voters who are allowed to sign only one petition but none at all if they voted or intend to vote in a major-party primary.

But the justices didn't stop there. The key to the nineteenth-century culture of vibrant minor parties was the ability of a minor party to cross-endorse a major-party candidate, giving adherents the ability to cast a vote for the minor party's ideological position while playing a genuine role in the choice of who wins the election. Often a cross-endorsing minor party would poll the deciding votes in an election, opening the way to negotiations on assimilating its ideological positions into the major-party platforms. The power of minor-party cross-endorsements was not lost on the leaders of the major parties. From 1900 to 1910, forty-one states under the control of one or the other of the major parties outlawed cross-endorsements, putting an end to vibrant minor parties in the twentieth century. In 1997, six justices upheld a Minnesota cross-endorsement ban against a minor party that sought to endorse the candidate of the Democratic Party and a Democratic candidate who wished to accept the minor-party endorsement.[43] To make things even worse for democracy, the justices formally recognized a legitimate state interest in preserving the duopoly power of the two major parties.

So under current constitutional ground rules, the two major parties are treated as autonomous private associations whenever political bosses want to prevent outsiders from challenging their powers, but then they morph into protected wards of the state when a minor party threatens the duopoly of the two major parties.

Madison would be aghast.

The Supreme Court has even rejected the last gasp of the alienated voter, the ability to cast a write-in protest ballot. In 1992, a voter in Honolulu wishing to cast a write-in ballot (unfortunately, for Donald Duck) argued that casting a write-in ballot is the quintessential act of political protest. The Supreme Court majority, utterly deaf to Madison's music, rejected the idea that voting is a First Amendment–protected exercise of political expression and association, viewing the casting of a ballot as nothing more than an instrumental means of choosing a public official to govern.[44] Because Donald Duck can't govern, reasoned the Court, you have no First Amendment right to vote for him—or anyone else who can't possibly win. Some instrumental choice: the nomination is rigged by party bosses, the general election is gerrymandered into insignificance, third parties have been strangled, and you can't even cast a write-in protest vote.

FUNDING DEMOCRACY

That brings us, may the gods help us, to the Supreme Court's treatment of campaign finance. As we've seen, by applying the equality-driven law of democracy, the Supreme Court has set the dial on the interplay between motive and democracy at about the worst possible place, encouraging cynics to seek to suppress the vote but discouraging idealists from seeking to undo the continuing political consequences of past racial discrimination. In the political gerrymandering cases, the Court has announced itself powerless to act while political leaders of the two major parties cement incumbents into office, unfairly draw electoral lines to benefit the party in power, and turn genuinely contestable legislative elections into an endangered species. In the major party duopoly cases, the Court has surrendered control of the major party nominating process to the political leaders of the two major parties, blocked minor parties from challenging the major parties' hegemony, and failed even to protect write-in protest voting. But it is in the campaign financing cases that the Supreme Court has reached its democratic low point. If a sworn enemy of democracy had been given the task of designing our campaign funding system, that enemy could not have done a better job of sabotaging Madison's music than Frankfurter's armchair political scientists wearing black judicial robes.

In 1974, in the wake of Watergate and the ugly campaign-spending scandals during the Nixon administration, political momentum built in Congress for an effort to reform the excessive role of big money in American politics. Instead of a genuine reform bill, though, Congress sought to purge almost all money from elections, a "reform" that just happened to coincide with the best interests of powerful incumbents. Election spending by presidential candidates was capped at two thirds of the paltry amount spent in 1972 by George McGovern in the worst presidential loss of the twentieth century. Congressional campaign spending was similarly capped at unrealistically low levels. Campaign contributions were limited to $1,000 per candidate per election. Election spending by independent supporters of a candidate was capped at less than the cost of a quarter-page ad in the *New York Times*. Finally, candidates of the two major parties were to receive discriminatory subsidies that were unavailable to independents and third parties.

In short, under Congress's 1974 "reform" agenda, it would have been illegal to spend enough money to oust an incumbent, and the duopoly of the two major parties would be reinforced. I joined a team of ACLU lawyers challenging the reform statute on behalf of, among other folks, James Buckley, the Conservative Party senator from New York. I focused my efforts on the unfairness of using discriminatory public subsidies to further cement the hegemony of the two major parties. Predictably, that argument lost. The Supreme Court didn't break a sweat in upholding the discriminatory subsidies. Only Chief Justice Rehnquist agreed with me. The Court also upheld the ceiling of $1,000 (now $2,600) on campaign contributions to a candidate in connection with a given election. Because most election cycles include two elections—a primary election and a general election—the current de facto ceiling in any election cycle is usually $5,200 per candidate. The *Buckley* Court also upheld aggregate ceilings on the total amount that any donor could contribute to all candidates and political parties in a given election cycle (now $123,200), but the current Supreme Court, reversing that part of *Buckley*, struck down the aggregate limits, leaving only the individual candidate ceiling of $5,200 in effect.[45] It is now possible, therefore, for a single billionaire to contribute unlimited sums to political parties and multicandidate committees, as long as no candidate gets more than $5,200. Given the substantial number of eligible candidates and other eligible political entities, by my count, a donor can now cut a check to party officials for up to $3.2 million in connection with each election cycle, and leave it to them to distribute the largesse.[46]

Having upheld limits on campaign contributions to individual candidates, the *Buckley* Court then went on to strike down Congress's effort to place ceilings on how much a candidate, or an independent supporter or opponent of a candidate, could spend on trying to influence the outcome of an election. The net result of upholding the half of the law limiting contributions while striking down the other half regulating spending was a campaign finance system that no rational person would have chosen and that not a single member of Congress had supported.[47] Without considering its impact on democracy, the *Buckley* Court created a hybrid campaign finance system for candidates and political parties that limits the supply of campaign cash raised through contributions, but leaves demand wholly unregulated. In effect, the justices built a campaign finance system that unwittingly replicates the nation's catastrophic approach to heroin and cocaine—concentrate all your efforts on interdicting supply but pay little or no attention to reducing demand. It doesn't work for drugs. It doesn't work for campaign financing.

Worse, because independent spending was left wholly immune from regulation, ideological outliers unconnected to the candidates or the two major political parties were given a huge financial advantage. Welcome to the Koch brothers, who have spent countless millions seeking to control our political agenda and influence our elections. If anything good can be said about the Supreme Court's recent invalidation of aggregate contribution limits, it is that the 650 billionaires who hit the aggregate contribution ceiling in the last election can now purchase undue influence directly from a political party, so now party officials can get their hands on some of the big money that was being spent independently. Maybe that will enable party leaders, who tend to seek to build broad coalitions needed to win elections, to stand up to big-spending ideologues like the Koch brothers. But that's where the good news ends. It's now a regime of "one dollar, one vote." Billionaires have a choice: they can buy undue influence independently, à la carte, or purchase it directly from party leaders in a prix fixe deal.

The *Buckley* Court's decision to approve stringent limits on campaign contributions to individual candidates but strike down *all* limits on campaign spending rests on a series of fiercely contested propositions of law that, taken together, have been a democratic disaster. First, the Supreme Court ruled that the act of spending money to elect a candidate is a form of "pure speech," entitled to the highest level of "strict scrutiny" free-speech protection. Eight years before *Buckley*, the Supreme Court had ruled that the act of burning a draft card to protest the Vietnam War was not pure speech but rather "communicative conduct" entitled to only a watered-down level of First Amendment protection.[48] Sixteen years after *Buckley*, moreover, the Court ruled that the act of attempting to cast a write-in protest vote isn't even communicative conduct, much less pure speech, and is not entitled to any First Amendment protection at all. Why the *act* of spending gobs of money to sway an election is "pure speech" but the *acts* of burning a draft card and casting a write-in protest ballot are not is a secret known only to certain members of the Supreme Court.

Deciding whether a political contribution is pure speech or communicative conduct is more than just an exercise in semantics. The level of First Amendment protection depends on which box you check. If, like a majority of the Supreme Court, you check the pure-speech box, you trigger First Amendment strict scrutiny, a lethal form of judicial review that requires the government to prove that the regulation at issue is the "least drastic means" of advancing a "compelling" government interest in preventing a grievous and immediate harm. The government almost never wins a First Amendment strict-scrutiny case. On the other hand, if you choose the communicative-conduct box, the regulation will be upheld if it is a "narrowly tailored," good-faith effort to advance a "substantial" governmental interest unrelated to the suppression of speech. As the draft card–burning case illustrates, the government usually wins under the less stringent standard of review. Unlike the Fourteenth Amendment equality cases discussed earlier, which require a showing of impermissible purpose, First Amendment strict-scrutiny cases are decided on the basis of the law's *effect*, not its *purpose*. Good intentions just don't count. Not surprisingly, in the thirty-eight years since unlimited campaign spending was equated with pure speech, no effort to limit campaign spending has breached the strict-scrutiny wall.

To defend the *Buckley* Court's position that money literally "talks," Justice Brennan compared a political campaign to an automobile and campaign spending to the gas in the tank. Because a candidate's campaign can travel only as far as the cash in its tank will take it, Justice Brennan reasoned that campaign spending is so integrally related to campaign speech that it must receive identical First Amendment protection. But an election is not a drive in the country. It's a race. Who'd bother to get excited about a race that depended on which pit crew had more gas? Moreover, education is also crucial to being able to speak effectively, as is access to mass media, but no one argues, alas, that poor people have a First Amendment right to an adequate education or access to the mass media.

Justice Stevens, who didn't participate in *Buckley*, never accepted the Court's decision to treat money as pure speech. Despite his repeated protests, however, the flawed analysis that equates the unlimited spending of money with pure speech has been cemented into Supreme Court precedent, making it all but impossible to stem the tide of big money engulfing our democracy.

Second, the *Buckley* Court held that preventing massive wealth-driven electoral inequality is not a "compelling governmental interest" that would justify placing reasonable limits on runaway campaign spending by the superrich. Defenders of campaign finance reform had argued that even if spending money is equated with pure speech, maintaining a modicum of political equality between the 1 percent and the rest of us is a sufficiently important interest to qualify as "compelling," even under First Amendment strict scrutiny. The Supreme Court has never confronted that argument head-on. Instead, the majority has argued that limiting the electoral spending of the superrich is not the "least drastic means" of dealing with economically driven political inequality. Subsidizing the weak speaker, reasons the Court's majority, is a less drastic way to advance political equality. But in a move that smacks of hypocrisy, the five Republican justices then ruled that public campaign subsidies cannot be "matched" to the spending of a privately funded candidate because that would "penalize" the private candidate for exercising his First Amendment right to raise and spend unlimited amounts of money. Why it is an unconstitutional "penalty" to make a wealthy candidate operate on a level electoral playing field is another secret known only to the five Republican members of the Supreme Court.

How can it be that protection of the two major parties from competition justifies laws preventing minor parties from cross-endorsing a major party candidate or from inviting members of the major parties to vote in the minor parties' primaries, but laws seeking to preserve a modicum of political equality between the massively wealthy and the rest of us are unconstitutional?

Even worse, the Court ruled that spending (or, as the Court puts it, *expending*) money, either as a candidate or as an "independent" supporter or opponent of a candidate, is a "direct" exercise of "pure speech" that is entitled to the highest level of First Amendment protection, but *contributing* money to a candidate is an "indirect" form of speech, entitled to slightly less First Amendment protection.

Building on that paper-thin distinction, the Court ruled that preventing actual or apparent electoral "corruption" is a compelling governmental interest that justifies limiting the size and source of campaign *contributions* (viewed as a less protected indirect form of speech), but does not justify limiting campaign *expenditures* (viewed as direct "pure speech") by candidates or by independent wealthy supporters or opponents. The Court defended this razor-thin distinction by arguing that a contribution is usually preceded by contact between the candidate and the prospective donor, creating fertile ground for corrupt quid pro quo deals, whereas independent expenditures usually take place without any contact between the candidate and the supporter. The absence of prior contact, argues the Court, insulates such expenditures, no matter how large, from the risk of corruption. In the only field, though, the justices really know anything about—judging—the Court recognizes that when a litigant independently *expends* millions of dollars to get a judge elected, the judge cannot sit on the litigant's case because a grateful judge might tilt, even subconsciously, in favor of his massive benefactor.[49] Why a similar risk does not infect grateful legislators, mayors, or presidents is yet another secret known only to a majority of the justices.

By treating independent campaign *expenditures* much more favorably than campaign *contributions* to a candidate, the Court undermined the ability of candidates (and political parties) to define their own political agendas, licensing "independent" ideological outriders to spend unlimited funds to dominate the electoral agenda, while candidates must struggle to raise tightly regulated contributions. In the end, therefore, the *Buckley* Court upheld limits on the size of campaign contributions, upheld the discriminatory presidential public financing scheme, but struck down Congress's effort to place ceilings on electoral spending by candidates and independent players supporting or opposing the candidate. The decision left us with a judge-made campaign finance system that turns American democracy over to ideologues in the top 1 percent of the economic tree, a system that no legislator has ever supported and one that would astound the Founders.

Over the next thirty-eight years, the Court's Republican majority repeatedly doubled down on each of the four mistakes, leaving us today with a campaign financing system that can be described only as grotesque. Candidates are trapped in a financial arms race, unable to stop raising campaign money because they fear being outspent by an opponent, but they're forced to raise the desperately needed money in dribs and drabs from contributors subject to a statutory maximum of $5,200 per candidate. In the campaign finance world the Supreme Court has made, ideological outriders unconnected to the campaign exercise disproportionate influence because they are constitutionally guaranteed the right to raise and spend as much money as they wish. The unending search for high-dollar "independent" supporters has shifted the balance of power from the candidates to wealthy outsiders who police the candidate's views by not so subtly threatening to turn off the money machine. And into that already deeply dysfunctional world, the five Republican justices have now parachuted the vast trove of corporate wealth, vesting massive for-profit corporations with the free-speech right to spend unlimited campaign funds on the eve of an election, as long as the spending is "independent" of the candidate's campaign.[50]

Tell the truth. If you tried, could you have come up with a worse way to structure and finance our democracy? If the answer is yes, you may be a candidate for the next Republican Supreme Court vacancy.

A SNAPSHOT OF OUR DYSFUNCTIONAL DEMOCRACY IN ACTION

The first decade of the twenty-first century opened and closed with three bitterly contested Supreme Court decisions that illustrate the limits of grounding constitutional protection of American democracy solely on the Equal Protection Clause of the Fourteenth Amendment rather than Madison's democracy-friendly First Amendment. In *Bush v. Gore*, five Republican justices awarded the 2000 presidential election to the Republican candidate, George W. Bush, by declining to permit Florida to complete a recount of disputed presidential ballots ordered by the Supreme Court of Florida. The Republican justices claimed to fear that continuation of the court-ordered recount would delay the state's formal certification of Florida's Electoral College winners beyond a "safe harbor" date insulating timely state certifications from congressional challenge. Had the Florida recount continued past the "safe harbor" date, and had Al Gore been declared the winner, the fear was that the Republican-controlled state legislature would have designated its own slate of Bush electors, forcing Congress to choose between conflicting judicial and legislative slates.[51]

In *Crawford v. Marion County* in 2006, six Justices upheld an Indiana voter ID law ostensibly aimed at preventing voter fraud despite a showing that the photo-ID requirement would disproportionately disenfranchise poor, unsophisticated voters, and that no case of fraudulent identity had ever been reported in an Indiana election.[52]

And in *Citizens United v. FEC* in 2010, five Republican Justices ruled that for-profit corporations enjoy a First Amendment right to spend unlimited sums to affect an election, reinforcing the stranglehold on the democratic process that the Court had already given to the superrich in *Buckley*.

Critics have launched powerful critiques of all three cases. Many have noted the artificially rigid equality analysis in the *Bush v. Gore* majority opinion, which destroyed a presidential election in order to save it, and the majority's radical departure from traditional federalism principles in depriving Florida of the final decision about whether to take the risks inherent in continuing its court-ordered recount beyond the "safe harbor" date. Others have noted the toothless standard of review in *Crawford* in an area where precedent—and respect for Madison's music—seemed to require a much more searching review of Indiana's justification for imposing yet another disproportionate burden on the poor's right to vote. If possible, *Citizens United* is even more vulnerable to doctrinal critique.

Justice Kennedy, writing for five justices, assumes that seven isolated and truncated words in the Free Speech clause, "Congress shall make no law abridging speech," provide the only relevant legal guidance. He then begs the central question in the case by asserting that the case involves the constitutionality of discriminating between two *similarly situated* categories of speakers—corporate speakers and individual speakers. Experience teaches that discrimination between similarly situated speakers is often motivated by hostility toward the disfavored speaker, so Justice Kennedy was surely correct in recognizing that courts are justifiably suspicious about government regulations treating First Amendment speakers differently. But the threshold issue in *Citizens United* was whether corporations (especially huge for-profit corporations) and human beings are "similarly situated" First Amendment speakers in the first place. The favored status of the for-profit business corporation—an artificial state-created legal fiction vested with unlimited life, entity shielding, limited shareholder liability, negotiable shares, and highly favorable rules encouraging the acquisition, accumulation, and retention of other people's money—raises important questions about whether corporate and noncorporate speakers really are "similarly situated."

Justice Kennedy's opinion in *Citizens United* simply begs that crucial question. He ignores the fact that more than a century ago, the Court ruled that for-profit business corporations fall outside the protection of the Fifth Amendment's right to remain silent because corporations lack the attributes of human dignity that underlie the privilege against self-incrimination.[53] That's still the law.[54] Justice Kennedy himself has ruled that big corporations can't take the Fifth. Where huge for-profit corporations are concerned, why should the First Amendment's Free Speech clause be read so differently from the Fifth Amendment's right to remain silent?[55]

It is no answer to point to the Court's nineteenth-century decision to treat corporations as legal "persons" for the purposes of constitutional protection under the Due Process and Equal Protection clauses of the Fourteenth Amendment. Since we invented the for-profit business corporation to unleash its economic potential, it makes good sense to hold that the investors in a corporate enterprise enjoy corporate constitutional protection against irrational or discriminatory economic regulation of the enterprise. It is, however, a huge and unsupported jump to vest for-profit corporations with noneconomic constitutional protections that flow from respect for human dignity—like free speech, religious conscience, or the right to remain silent. A robot has no soul. Neither does a for-profit business corporation. Vesting either with constitutional rights premised on human dignity is legal fiction run amok. Corporations can prey, but they can't pray.

Nor is it persuasive to argue that because for-profit press corporations like the *New York Times* and the components of Rupert Murdoch's press empire enjoy First Amendment protection, for-profit corporations having nothing to do with the press must also be vested with First Amendment rights to spend unlimited sums on electoral speech. When it comes to spending corporate treasury funds for electoral speech, press corporations are treated just like any other corporation. Congress has forbidden them from doing it. Press corporations receive favored First Amendment protection only for their press activities. The unique constitutional protection afforded to the business of the press—it's the only business mentioned in the Constitution—flows from Madison's insertion of a separate Free Press Clause into the First Amendment. Madison recognized that free speech in a robust democracy requires an institution devoted to its widespread dissemination. That institution is the press. Respect for the structure of Madison's First Amendment renders it impossible, therefore, to transpose the instrumental protection of the press into a general protection of speech by huge profit-making corporations having nothing to do with the business of disseminating speech to mass audiences.

Nor is commercial speech by corporations a persuasive analogy. The fact that the Supreme Court has recognized a limited First Amendment right to commercial speech not only fails to support a general right of corporate electoral free speech; it cuts strongly against recognizing such a right. Precisely because business corporations lack the dignitary status needed to justify a constitutional right to free expression, the Supreme Court has recognized that commercial free-speech rights belong not to the advertiser speakers but to the consumers, the hearers, enabling them to receive information needed to make rational market choices. Consumer-centered commercial free-speech protection is confined to speech that actually helps consumers to make rational market choices, so commercial speech may be regulated in ways that would never be permitted in the first-class political-speech compartment—most important, on grounds of truth or falsity, and to prevent harm to consumers and the market.[56]

Finally, the fact that grassroots political groups organized as nonprofit corporations enjoy free-speech rights says nothing about whether huge, multishareholder for-profit corporations should be treated the same way. Grassroots nonprofits are relatively small groups of flesh and blood persons who have associated in corporate form to advance a political idea. Because all members of the group share a common interest in pursuing a defined political goal, allowing the nonprofit corporation to speak for them is a far cry from letting Citibank's managers decide which candidate Citibank's shareholders, depositors, and employees should support in a particular election.[57] Justice Kennedy seems to have been clearly wrong, therefore, in assuming that corporations and human beings are "similarly situated" speakers.

Justice Kennedy rejected the argument that letting corporations throw a ton of money on the electoral scales would give them excessive influence over the grateful winner, noting that the Court has consistently ruled (incorrectly, I believe) that independent expenditures on behalf of a candidate do not pose a risk of corruption because no communication between candidate and supporter occurs prior to the expenditure. Never mind what happens after the election when the successful candidate is deeply beholden to his financial angel. Never mind that when elected judges are concerned, Justice Kennedy himself recognizes an unacceptable risk of bias.

While it is tempting to continue to pound on the three cases' doctrinal shortcomings, critics like me can never prove that, viewed solely as equality cases, they were wrongly decided. In *Bush v. Gore*, seven justices, including Souter and Breyer, were persuaded that unconstitutionally unequal criteria were being applied in different Florida counties in connection with the recount of the contested presidential ballots. They disagreed only with the five-justice majority's decision to prevent Florida from continuing the recount beyond the safe-harbor deadline under corrected, uniform criteria. Even the intensely political decision by five Republican justices to end the Florida recount, while deeply problematic as a matter of federalism and disastrous as a matter of democracy, was ostensibly based on a fear that unless Florida acted immediately to certify a winner, the congressional safe-harbor period designed to insulate state presidential electoral results from congressional challenge would expire, possibly setting off a congressional free-for-all that might have resulted in disenfranchising the entire state, as well as destabilizing the American presidency in a world dependent on the anchor of American power.

In *Crawford*, six justices held that preventive antifraud protections like photo IDs for voters are constitutional even though they fall with disproportionate severity on the poor and were not shown to be necessary to deal with an existing problem. I think that the Court applied an unduly weak standard of review in *Crawford* (much weaker than the standard used to test the Florida recount in *Bush v. Gore*, and much weaker than the standard envisioned by Justice Brennan), but that's a risk you take when you invoke the notoriously unstable Equal Protection Clause and require proof of an impermissible purpose.

Finally, in *Citizens United*, longtime First Amendment stalwarts including the ACLU have applauded Justice Kennedy's opinion as a great victory for free speech because it resulted in a net increase in the amount of speech in circulation.

Thus while I believe passionately that all three cases got the legal doctrine wrong, I cannot deny that reasonable people with different values might disagree. There is, however, a level of critique applicable not only to *Bush v. Gore*, *Crawford*, and *Citizens United*, but to the full range of judicial decisions that have shaped the contours of American democracy for the past half century—a critique based on Madison's democracy-friendly First Amendment. As the heated exchange between Chief Justice Roberts and Justice Breyer in *McCutcheon*, the case invalidating aggregate limits on massive campaign contributions, demonstrates, under current constitutional ground rules American judges confronted with a case having significant implications for the functioning of American democracy are not required—indeed, they may not even be permitted—to ask whether the outcome is good or bad for democracy. Rather, at least since Justice Brennan's fateful strategic decision not to confront Felix Frankfurter directly in the "one person, one vote" cases, American judges are expected to resolve democracy cases by pigeonholing them into one or another formal legal category, such as Equal Protection, Free Speech, or Freedom of Association, having nothing intrinsic to do with the quality of democracy. The fact is that for more than fifty years Supreme Court justices operating inside doctrinal silos have shaped the quality of American democracy without once asking what kind of democracy they were building. The result has been and is an accidental, highly dysfunctional political system cobbled together by judges wearing blinders. American democracy has become that accidental house I mentioned earlier, an M.C. Escher nightmare of illusory passages and stairways to nowhere. It is long past time to bring concern over the quality of our democracy back into the judicial equation.

American judges are fully capable of recovering the music in Madison's democracy-friendly First Amendment, just as they have been capable of developing judge-made rules governing the separation of powers and American federalism. The United States Constitution rests on three structural pillars: *separation of powers* between the legislative, executive, and judicial branches of government; principles of *federalism* allocating power between the state and federal governments; and Madisonian *democracy* providing for robust, egalitarian self-government. It is tragic that the Supreme Court has been willing and able to forge a constitutional jurisprudence of federalism and separation of powers, despite the lack of explicit guidance in the constitutional text, but has shied away from giving constitutional meaning to the textual protection of democracy that is the essence of Madison's First Amendment.

When cases such as *Bush v. Gore*, *Crawford*, and *Citizens United* are viewed through the lens of Madison's democracy-centered narrative, they are revealed as judicially imposed democratic disasters. Cutting off the Florida recount at the insistence of five Republican justices resulted in a judicially imposed Republican president. Forcing poor voters to obtain a voter ID in a political system like Indiana's, where voter fraud is unknown, is merely a cynical device to suppress their vote. Finally, unleashing unlimited electoral spending by for-profit corporations exacerbates the already excessive power exercised by the superrich over our political life. From a democracy standpoint, it can't get much worse.

Properly read, Madison's great First Amendment poem to democracy would never accept a judicially imposed president, the cynical disenfranchisement of the weak, the elimination of contested legislative elections, or the rule of "one dollar, one vote."

6

The Democracy-Friendly First Amendment in Action

Remember that Madison's First Amendment narrates the odyssey of a democratic idea, (1) born in the conscience of a free citizen protected against government interference by the Establishment and Free Exercise Clauses and proceeding through: (2) *freedom of speech* (the public articulation of the idea); (3) *freedom of the press* (mass dissemination of the idea to the general public); (4) *freedom of assembly* (collective action on behalf of the idea); and (5) *freedom to petition for a redress of grievances* (insertion of the idea into the formal processes of democratic lawmaking). Remember, as well, that Madison's Ninth Amendment authorizes American judges to use a disciplined mix of text, analogy, and necessity to recognize nontextual rights in the "equity" of the First Amendment. That's just what Justice Harlan did when he recognized the existence of nontextual protections of freedom of association and freedom of secular conscience immanent in Madison's constitutional text.

MADISON'S FIRST AMENDMENT RIGHT TO VOTE

When you put Madison's carefully structured textual depiction of democracy in the First Amendment together with his Ninth Amendment grant of power to judges to use the equity of the statute to define nontextual rights needed to make the process work better, the result is judicial recognition of a First Amendment right to vote. We should replace or at least supplement the equality-based approach to protecting democracy used by the Supreme Court for the past fifty years with a First Amendment–based constitutional right to vote, run for office, and receive fair legislative representation. The Supreme Court has often recognized the rhetorical relationship between voting and the First Amendment—often by referring to the right to vote as a precondition to the enjoyment of all other rights. It has even tiptoed up to treating the right to vote and to run for office as rooted in the First Amendment.[1] But the Court has never formally treated voting as the ultimate act of political expression and association. Instead, it has clung to equality as the only constitutional basis for enforcing rights to participate in the democratic process. That should not, however, prevent the current Court from rethinking the relationship between the text of Madison's First Amendment and a constitutional right to participate in the democratic process. Equality-based protection is useful, but it's no substitute for an individual First Amendment right to vote. Billie Holiday was right: "Momma may have, Poppa may have, / But God bless the child that's got his own."

Once the internal rhythm of the First Amendment is understood as the story of a democratic idea that is born in a free conscience (Establishment and Free Exercise) and moves through articulation (Speech), dissemination (Press), collective action (Association and Assembly), and formal presentation to lawmakers (Petition), a First Amendment right to participate in choosing the lawmakers is precisely the kind of implied right that should be recognized as part of the equity of the First Amendment. As we've seen, the Supreme Court has already used the Madisonian safety net built into the Ninth Amendment to recognize nontextual First Amendment rights to freedom of secular conscience and freedom of association, nontextual Fourth and Fifth Amendment mandates to exclude unlawfully obtained evidence and involuntary custodial confessions from criminal trials, nontextual rights derived from the Fifth and Sixth Amendments requiring the government to prove each element of a crime to a jury beyond a reasonable doubt, and an extratextual reading of the Due Process Clause of the Fourteenth

Amendment as imposing most of the Bill of Rights on the states. In recent years, the Court has recognized nontextual privacy rights in personal autonomy and gender equity derived from the Due Process and Equal Protection Clauses in order to protect a right to contraception,[2] a woman's right to choose whether to bear a child,[3] an extended family's right to live together,[4] a human being's right to express his or her own sexuality,[5] and a person's to enter into intimate personal relationships like marriage.[6] Finding a nontextual constitutional right to vote latent in the equity of the First Amendment's disciplined narrative of democracy in action should be a judicial walk in the park.

Shifting to a First Amendment–based protection of democracy would have immediate practical benefits. Most important, it would eliminate the need to prove improper purpose in challenging the constitutionality of government regulations that make it harder to vote or to run for office. The Supreme Court has made it clear that First Amendment speech protection is triggered by effect, not purpose. Under a First Amendment right to vote, there would be no more democratic fiascos like Louisiana's decades-long defense of a multimember judicial district for New Orleans designed to prevent the election of a black supreme court justice, or like Florida's mysterious reenactment of racist felon disenfranchisement laws to preserve a statewide Republican voting majority. No more games in Republican-controlled states where cynical legislators impose onerous voter ID laws, proof-of-citizenship requirements, or other restrictive laws governing the voting process that just happen to depress the vote among the poor. No more long lines at voting booths in poor neighborhoods likely to vote Democratic. Each such assault on democracy would violate the Madisonian First Amendment right to vote.

Not only would a shift to a First Amendment right to vote get rid of the need to prove improper purpose; it would also substitute First Amendment strict scrutiny for the often toothless standard of review currently used in many Fourteenth Amendment equality-based democracy cases. When the Supreme Court ruled that spending money was a form of pure speech, it sentenced campaign spending reform to a lingering death, because under First Amendment strict scrutiny any interference with pure speech requires the government to prove: that a "compelling" problem exists requiring immediate regulatory action; that the proposed government regulation will actually solve or abate the problem; and that no "less drastic means" short of government censorship is available to deal with the problem. Imagine what voting rights law would look like if every government regulation that depressed voter turnout or the ability to run for office had to run the gauntlet of First Amendment strict scrutiny. No more eleven-month waiting periods to vote in a major party primary. No more bans on cross-endorsements by minor parties. No more cynical hurdles designed to keep third parties and independents from challenging the legally reinforced major-party duopoly.

Instead, a robust democracy that dances to Madison's music.

ENDING "ONE DOLLAR, ONE VOTE"

As we've seen, from the standpoint of democracy, campaign finance law can't get much worse. Billionaire oligarchs have a First Amendment stranglehold on the electoral process. Wealthy ideologues on the left and right dominate the electoral agenda. Huge for-profit corporations are guaranteed the power to pour unlimited sums into buying political influence. Public officials and candidates spend most of their time trolling for support from wealthy donors, who often view campaign contributions as economic investments. Political investors can now choose whether to buy influence directly, with checks to specific leaders, or indirectly, as independent spenders.. Election winners repay their wealthy supporters with excessive political influence; election losers mortgage their souls trying to persuade investors to bankroll their comebacks. Giant loopholes in the disclosure rules let wealthy individuals and corporations spend huge sums in secret to manipulate unwitting voters, and well-meaning legislators are forbidden to break the economic stranglehold of the rich by using the most efficient form of campaign subsidy—matching public funds tailored to the sums raised by privately funded opponents.

Bad as things are, though, there is a beam of sunlight. The law that has generated our appalling current campaign finance structure rests on constitutional quicksand. Five members of the Supreme Court have brought American democracy to this parlous state by tearing the Free Speech Clause from the rest of the First Amendment's carefully structured text and reading it as though it were a freestanding legal command without context or roots in a comprehensive First Amendment devoted to the celebration of democracy. Worse, the five Republican justices distort the very slice of the text they claim to revere, treating the Free Speech Clause as if it read "Congress shall make no law . . . abridging speech." By ignoring the words *the freedom of*, the five Republican justices have turned the clause into a simplistic deregulation device that disables the government from protecting the very democracy the Free Speech Clause was intended to serve.

The term "the freedom of speech" as used in Madison's First Amendment has no intrinsic literal meaning. Like any abstract legal concept, it must be given precise meaning by human judgment. That's why threats, blackmail, extortion, false statements causing harm, obscenity, and "fighting words" are treated by the Court as outside "the freedom of speech." Once the governing text is expanded from seven to ten words, and once the ten words are read as part of Madison's great poem to democracy, there is absolutely no reason to include the act of spending unlimited sums of money to influence the outcome of an election as within "the freedom of speech." At a minimum, it would be demoted to "communicative conduct," entitled to significant First Amendment protection but subject to good-faith regulation aimed at advancing two substantial government interests in making democracy work—reinforcing the commitment to political equality recognized in the "one person, one vote" cases and preventing the reality or appearance of corrupting the political system.

Reinforcing political equality is unquestionably a substantial government interest. The Supreme Court has suggested that it is even "compelling." Once the act of spending money is demoted from "pure speech" to "communicative conduct," the government would be permitted to place reasonable limits on campaign spending without being obliged to exhaust impracticable "less drastic means," like subsidies, especially now that the Supreme Court has placed the most efficient form of subsidy—matching grant—constitutionally off limits. Actually, using subsidies instead of spending limits would become much easier, because under a democracy-friendly First Amendment it would be impossible to characterize a matching campaign subsidy system aimed at leveling the electoral playing field as a "penalty" on wealthy candidates.

Reasonable campaign spending limits would also prevent electoral corruption in at least two important ways. It would prevent "independent" supporters from pouring so much money into a campaign that the winner can't help feeling a sense of obligation (and a hope of future support) that causes her to tilt in the direction suggested by the huge supporter. We already recognize such a possibility in the contribution process. That's why the size of a contribution is limited. We already recognize such a possibility in the context of judicial elections. That's why judges can't sit on cases involving folks who spent a fortune to get them elected. The same reasoning calls for reasonable limits on all campaign spending by wealthy independent donors.

Equally important, a generous campaign spending cap would end the current campaign spending spiral that drives each candidate into a never-ending effort to raise funds out of fear that he will be outspent by an opponent. As we learned during the Cold War nuclear standoff with the Soviet Union, such a spiral forces both parties into frenzied action designed to avoid yielding an advantage to the other, even when neither wishes to act. A generous spending cap would permit both sides to relax and to focus on substance once the cap was reached. It would also eliminate the potentially corrupt bargaining power exerted by a supporter as a campaign draws to a close and the candidate gets really desperate. In fact, a generous spending cap would make all contributions fungible, allowing a candidate to spurn support from a donor seeking undue influence because the cap could be achieved using alternative sources.

Demoting campaign spending from pure speech to communicative conduct would not deprive it of all First Amendment protections. No regulation could be "viewpoint driven" in an effort to weaken disfavored speech. Spending limits could not be unreasonably low. But reasonable efforts to cap campaign spending at a generous level (far higher than the unreasonably low ceilings imposed in the 1974 act that were struck down in *Buckley*) would ensure vigorously contested political campaigns without surrendering our democracy to the tender mercies of the superrich.

REDISCOVERING THE IDEA OF CONTESTED LEGISLATIVE ELECTIONS

Madison's democracy-friendly First Amendment would also provide a desperately needed antidote to the epidemic of political gerrymandering that has sucked the air out of our state and federal legislative elections. Widespread gerrymandering at every level of American government has made it almost impossible to topple a legislative incumbent powerful and wily enough to tailor-make a district that can't be lost. Constant gerrymandering of legislative districts virtually guarantees the reelection of incumbents and gives the party in power a disproportionate share of the legislative seats. In the 2012 elections for the House of Representatives, for example, Republicans won a comfortable 234–201 majority, despite being outpolled nationally by more than one million votes in House races. While a slice of the extra one million votes was in urban districts overwhelmingly won by Democrats, as many as 15 seats of the Republican 33-seat margin are traceable to the adroit drawing of congressional district lines to maximize Republican voting power. And 2012 wasn't an aberration. Using the criteria of the American Political Science Association, partisan gerrymandering by both parties has resulted in a House of Representatives where only about 40 seats—fewer than 10 percent of the membership—are chosen in a genuinely contested general election. No wonder the House is so dysfunctional. Most members don't have to worry about being reelected. No wonder so many people don't bother to vote in midterm "elections." They know almost all of the outcomes in advance.

Under the current equality-driven constitutional law of democracy, five members of the Supreme Court insist that there is nothing judges can do to prevent politicians from slicing and dicing the electoral map to ensure the reelection of incumbents, moving voters around like pawns on a chessboard to maximize the advantage of the party in power. In order to know whether political line drawing is unconstitutionally unequal, the majority justices argue, you need an objective baseline from which to measure whether the political gerrymander at issue deviates too far from representative fairness. The five Republican justices claim to be unable to find such a baseline.

The four Democratic justices argue that a fair baseline exists, but they can't agree on what it is. Several of them argue that a reviewing court could ask whether the statewide outcome of an allegedly gerrymandered legislative election roughly reflects the political preferences of the electorate measured by statewide pre-election party registration figures. If the deviation is too great—say, more than 10 or 15 percent—a court could order that the electoral lines be redrawn to more fairly reflect the political complexion of the electorate. The five Republican justices reject such a test, arguing that pre-election registration figures are an inadequate measurement of a postelection fair political outcome because the very essence of democratic politics is change. Alternatively, the Court could focus on particular districts and ask whether the only plausible explanation for the district's configuration is an effort to maximize the voting power of supporters of one political party. The Supreme Court majority rejects such a test because, in the Court's view, politics plays an inevitable and appropriate role in the apportionment process (for example, ensuring minimal representation for long-established interest groups like farmers, industrial laborers, or adherents of a hopelessly outvoted major party), making it impossible to know when politics is exerting too much influence.

If we change the equality lens, though, and view massive political gerrymandering from the perspective of a democracy-friendly First Amendment, one thing jumps out of the fog of statistics and partisan blather. A successful partisan gerrymander almost always results in the minimization—often the elimination—of contestable legislative elections.[7] No savvy incumbent politician designs a district he can lose. No effective partisan gerrymander results in really close races that the party in power can actually lose. The whole purpose of the gerrymander is to rig the outcome of as many elections as possible by careful line drawing, packing your opponents into a few "landslide districts" where they'll win a few seats with 80 percent of the vote, but drawing the rest of the lines so that your supporters will win in a series of elections with just over the statistically safe registration edge of 55 percent to 45 percent. The measure of a successful gerrymander is its elimination of contestable elections and its assurance of a steady legislative majority for the party in power.

Witness what the Republicans have done in North Carolina. In 2012, the popular vote for House members in North Carolina was 51 percent Democratic to 49 percent Republican. But North Carolina's House delegation is nine Republicans and four Democrats because the Republican legislature drew district lines that packed the Democratic voters into four landslide districts, allowing Republicans to microconstruct nine noncontestable Republican districts. Not a single contestable election takes place in a closely divided state.

North Carolina isn't alone. Democrats also polled more than 50 percent of the House votes in Arizona, Michigan, Pennsylvania, and Wisconsin but failed to elect a majority of the House members in those states because of Republican line-drawing artistry. In the seven states most intensively gerrymandered by the Republicans, in 2012 Republicans won the popular votes for the House with just over 50 percent but outelected the Democrats 73–34 with almost no contestable elections. By my calculations, if the gerrymandered lines stay where they are, Democrats would have to poll 58 percent of the national popular vote to win a one-vote majority in the House of Representatives in the 2014 elections.

Democracy is all about contestable elections. Not surprisingly, they're at the core of Madison's First Amendment. A genuinely free, contestable election is the defining event toward which each clause of the amendment converges. Contested elections permit citizens exercising free thought, speech, press, association, assembly, and petition to pass effective electoral judgment on the performance of their representatives. It is irrational to argue that every clause receives First Amendment protection on its own, but the point at which they all converge—a contestable election—is left unprotected, twisting slowly in the political wind. When, as in contemporary America, virtually all district lines are carefully drawn by partisan hands so that everyone knows in advance who will win, elections become a sham, rendering the antecedent protections of free thought, speech, press, collective action, and petition meaningless. The resulting governing process does not deserve to be called a democracy and could never be upheld under a First Amendment that recognizes Madison's music.

It would be easy for a Supreme Court capable of hearing Madison's music to supplement the equality-driven "one person, one vote" principle with a democracy-driven First Amendment protection of contested elections. The problem of identifying a fair representative baseline disappears. Even a Republican justice should be able to figure out that politicians have done away with contestable House elections in North Carolina.

Of course, given geographical concentrations of voters with similar political preferences (often in cities), genuinely contested elections may not be possible everywhere—unless we adopt proportional representation or experiment with democracy-friendly multimember or at-large districts. But the Supreme Court should be able to apply a First Amendment rule that forbids systematic electoral line-drawing that purposefully eliminates contested legislative elections from the American democratic process. If elections were less predictable, maybe more people would vote. And maybe legislators would make better laws

BREAKING UP THE REPUBLICRAT CARTEL

The Supreme Court took a wrong turn in campaign finance law when it tore the Free Speech Clause from its democracy-centered First Amendment roots and misread it as a flat ban on regulating campaign spending. A narrow majority of the Court has gone even further afield in its misuse of a nontextual sliver of the First Amendment—freedom of association—to impose a Republicrat duopoly that allows major-party political bosses to snuff out intraparty insurgencies and prevent third-party challengers from threatening their hegemony.

As usual, the mistake was to tear a piece of the First Amendment from its democracy-reinforcing context and treat it as a freestanding command. Only this time, the rootless command isn't even a part of the text. It's the nontextual protection of freedom of association that was read into the text by Justice Harlan in 1958 in order to reinforce its democratic narrative. Justice Harlan was surely right in recognizing freedom of association as a nontextual First Amendment right. Freedom of association fits all the criteria for a proper application of the equity of the Bill of Rights under Madison's Ninth Amendment safety net. It is analogous to the textual right of free assembly, harmonious with the rest of the First Amendment's text, and crucial to the story of the evolution of a democratic idea that is the organizing principle of Madison's First Amendment. In 1958, protection of the NAACP against hostile attacks by Alabama was an essential democratic way station for the evolution of the luminous political idea that ended American apartheid—a way station that was not adequately protected by the textual protections of speech, press, or physical assembly.

Unfortunately, instead of deploying freedom of association in defense of robust democracy, the Court has used it as a device to frustrate efforts to broaden democracy. For example, the Court has refused to recognize voting and running for office as quintessential exercises of First Amendment political association, leaving both fundamental building blocks of self-government to fend for themselves in the rough and tumble of partisan politics, weakly protected by the Equal Protection Clause. To make matters worse, the Court has twisted associational freedom to treat the nominating procedures of the Republican and Democratic parties as hermetically sealed exercises of like-minded people, as though a small group of ideologically identical neighbors were meeting to choose a spokesman. While the two major parties do differ in philosophy and program, each is hardly a sealed group of like-minded citizens. Rather, as in any complex modern democracy using "first-past-the-post" elections in defined constituencies, the two parties function as competing coalitions of loosely connected interests, open to—indeed, eager for—outsiders who wish to affiliate, however loosely, in an effort to cobble together a winning electoral majority. The Court's erroneous fixation on the ideological boundaries of the major parties has caused it to block efforts to open their nominating processes to the entire electorate. When California opened them to the whole electorate, voter participation spiked by more than 10 percent, and moderates won a fair share of nominations. After the Court's majority had explained why letting outsiders help choose the nominees violates party members' free-association rights, participation in California primaries plummeted, and the extreme ideological wing of each major party retook control of the nominating process. In short, the Court has invoked freedom of association not to broaden democracy, but to turn too many primaries into playgrounds for extremists.

Recognizing a democracy-friendly First Amendment would require the Court to take a second look at the function of big-tent major parties in a mass democracy. Once the two major parties were recognized as vaguely defined, shifting coalitions, the Court would strike down yearlong ideological waiting periods for voting in a major-party primary but uphold efforts to open the nominating processes to the entire electorate.

The Court's failure to consider the democracy-reinforcing function of freedom of association has also made a shambles of the law governing minor parties. In a complex modern democracy, minor parties rarely elect candidates. By definition, they lack the mass support needed to win an election. But they do play the crucial function of injecting new ideas into the political process, forcing the major parties to react, by either assimilating them into the party platform or urging their rejection by the electorate. Freedom of association, properly understood as reinforcing democracy, could protect minor parties by assuring them inexpensive access to the ballot without depleting the funds needed for the campaign; allowing them to invite disaffected members of the major parties to participate in choosing protest candidates; and, most important, permitting them to cross-endorse major party candidates, allowing the supporters of a minor party to play a role in selecting the winner of an election while expressing support for the minor party's ideological position.

The robust third-party culture of the nineteenth century rested on ease of ballot access and the ability to cross-endorse. The Supreme Court has wiped out both, leaving a Republicrat cartel that stifles new ideas that might threaten the status quo. A Supreme Court willing and able to hear Madison's democratic music would use it to break the cartel, not reinforce it.

THE MODERN PETITION CLAUSE: ON SETTING DEMOCRATIC AGENDAS

The Supreme Court has virtually erased the Petition for a Redress of Grievances Clause from the modern First Amendment, insisting that it does no work that is not already done by an imperial Free Speech Clause that has simply swallowed the rest of the First Amendment.[8] The emergence of an imperial Free Speech Clause that purports to supplant the separate clauses protecting free exercise, free press, freedom of assembly, and the right to petition is a classic example of how failure to hear Madison's music distorts First Amendment jurisprudence. If the seven truncated words of the Free Speech Clause do all the heavy lifting in all those areas, why did Madison bother with redundant press, assembly, and petition clauses?

In fact, each clause protects an essential phase of Madison's democratic narrative. The religion clauses protect the interior spaces of the mind, where an idea develops. Free speech protects its articulation; a free press, its mass dissemination. Freedom of association nurtures the idea's growth into a political movement, where free assembly takes over, protecting its mass mobilization. The Petition Clause concludes Madison's narrative, protecting the idea's introduction into the formal democratic lawmaking process, forcing the legislature to place the issue on its agenda.

The legislative agenda-setting function of the Petition Clause is a watered-down version of an even stronger idea considered and rejected by the Founders that would have permitted constituents to "instruct" legislators to take certain action. That was too much for Madison and his friends in the summer of 1789, but not before a full-dress debate considered and rejected the idea of "instruction."[9] Instead, drawing on British parliamentary history, the Founders compromised on a "petition" mechanism to ensure that the legislature would be confronted by issues of great concern to constituents.

Viewed as the culmination of Madison's democratic narrative, the Petition Clause plays a crucial structural role, linking a vigorous private democratic culture protected by speech, press, association, and assembly to the formal processes of democratic lawmaking. Unlike the stronger idea of instruction, petition does not require legislators to vote one way or another. But properly understood, the Petition Clause does require the democratic legislature at least to *consider* issues of great importance to constituents. Although the Petition Clause has fallen on hard times these days, it played a major role in debates over slavery in the pre–Civil War period. Beginning in 1831, Northern abolitionists adopted a British strategy and flooded Congress with petitions seeking legislative action limiting or abolishing slavery. In Britain, the petition process triggered an 1833 vote in the House of Commons abolishing slavery in most of the British Empire. In the United States, however, Congress was dominated by pro-slavery members, who used a series of blocking techniques—"gag rules"—to keep antislavery petitions from being read on the floor of the House. When John Quincy Adams, after serving as our sixth president from 1825 to 1829, was elected to the House in 1830, he became a champion of the petition process, almost starting a riot when he attempted to read a petition from twenty-two slaves seeking freedom. The petition movement crested in 1837 and 1838, when more than 130,000 petitions challenging slavery were lodged with Congress. The proslavery forces responded by enacting a House rule formally excluding the abolitionist petitions, overriding Adams's argument that the First Amendment required Congress to consider them. That in turn triggered a popular response, sweeping the antislavery Whigs into power for the first time. In 1844, Adams was successful in persuading Congress to abolish the gag rule, leading to intense legislative engagement that culminated in the Missouri Compromise banning slavery in the territories but allowing it to flourish in the South. The ban on slavery in the territories as part of a grand compromise seeking to avoid civil war was declared unconstitutional by the Supreme Court in 1857 in the infamous *Dred Scott* case, ending efforts to deal with slavery through democratic means and rendering the Civil War inevitable.

Under a Madisonian reading of the First Amendment, once the Petition Clause placed an item on the legislative agenda, Congress would be obliged to confront it. Properly understood, therefore, the clause is much more than just a colony of the imperial Free Speech Clause. Read as an integral part of the first stanza of Madison's poem, it could loosen the current gridlock in both houses of Congress. The Senate, grossly malapportioned by design, operates under a filibuster rule permitting forty-one senators representing about 11 percent of the population to prevent a vote on the merits of legislation favored by representatives of 89 percent of the population. The House of Representatives currently operates under a self-imposed rule forbidding a vote on any legislation that has not been preapproved by a caucus of the majority party's members, currently allowing 118 House Republicans, many elected from gerrymandered districts, to prevent the 435-member House from voting on crucial legislation. Properly read, Madison's Petition Clause might well provide a popular mechanism to force up-and-down votes in both Houses, presenting the electorate with a clear voting record on which to judge their representatives at the next (contestable) election.

A MODEST NONCONSTITUTIONAL PROPOSAL FOR A SINGLE-TIER DEMOCRACY

We don't have to wait for a fifth Supreme Court vote to do something about our three-tier democracy. We can dance to a version of Madison's democratic music without the permission of judges. American democracy currently is dominated by the top 1 percent of the economic tree, those who privately fund the electoral process. We could eliminate the first tier tomorrow by publicly funding our elections. It costs money to buy access to the voters. It costs money to organize supporters. It costs money to run a campaign staff. Most of the time, we offload the expense to rich volunteers (individual and corporate) who are only too happy to cover the costs of democracy off the books because in return they get strings to pull like puppeteers. For many in the first tier, political spending is just another investment—with the chance of a massive economic return. Until we acknowledge that the cost of democracy should be an on-the-books expense requiring public funding of the campaign process, the first tier will continue to dominate our politics.

Although the Supreme Court has slammed the door on the most efficient public funding approach—matching funds geared to the amounts raised by privately funded candidates—it has left open at least two approaches. First, we could provide a dollar-for-dollar electoral tax credit up to $250. That would give most people a free $250 to put into the democratic process without a government bureaucracy to collect or distribute the money. Imagine campaigns geared to persuading ordinary people to commit some or all of their tax-subsidized $250 to a candidate who promises to respond to *their* needs, instead of kowtowing to the 1 percent. Another approach might build on New York City's public campaign funding program. Since 1988, New York City has offered multiple matches of small donations as a form of campaign subsidy, enabling underfunded candidates to raise a significant campaign chest with a small donor base. In return, the candidate must agree to a generous spending cap. It works. In recent years, New York City campaigns have centered on issues, not overblown and expensive media spectacles. Unless his name is Bloomberg, one candidate rarely is able to dominate a campaign by dramatically outspending an opponent. And most important, the winner doesn't owe anything to moneyed interests.

Tax credits and multiple matches aren't the only ways to subsidize clean elections. Once we commit ourselves to eliminating electoral control by the first tier of supercitizens, the imagination of a free people will quickly show us the way to yet other techniques for public funding—including subsidized access to mass electronic media at or below market rates. It'd cost some money. But we'd get our democracy back.

The third tier of American democracy is the domain of the poor. Not long ago, poor people didn't vote because they couldn't afford the poll tax, because they were illiterate, because they were newcomers, because they didn't satisfy a property qualification, or because they were the wrong gender, color, or ethnicity. Today, although those formal barriers no longer exist, the folks at the bottom of America's economic ladder still do not vote in anything like their actual numbers, virtually surrendering their ability to use politics to improve their lot. We could eliminate the third tier entirely by recognizing a civic duty to vote, similar to the duty to serve on juries, register for the draft, go to school, buy health insurance, become vaccinated, pay taxes, wear motorcycle helmets, or cooperate with the census. Australia, among a number of democracies that view voting as a civic duty, boasts voter turnouts of 95 percent. We have not reached 65 percent in a presidential election for more than a hundred years and often fall below 50 percent. A 61 percent turnout was cause for celebration in 2008. Turnout in the crucial 2010 legislative elections barely reached 40 percent. We celebrated another turnout in 2012 that barely topped 60 percent.

Defenders of the current system argue that imposing a legal duty to vote would violate the First Amendment. Once formal barriers to voting have been removed, opponents of compulsory voting argue that the decision not to vote is an individual's choice, entitled to as much respect as a decision to participate in the political process. There is, of course, great irony in arguing that the First Amendment guarantees the right *not* to vote but doesn't guarantee the right *to* vote. Despite the irony, though, it is true that any form of compulsory voting would risk forcing some nonvoters to act inconsistently with their political beliefs. In order to avoid such an unpalatable result, any civic duty to vote should have a convenient escape hatch, allowing an individual to opt out of voting merely by expressing a desire to do so. Once such an easy opt-out is made available, I see no constitutional problem in operating an opt-out voting process instead of the current opt-in model. After all, a legal system that has rejected constitutional challenges to military conscription, compulsory jury service, compulsory schooling, compulsory vaccination, compulsory health insurance, compulsory cooperation with the census, and compulsory taxation to support programs with which the taxpayer profoundly disagrees can hardly draw a principled line at a civic duty to vote, especially one that can be so easily trumped by a convenient opt-out. We know from our experience with activities ranging from joining class actions to participation in 401(k) retirement plans that opt-in systems tend to yield low turnouts and that the turnout is lowest among the poor and less educated. And yet we insist upon operating an opt-in system for voting. A legislative switch to an opt-out system would virtually eliminate the third tier without violating anyone's First Amendment rights.

If the idea of compulsory voting is a little too Orwellian for your taste (even with a no-questions-asked opt-out clause), the size of the third tier can be dramatically decreased by lowering the hurdles associated with voting. No democracy makes it harder to vote than we do. We require prospective voters to carry out three preliminary tasks before casting a ballot. First, a prospective voter must ascertain the place and method of registering and voting. In years past, officials bent on preventing blacks from voting made it as hard as possible to find the registration office. Nowadays, nobody actually hides the registration office, but the radically decentralized nature of our election administration often makes it difficult to identify exactly where to go to register to vote, much less where to go to actually cast a ballot. Our bewildering array of precincts, election districts, and assembly districts can create an electoral maze. While great progress has been made in simplifying registration—postcard registration is now widely available, and the forms have been standardized in federal elections—the process of learning where to register and vote can seem daunting to a poor, unsophisticated person thinking about voting for the first time.

Second, in the United States, the burden of placing one's name on the voting rolls in advance of the election must be borne by the prospective voter. In most states, it is not enough to be motivated to vote on Election Day. The motivation must have caused the prospective voter to take the preliminary step of registering, usually at least a month in advance of the election. No other democracy places such a preliminary burden on the voter. The United States did not begin doing so until the first decade of the twentieth century, which not so coincidentally triggered a decline in voter participation from 75 percent in 1896 to 44 percent in 1924. In virtually every other democracy, the duty of assembling the voter registration rolls is placed on the government. In our system, the requirement of advance registration acts as an economic and social screening mechanism, disproportionately filtering less sophisticated, poorer voters out of the process. When we register young men for the draft, we don't count on voluntary compliance; we compel registration on pain of criminal sanction. When we enumerate the population for the census, we don't rely on voluntary registration; we use government officials to compile the data, and we compel cooperation with the process. When we register persons for jury service, we don't rely on voluntary registration; the government compiles the juror rolls and compels service. But when it comes to voter rolls, the government neither requires registration nor makes any effort to compile the necessary information.

Finally, once registration hurdles are surmounted, we require prospective voters to vote on a workday, often using vintage voting equipment and appallingly outdated information technology, causing lines that can last for hours, especially in poor, black, and Latino precincts. Affluent election districts update their election technology, lowering the error rate and eliminating long waits to vote. Inner-city election districts, strapped for funds, often use the oldest, least reliable voting technology, and experience numbingly long lines, which discourage all but the most highly motivated. When you add cynical voter ID laws or proof of citizenship requirements designed to create yet one more hurdle for the poor, the democratic process loses much of its moral legitimacy.

Extremely low voter participation in the United States is not caused by some perverse form of American exceptionalism. It is the predictable cumulative impact of legally imposed transaction costs on voting. Were we to simplify and update election administration, require the government to assemble the voting rolls, permit Election Day registration, and make Election Day a holiday, the problem of a morally unacceptable third tier would dramatically diminish. Nonparticipation would continue, of course. But it would be at a far lower rate, and, most important, it would no longer be radically skewed by race and class.

Ask yourself this very troublesome question: is the real reason we tolerate so many unnecessary hurdles to voting that, deep down, we don't want the poor to vote? Have we found the ideal hypocritical way to limit the franchise—formally guarantying everyone the right to vote, but under such a lukewarm, indeed hostile, standard of legal protection that we tolerate, indeed invite, regulatory hurdles that predictably disenfranchise the poor in large numbers, allowing us to blame them, not us, for the continued exclusion of the poor from American political life?

The justices all claim to understand Madison's central First Amendment message: that vigorous political speakers and well-informed voters are the indispensable core of a robust democracy. Indeed, in recent years, Justice Breyer has argued in dissent that the underlying purpose of the First Amendment, indeed the entire Constitution, is to make democracy work. In the name of protecting vigorous speakers, however, the current Court has uncoupled the Free Speech Clause from its democracy-supportive context, ignored three of the ten words in the clause, and construed the remaining seven to elevate the interests of wealthy speakers over the interests of everyone else. The challenge is to build on the Court's rhetorical acceptance of the relationship between informed voters and democracy, to develop a democracy-friendly First Amendment based on all forty-five words of Madison's full text. Read with careful attention to the parts and the whole, as one would read a great poem, those forty-five words effectively protect the essentials of a democracy: the right to vote, the right to be a truly informed voter as opposed to a pawn, the right to enjoy fair representation via contested elections, and the right to participate equally in a democratic process free from manipulation by the very rich.

7

Mr. Madison's Neighborhood

Madison's First Amendment doesn't stop with the protection of electoral speech or even with the protection of formal democracy. The Founders understood that a robust democracy cannot live on political speech alone. That's why Madison begins his poem in the apolitical interior of the human spirit with freedom of religious (and eventually secular) conscience. He knew that the habits of thought that enable free people to govern themselves justly and well—respect for individual dignity, a healthy sense of self-worth, curiosity about and respect for others, skepticism about absolutes, toleration of disagreement, and openness to change—cannot thrive without a steady flow of unfiltered information, ideas, and opinions about art, philosophy, literature, science, technology, history, ethics, economics, psychology, sociology, sex, leisure, and business. Would-be tyrants have always understood that control over speech about the full range of human experience—not just politics—is crucial to the maintenance of authoritarian rule. It's no coincidence that Hitler and Stalin (to say nothing of Mao Tse-tung and Pol Pot) abhorred literary or artistic innovation. They knew that freedom to imagine and depict the world in new, even disturbing, ways nourishes an indispensable core of individuals who chafe at imposed orthodoxy, especially state-imposed political conformity.

I've argued earlier that the inside-to-outside order of the First Amendment's six textual clauses tells us a good deal about how laws governing the relationship between speech and democracy should be structured. Can their careful order also guide us in establishing legal ground rules governing speech generally? Again I believe that the answer is yes. The protected freedoms of the First Amendment—conscience, expression, press, association, assembly, and petition— not only depict democracy in action, but also celebrate a partnership between free speakers and free hearers that is the bedrock on which democracy rests. The first three clauses—Establishment, Free Exercise, and Speech—protect an autonomous, intellectually committed speaker, free to shape her own destiny, personality, thoughts, and beliefs and to express those thoughts and beliefs openly, even when they challenge deeply entrenched orthodoxies. Immanuel Kant, an eighteenth-century German philosopher whose respect for the inherent dignity of every human being profoundly influenced Madison and the other Founders, would smile. If Madison had stopped after the first three clauses, the First Amendment's structure would be almost entirely speaker centered, a one-dimensional celebration of the Kantian self as speaker. Unfortunately, that's just about where the current Supreme Court stops, with an imperial Free Speech Clause that subsumes the final three clauses—Press, Assembly, and Petition—which celebrate the speaker's interaction with a "neighborhood" of Kantian hearers, who must also be free to shape their own identities and preferences. The full First Amendment is a story about the interaction between free speakers and free hearers in a democracy. The challenge is to forge coherent First Amendment doctrine that respects both speakers and hearers.

WHO LIVES IN MR. MADISON'S FIRST AMENDMENT NEIGHBORHOOD?

Five kinds of people live in Mr. Madison's metaphorical First Amendment neighborhood—*speakers*, *hearers*, *conduits* (whose principal function is to transmit the speech of others to larger audiences), *speech targets* (persons discussed or described in the speech), and *government speech regulators* (you can tell them by their shifty eyes and black hats).

ARISTOCRATIC SPEAKERS

The current Supreme Court, fixated on seven deracinated words from the First Amendment ("Congress shall make no law . . . abridging . . . speech"), has anointed speakers as the neighborhood aristocrats. Beginning with the great Holmes and Brandeis dissents in the 1920s, nourished by Justice Jackson's luminous rhetoric in the 1943 case exempting Jehovah's Witnesses schoolchildren from a duty to salute the flag each morning, and culminating in the "Fuck the Draft" and flag-burning decisions of the late twentieth century, modern First Amendment doctrine has become increasingly speaker centered to the virtual exclusion of everyone else in the neighborhood.[1]

Speakers often defend their privileged position by invoking their status as autonomous human beings blessed with free will. Citing Immanuel Kant, John Milton, and John Locke, three great theorists of individual dignity, speakers insist, correctly, that truly autonomous human beings must be empowered to speak freely in order to shape their own identities and form their own preferences, shielded from the dead hand of the state. Once the celebration of a Promethean vision of the heroic speaker raging at the gods is exhausted (it can take days), aristocratic speakers retreat to a somewhat less lofty position. The free flow of ideas and information generated by autonomous speakers, they argue correctly, is essential to the ability of hearers to make the informed decisions on which the efficient functioning of choice-dependent institutions like democracy, markets, and scientific inquiry depend. The ghost of Galileo is usually trotted out to demonstrate both the affront to human dignity and the adverse impact on scientific inquiry imposed by the Church's censorship of his work in the seventeenth century.[2]

At this point, the Supreme Court usually breaks down and

embraces the aristocratic speaker without asking whether the particular speech before the Court actually enhances a hearer's capacity for informed free choice or whether the other inhabitants of Mr. Madison's neighborhood are also entitled to be treated as dignified human beings.

HAUTE BOURGEOIS HEARERS

Hearers are the neighborhood haute bourgeoisie—respectable, even admired, but a clear cut below the aristocracy of speakers. When the communicative interests of speakers and hearers point in the same direction, as they do most of the time, First Amendment protection is at its strongest. Those are the easy free-speech cases. However, when the interests of speakers and hearers diverge, the edge usually goes to speakers. It takes a very thick skin to be a hearer in today's version of Mr. Madison's neighborhood. Apart from overt threats and intense face-to-face verbal assaults ("fighting words"), an unwilling hearer has almost no right to be shielded from false, offensive, denigrating, or even frightening speech. For example, according to the Supreme Court, a black family newly arrived in the neighborhood has no right to be protected against a speaker burning a cross on the sidewalk across the street from the family's house, unless the government can prove beyond a reasonable doubt that the cross burning was actually intended to threaten or intimidate the family.[3] Merely intending to denigrate the newcomers or express opposition to their presence in the community isn't enough. You can't even tell the jury that burning a cross is presumed to be an attempt at intimidation.[4] Under current Supreme Court doctrine, the black family's First Amendment role as involuntary hearers is to act as a piñata for the privileged speaker, even when it hurts—a lot. Similarly, Holocaust survivors living in Skokie, a largely Jewish suburb of Chicago, had no right to be shielded from Nazi marchers who chose to display swastikas and other Nazi regalia in the Jewish suburb precisely because the symbols would upset the elderly Jewish victims.[5] Finally, consider a woman who has reached an agonizing decision to terminate a pregnancy. According to the Supreme Court, as a hearer in Mr. Madison's neighborhood, she is fair game for so-called counselors who insist on approaching her and trying to talk her out of going through with her decision even as she is walking through the doors of a health facility. It did not seem to occur to any of the justices that a woman preparing to face a physical and emotional ordeal might be entitled to a few moments of privacy, free from the reach of the neighborhood's aristocratic speakers.

In fairness, the Court occasionally drops a crumb to a beleaguered hearer. Face-to-face threats and gross insults can be prohibited,[6] but the protection probably doesn't apply to hate speech directed to the general public. If I were a hearer, I wouldn't get too excited about my "fighting words" protection, though; the Supreme Court hasn't used it since 1942. Unreasonably noisy speech can be ordered to be toned down.[7] Prospective voters are assured a quiet zone as they approach the polls.[8] Consumers may be protected against egregiously false, misleading, or particularly distressing commercial advertising.[9] Commercial mail or phone solicitations can be banned in certain contexts.[10] Demonstrators marching in front of a target hearer's home must keep moving.[11] In some states, women approaching an abortion clinic may be afforded "free access" corridors or floating "buffer zones," sparing them face-to-face confrontation with antiabortion protesters but permitting demonstrators to line up on either side of the corridor to shout and display disturbing messages that the women do not wish to hear or see.[12] In many states, women seeking an abortion have no access corridor at all but must wade through a sea of vilification. The Supreme Court has even held that, under the First Amendment, a woman entering a medical facility to obtain an abortion is fair game for antiabortion "counselors" who are constitutionally entitled to approach her and earnestly try to talk her out of the abortion even when she doesn't want to talk to them.[13]

Hearers may occasionally assert an independent right to receive information. In 1965, Congress required the addressees of "communist political propaganda" mailed to them from abroad by foreign governments to put their names on a post office list affirmatively requesting delivery. The Supreme Court invalidated the requirement, even though it found that the foreign government (the speaker) had no First Amendment rights. Instead, the Court ruled that the addressee/hearer had an independent First Amendment right to receive the magazines in question free from government interference—a First Amendment "right to know."[14] That's actually where First Amendment protection of commercial and corporate speech comes from. If you read the Supreme Court's corporate or commercial free-speech opinions closely, you'll find that the justices are careful not to say that corporations have independent First Amendment rights. Instead, the Court allows the corporate speaker to borrow the hearers' First Amendment rights to receive the information. Unfortunately, unlike the 1965 case, in which the hearers were seeking access to the speech in question, nobody bothers to ask the hearers in corporate or commercial speech cases whether they actually want to hear the speech. No one even thinks of providing unwilling hearers in those kinds of cases with a means to avoid unwanted communications premised on the hearers' so-called right to know. It's like a right to be fed spinach whether or not you actually want to eat it. The Supreme Court simply assures the "lucky" conscripted hearers that unlimited corporate electoral speech and annoying commercial advertising is actually good for them—like spinach.

When a right to know would have real benefits for hearers, though, as in challenges to government secrecy or efforts to increase the variety of voices in mass media, the Court usually shuts it down. In secrecy cases, it defers to the government's assertion of national security interests. In mass-media cases, it defers to corporations' private property interests. In the end, the hearer's so-called right to know is almost always turned into a device for forcing hearers to be subjected to speech they don't want to hear, but it rarely gives them access to important speech they do want to hear.

ARRIVISTE CONDUITS

Conduits, especially major newspapers, television and cable networks, and Internet providers, are the neighborhood arrivistes. The conduit's principal role in the neighborhood is to function as a skilled tradesman who builds and runs complex machinery transmitting the speech of others to a larger audience. Think of the highly skilled artisans who owned and operated the printing presses in Madison's time. Today's conduits have persuaded the Supreme Court to let them dress up as aristocratic speakers, even though all they do is run a big machine that transmits the speech of others to a mass audience.

Madison gave conduits their own clause—the Free Press Clause—designed to permit skilled tradesmen to transmit the speech of others to larger audiences free from government interference. But the current Court usually ignores Madison's Free Press Clause, treating it as just another colony of the imperial Free Speech Clause, which does all the legal work. Thus under current law, the press is treated as just another group of speakers with no special institutional rights or responsibilities. But why did Madison bother to include a separate Free Press Clause? If it were read properly, conduit protection under the Free Press Clause might differ significantly from speaker protection under the Free Speech Clause. If we decoupled the two clauses, the press might be granted a special First Amendment institutional role to seek out and offer voice to weak speakers whose own voices have been silenced—for example, by imprisonment or other form of government muzzling.[15] Recognizing a special institutional role for the press as conduit would also argue for rules that insulate the press from being forced to reveal sources or from liability for innocently distributing the speech of others. It might even facilitate press access to government secrets. On the other hand, press conduits might be subject to regulations designed to ensure access to the mass media for otherwise blocked or unheard voices.[16] Until we separate the conduit from the speaker, though, the Free Press Clause will continue to languish as a backwater of the imperial Free Speech Clause.

SLUM-DWELLING TARGETS

Speech targets—the people being talked about—are the neighborhood slum dwellers. A speech target's interest in being described accurately and with dignity is almost always subordinated to the interests of aristocratic speakers and conduits masquerading as speakers. Under existing First Amendment rules, false speech that harms the reputation of a speech target in the public eye (the "public figure") is immune from punishment unless it was uttered with "actual malice," which usually translates into subjectively knowing that the speech is false. False speech about public figures uttered without actual malice, even when the speaker or the conduit has been grossly negligent in checking the facts, slips under the law's radar.[17] Under existing ground rules, therefore, powerful speakers and conduits can unfairly ruin a speech target's reputation with false charges as long as no one can prove they know they're spreading lies.

THE LOCAL MOTORCYCLE GANG

Government speech regulators are the neighborhood motorcycle gang, eager to terrorize the entire neighborhood if allowed any traction at all. Much of our modern free-speech law glorifying the speaker has little to do with making institutions of choice work better or advancing the human dignity of the speaker or anyone else. Make-weight arguments about human dignity or institutional efficiency are really designed to reinforce and justify the Court's almost pathological mistrust of the ability of a government official to regulate speech fairly. Modern free-speech law rests on a slippery slope so precipitous that any step toward government speech regulation aimed at controlling dysfunctional speakers, improving the quality of choices for hearers, or reinforcing the Kantian dignity of hearers and speech targets is demonized by the Supreme Court as a first step toward tyranny. The result is a First Amendment jurisprudence that claims to be built on improving the functioning of our institutions of choice and reinforcing our commitment to human dignity but is paralyzed by fear of government regulatory abuse. It has spawned a speech culture that can be corrosive of the very values of institutional efficiency and dignity it is supposed to serve.

Like the privileged of most neighborhoods, aristocratic speakers defend their status by fearmongering, reminding us that government speech regulators have generally behaved very badly, often using the state's monopoly of force to crush dissenters. The only safe solution, argue the First Amendment speaker aristocrats, is a set of prophylactic rules, both substantive and procedural, designed to prevent the government motorcycle gang from getting any traction at all.[18] It's true, of course, that governments have a terrible censorship track record, but the modern Supreme Court's demonization of the government speech regulator has at least two flaws. Many of the worst examples of government censorship come from totalitarian governments or authoritarian institutions like the Catholic Church before the Enlightenment. But today, Great Britain, Germany, and France regulate the flow of speech in a few narrowly defined settings, including campaign finance, hate speech, and libel without falling into totalitarian hell. Perhaps more important, pulling the government speech regulator completely out of the game does not mean that the flow of speech will become unregulated. If government is disabled from doing the job, someone else will direct the speech traffic in Mr. Madison's neighborhood—probably one or more powerful private speakers or conduits. Which of the following three scenarios should frighten you most as a good Madisonian democrat: the prospect of government regulation of campaign spending in an effort to protect political equality, rules requiring limited access to the mass media for voices unable to purchase commercial airtime, or the situation in today's America, where a relatively few corporations and billionaires own every single engine of mass communication—newspapers, publishers, bookstores, television stations, cable networks, movie studios, theaters, and Internet platforms?

IS THE NEIGHBORHOOD RIPE FOR A LITTLE URBAN RENEWAL?

The relationships between and among the five inhabitants of Mr. Madison's neighborhood give contemporary free speech law its content and texture. Like any long-established neighborhood, it may need some urban renewal. Four recent Supreme Court cases illustrate the current Court's glorification of the speaker, despite the fact that half of the First Amendment is about empowering hearers and other members of the First Amendment community.

In the first case,[19] the Court reversed the criminal conviction of a would-be local politician (newly elected to a local three-person water board) for falsely asserting during a town meeting that he had been awarded the Congressional Medal of Honor. Focusing on the dignitary right of a speaker to self-definition, the Court observed that even inveterate liars are entitled to fantasize about themselves in public, including when performing a public duty. That's Kant on stilts—a dignitary right to lie. But that was just window dressing. The real basis for the Court's opinion was a fear that criminalizing willful lying in the absence of proof of tangible harm would place a dangerous weapon in the hands of government officials, who might be tempted to react to vigorous criticism by cynically branding it as an indictable lie. Think what Putin could do with such a law. That's a classic example of fear of the motorcycle gang forcing us to tolerate speech that is unsupported by any plausible concept of human dignity and that cannot possibly be thought to aid hearers in making our institutions function better. The Court's rhetorical elevation of lying to a mystical exercise in Kantian dignity is typical of our front-end approach to useless or harmful speech. Throughout our First Amendment jurisprudence, we deal with fear of government abuse by elevating useless or harmful speech to underserved heights of protection. Why not focus instead on the back end, by acknowledging the unprotected nature of the speech while limiting available sanctions to minimize the chances of government abuse—a kind of cruel and unusual punishment clause just for speech. Maybe we should just limit the weapons available to the motorcycle gang. Instead of turning an inveterate liar into Prometheus raging at the gods, why not make sure that no one was actually harmed by his conscious lie, and then let him off with an apology or a small fine?

In the second case,[20] eight members of the Court voted to reverse a jury's award of compensatory damages for intentional infliction of emotional distress against a group of antigay religious fanatics who staged a raucous demonstration on public land one thousand feet from a church during the funeral of a young soldier killed in Iraq in the line of duty. The demonstrators, who already had picketed some six hundred military funerals, waved graphic placards and claimed that the soldier's death was a just punishment from their god (not mine) for America's toleration of homosexuality. The funeral procession passed within two hundred to three hundred feet of the demonstrators. The jury awarded $2.9 million in compensatory damages and $8 million in punitive damages for intentionally inflicting emotional distress on the family as it buried a son. The justices reversed, ruling that, because the demonstration was on public land and was not visible from the church, First Amendment freedom of speech included a speaker's right to hijack the funeral of a young soldier as a backdrop for their bigotry, despite the additional anguish imposed on the soldier's family.

In the third case,[21] the Court invalidated a ban on the sale to children of violent video games that depict digitally simulated acts of misogyny, rape, torture, and murder. Justice Scalia, writing for the Court, insisted that no First Amendment difference exists between Dante's graphic verbal depiction of violence in the *Inferno* and interactive video-game simulations of rape and murder. The justices reasoned that because the government is unable to prove conclusively that children are adversely affected by reading Dante or playing computer video games in which they act out scenes of misogyny, the speakers (the for-profit corporations that develop and sell violent video games to minors) were immune from government regulation.

Finally, the Court struck down a federal statute banning videos depicting the wanton torture and violent killing of small animals,[22] holding that the statute's inapt description of the scope of its coverage might be read someday by a foolish member of the motorcycle gang to criminalize documentaries about hunting. Because, reasoned the justices, hunting documentaries are protected under freedom of speech, the entire statute must be invalidated, even the ban on depicting violent cruelty to animals. In short, to deflect a hypothetical future assault on speech about hunting that will probably never happen, the Court provided a windfall to the distributor of videos depicting cruelly abused dogs fighting to the death.

These four cases assemble a motley collection of "dignitary" speakers: (1) an inveterate liar using false statements about winning the Congressional Medal of Honor to increase his local political clout, (2) a group of antigay religious fanatics trashing the funeral of a dead soldier to make a bigoted statement, (3) the developers of violent video games pitching misogyny, torture, and murder to kids for fun and profit, and (4) the makers of videos depicting the warped torture and brutal killing of small animals. It's possible, of course, that all four cases were rightly decided. After all, the prosecutor forgot to allege that the lie about winning the Medal of Honor was designed to bolster the liar's local political influence. The religious bigots picketing the soldier's funeral were just out of earshot of the church. The link between a child's exposure to violent video games and adverse changes in the child's values and personality, while plausible, cannot be conclusively proven. And the animal-crush-video statute was very poorly drafted. But that's not how the Court's opinions read. In each case, rather than conceding that the speech in question was of no value, ruefully explaining why the particular effort at regulation before the Court was technically deficient, and advising how future similarly valueless speech should be dealt with, the Court's tone was positively triumphant about protecting "the freedom of speech" of four appalling speakers, not one of whom provided information of use to hearers, and not one of whom had any respect for the dignity of the rest of the folks in Mr. Madison's neighborhood.

Don't get me wrong. I get nervous about government censorship. But I also get nervous about the Court's fixation on speakers who run roughshod over the others who live in the neighborhood. Recognizing a community of speakers *and* hearers doesn't mean the overthrow of the speaker. But is it really necessary or wise to raise appalling speakers above the law just because we mistrust government's ability to regulate them fairly? Why don't we spend more energy worrying about minimizing the chances of improperly motivated government censorship? How did we get to such a place?

A TALE OF TWO FREE-SPEECH CLAUSES: DEREGULATORY AND ASPIRATIONAL

In today's America, robust constitutional protection of free speech is neither a Republican nor a Democratic idea; it's a consensus American idea. And that's a wonderful thing. But as I've noted earlier, it can be a false consensus. All nine Justices agree about the importance of robust free-speech protection, but their agreement masks an important difference in their readings of the First Amendment. The five Republican justices tend to tear out seven words—"Congress shall make no law . . . abridging . . . speech"—and read them as a deregulatory command forbidding any government interference with communication, at least by rich and powerful speakers. After preventing the government from regulating speech in most settings, the Republicans appear comfortable letting powerful corporations decide what gets said to whom.

The four Democratic justices tend to approach the First Amendment as an aspirational partnership between speakers and hearers aimed at preserving human dignity and improving the efficient functioning of institutions dependent on informed free choice. The Democrats also subordinate the rest of the First Amendment to an imperial Free Speech Clause, but at least they use all ten words—"Congress shall make no law . . . abridging *the freedom of* speech," letting the words *the freedom of* act as a filter to allow narrow government regulation of speech in aid of their aspirational vision of the ideal free-speech community.

Because any government regulation of speech usually impinges on human dignity and threatens the free market in ideas, the Democratic aspirational approach to the First Amendment usually dovetails with the Republican deregulatory approach, creating a powerful bipartisan consensus First Amendment. In the many settings where the deregulatory and aspirational approaches overlap, constitutional protection of the speaker usually trumps all competing values. Such a left/right consensus about the importance of free speech is relatively recent. For much of the nation's history, free speech was just one of a number of important values that jostled with each other in the formulation of constitutional law. Free speech usually lost.[23] Until recently, a desire for vigorous Supreme Court enforcement of a robust First Amendment was a trademark of the American left and the bête noire of the American right. For most of the twentieth century, left-wing reformers, certain that their ideas were on the winning side of history, viewed robust free speech as an agent of change capable of destabilizing an oppressive and unequal status quo. To the reformist American left, more speech meant more—and faster—social and economic change. The future potential impact of a deregulatory First Amendment on the weak and the poor was deemed a small price to pay for the ability to invoke a robust free speech principle today in support of a more equal world.

Unlike the confident left, many mid-twentieth-century American conservatives, appalled by the excesses of fascist lunatics, their faith in unregulated economic markets battered by the great Depression of the 1930s, and confronted by an almost unbroken phalanx of academic support for leftist programs, did not look to the future with intellectual confidence. The Republican Party's shameful role in the infringement of free speech in the 1940s and

1950s—supporting McCarthyism, urging censorship of politically radical or erotically suggestive speakers, books, and movies, and applauding the successful effort to outlaw the American Communist Party—reflected the fear of many conservatives that uncensored speech and uncontrolled freedom of political association posed an unacceptable risk to the status quo and would lead to political, social, and economic chaos.[24]

The result was Republican support for a weak First Amendment built around the "bad tendency" doctrine, authorizing government to censor controversial speech based on its perceived tendency to lead to social harm. Under the bad-tendency test, a plausible suspicion that speech might increase the likelihood of harm was sufficient to ban the speech.[25] That's what sentenced the opponents of World War I such as Eugene Debs to prison. That's also what led to the successful criminalization of the American Communist Party in 1951. In the late 1950s and the 1960s, the Warren Court, with a comfortable 6–3 Democratic majority (7–2 if you count Earl Warren as an honorary Democrat), rejected the bad-tendency test, laying the foundation for the modern First Amendment. In 1958, Justice Harlan discovered freedom of association. In 1964, the Court ruled that "public figures" must prove "actual malice" before suing a newspaper for libel. Throughout the 1960s, with the glaring exception of draft-card burners, the Court repeatedly shielded civil rights demonstrators and opponents of the Vietnam War from arrest and prosecution.[26] The process culminated in 1969,[27] when eight justices (five Democrats, if you include Earl Warren, and three Republicans) formally repudiated the old "bad tendency" doctrine in favor of a new constitutional standard—the "clear and present danger" test, originally articulated in the 1920s in the great Holmes/Brandeis opinions in *Abrams* and *Whitney*. The 1969 Court held that ranting by Ku Klux Klan leaders threatening "revengeance" against the government at some unspecified future time could not be deemed criminal in the absence of proof that the speech was almost certain to cause very serious and imminent harm.

Thus, beginning in 1969, in order to be allowed to censor, the neighborhood motorcycle gang had to convince a skeptical judge that the speech in question posed a grave and imminent risk to a very important (often "compelling") governmental interest, a risk that could not be avoided by anything less drastic than censorship. The Court's new test would almost certainly have required the invalidation of Congress's successful attack on the leadership of the American Communist Party in the 1950s. Two years later,[28] in 1971, three Democratic justices (Douglas, Brennan, and Marshall) joined two Republicans (Harlan and Stewart) in reversing the disorderly conduct conviction of a young man who wore a jacket into a Los Angeles courthouse with the words FUCK THE DRAFT emblazoned on the back. The majority made it clear that an involuntary hearer's interest in being shielded from offensive speech cannot be deemed a compelling interest justifying government censorship. Sheltered behind the Court's clear-and-present-danger test and the Court's rejection of offensiveness as a justification for censorship, the American left breathed a sigh of relief and awaited its inevitable triumph. The right hunkered down and vowed to fight on the beaches.

But a couple of unexpected things happened on the left's First Amendment road to political paradise. First, during the last two decades of the twentieth century, the core of the American left's economic agenda imploded, while the American right enjoyed a remarkable intellectual renaissance.[29] The left's economic platform had been premised on varying degrees of governmental redistribution of wealth, ranging from rigid Marxism to European democratic socialism to the mild egalitarianism of the Kennedys to Lyndon Johnson's War on Poverty to the amorphous do-gooder policies of the Carter, Clinton, and Obama administrations. After the Berlin Wall fell in 1989, that agenda ran into an increasing sense in the United States that government—even democratic government—performs poorly as the economic linchpin of a society. Whether it was the gray tyranny of Communism, the horrors of Fascist and Nazi rule, the kleptocratic antics of authoritarian dictators, or the often disheartening bureaucratic ineffectiveness of well-meant democratically enacted government programs, many—including many on the left—simply lost faith in the efficacy and moral legitimacy of an agenda based on a strong, redistributive government.

A generation of conservative intellectuals stepped into the programmatic vacuum, worshipping the market, glorifying individual autonomy, and questioning the effectiveness, indeed the very legitimacy, of government.[30] Flush with faith in their ideas—and the confidence that such faith brings—the American right discovered the First Amendment. During the early 1970s, under a new Republican Supreme Court majority, an expansive conception of free speech became attractive to Republican justices, both because robust free-speech protection fit neatly into the right's skeptical, deregulatory approach to government generally, and because it encouraged vigorous transmission by powerful speakers of the right's newly energized collection of ideas. When the right's newly minted dedication to an expansive Free Speech clause was added to the reformist left's longtime preoccupation with free speech, the resulting coalition created what I call "the First Amendment era of good feelings,"[31] beginning in the 1960s with the civil rights movement and reaching its apogee in the 1989 and 1990 flag-burning cases.[32]

The flag-burning cases illustrate the First Amendment era of good feelings at its most intense. The Supreme Court asked why the government wished to suppress the symbolic burning or other "desecration" of an American flag. Because the government was unable to posit a compelling reason for banning flag desecration other than the distress felt by hearers and viewers, the Court's bipartisan majority invalidated both state and federal flag-burning statutes. In both cases, the justices followed the FUCK THE DRAFT case in declining to recognize the adverse emotional impact of flag burning on unwilling viewers as an adequate basis to suppress controversial speech.

During the First Amendment era of good feelings, the Republican and Democratic justices forged a strong free speech partnership. In 1976, four Republicans joined three Democrats to hold that the First Amendment protects the power of the superrich to spend big money to affect electoral outcomes,[33] giving the 1 percent a tangible reason to celebrate a muscular First Amendment. A coalition of four Republicans and three Democrats then recognized limited but important First Amendment protection for truthful, nonmisleading commercial advertising,[34] giving corporate management a strong stake in the First Amendment.

Even during the era of good feelings, occasional rifts appeared in the consensus. For example, four Republican justices, joined by Justice Stevens (a formal Republican but an honorary Democrat), outvoted the Court's three Democratic justices, joined by Chief Justice Rehnquist, to hold that for-profit corporations enjoy a First Amendment right to use corporate treasury funds to oppose a statewide referendum on raising taxes,[35] thus increasing corporate America's already substantial stake in protecting free speech. In the 1980s and 1990s, the Court's Republican majority invoked the First Amendment as a potent shield against government efforts to regulate massive private concentrations of communicative power, endearing the First Amendment to Rupert Murdoch and the other media barons who own and control most of the nation's mass media outlets.[36] To add insult to injury (literally), in the 1990s, the Court invoked the First Amendment to reverse convictions for hate speech, including cross burnings targeting vulnerable minorities.[37]

By 1990, some progressives began to suspect that they had made a bad First Amendment bargain. They began to realize that a free-speech doctrine that protects the rights of a couple of scruffy kids to burn flags, and provides tepid protection for carefully constrained street demonstrations, but that also protects uncontrolled campaign spending by the superrich—including corporations—abets concentration of media power in a handful of huge corporations, and shields bursts of verbal venom aimed at historically weak hearers seeking access to education and decent housing is hardly a prescription for progress. Some on the left began to view the bipartisan era as a Faustian bargain, far more likely to reinforce the status quo than destabilize it. By 2000, the First Amendment era of good feelings was over, but not before the bipartisan coalition had generated an enormously powerful body of precedent establishing an imperial Free Speech Clause.

After 2000, Republican and Democratic justices began to revert to type. The Republicans remembered the values of hierarchy, security, and control, shrinking public employees' rights to criticize the boss,[38] limiting the rights of high school students to display banners at school-supervised events,[39] all but destroying the protections of the student press,[40] attacking the free-speech rights of unions,[41] and limiting the ability of Americans to associate peacefully with foreign organizations labeled by the government as terrorist.[42] In each case, the three Democratic justices plus Justice Stevens (an honorary Democrat) dissented, urging the recognition of free-speech rights at the bottom of the hierarchy. On the other hand, the Democratic justices, realizing the danger to egalitarian values posed by a deregulatory First Amendment, stridently dissented from Republican majority opinions upholding uncontrolled electoral spending by corporations,[43] invalidating efforts to use matching funds to subsidize political campaigns,[44] and striking down aggregate limits on the amount a single person can contribute during a given election cycle.[45]

One important message emerges from the story of the evolution of the modern First Amendment: nothing about it is written in stone. The evolution of the current speaker-dominated amendment tells a story of constitutional interpretation in constant flux, as the justices seek to refine the meaning of "the freedom of speech" in response to an ever-changing America. Current First Amendment doctrine, which aggrandizes the speaker (including conduits dressed up as speakers), subordinates the hearer, ignores the speech target, and demonizes the government regulator, reflects the nation's existential struggle during the twentieth century against totalitarian challenges from the left and right; its own failure during the McCarthy years to live up to its First Amendment ideals; the political and social forces of the labor, civil rights, and anti–Vietnam War movements; and a libertarian reaction against intrusive (and bumbling) government of any kind. But the wheel turns. A steady diet of speaker-obsessed deregulatory free-speech doctrine has begun to expose its costs to Madisonian democracy and to the larger social partnership between speakers and hearers that supports it. The time may be ripe for a modest political shake-up in Mr. Madison's First Amendment neighborhood.

TAMING ARISTOCRATIC SPEAKERS

The structure of Madison's First Amendment reminds us that the speaker is—and should be—first among equals. Without free speakers, Madison's democratic machine never gets started. It's no coincidence that Madison begins his poem by celebrating the conscience and expressive power of the autonomous speaker, turning to the rest of the communicative community—hearers, conduits, speech targets, and regulators—only after the speaker has been celebrated and granted pride of place. But first among equals doesn't mean overweening tyrant. After all, half of the First Amendment—press, assembly, and petition—is about the rest of the neighborhood. The challenge is to find a way to respect the primacy of the speaker while preserving the dignity of everyone else.

I believe we can learn from Madison's recognition that respect for private property is a crucial guaranty of political freedom. The Contracts Clause and the Fifth Amendment's Due Process and Takings Clauses[46] are designed to ensure that government does not unfairly appropriate valuable assets belonging to members of the community. The hope is that by ensuring that even dissenting, politically weak, and unpopular individuals receive protection for their property, something close to a power equilibrium will emerge between the individual and the state.

Perhaps that lesson can be applied in Mr. Madison's neighborhood to block already privileged speakers from appropriating valuable assets belonging to other folks in the neighborhood. For

See pg. 102 on "right to know"

example, when in corporate or commercial speech settings the Supreme Court authorizes an otherwise unprotected corporate speaker to "borrow" the right to know belonging to hearers, the Court should make sure, first, that hearers are willing to lend their rights; and, second, that the borrowed rights will actually be used by corporate speakers to benefit their true owners, the hearers. Thus at the point where an otherwise unprotected speaker is relying on borrowed hearer rights, First Amendment doctrine should shift its priorities from speaker to hearer. In the commercial speech context, the Supreme Court gets the hearer-centered doctrine right most of the time, protecting truthful commercial speech about lawful options that will be of use to hearer/consumers in making efficient market choices, but declining to protect speech that is either useless or detrimental to consumers.[47] That's why commercial speech urging the performance of an unlawful act is unprotected. That's also why egregiously false and misleading commercial speech lacks First Amendment protection. Finally, it's why government commercial speech regulators are given regulatory breathing room in order to ensure that the hearers' interests remain paramount.

But the Court got it dead wrong in *Citizens United* and other cases in the corporate electoral speech area, where large profit-making corporations, lacking free-speech rights of their own, are permitted to borrow the hearers' right to know, and then are allowed to bombard hearers with false, misleading, and overwhelmingly one-sided speech. Despite its hearer-borrowed nature, the corporate speech doctrine is relentlessly speaker centered, with not a hint of concern for the interests of hearers except as a rhetorical flourish designed to further enable privileged speakers. It's time to turn "borrowed" corporate speech rights into a hearer-centered doctrine. That would mean limits on corporate speech that's objectively false and misleading or that encourages hearers to engage in unlawful or harmful behavior, such as violent video games sold to children. It would mean limits on the corporate electoral speech that currently forces hearers to absorb massive amounts of corporate propaganda that they do not wish to hear.

A free-speech doctrine that takes hearers into account would also involve thinking about when an otherwise unprotected speaker should be allowed to borrow the rights of others in the first place. For example, much speech depicting the violent torture and rape of women or the torture of animals falls outside most people's definition of "the freedom of speech." But when the neighborhood speech regulator tries to suppress it, she is often met by the argument that the poorly drafted regulation might also be used to outlaw hunting videos, Dante's *Inferno*, *Swan Lake*, or *Romeo and Juliet*. That's how the purveyors of animal snuff videos and kiddie porn usually get off. The unprotected speaker borrows the rights of future protected speakers and deploys the borrowed rights to extract an undeserved windfall. In settings where potential future speakers are unlikely to be able to defend themselves effectively, allowing unprotected speakers to borrow their rights today in order to destroy a flawed regulatory scheme that may be deployed against weak protected speakers tomorrow may well be a good idea. That's how the Warren Court often protected civil rights demonstrators. But when the potential future targets of a flawed regulatory regime are powerful speakers fully able to assert their own rights, or when the protected future speech is of no discernible social value, why allow today's unprotected speaker to borrow the rights of tomorrow's speakers at the expense of everyone else in the neighborhood?

TAKING HEARERS SERIOUSLY

Madison's First Amendment is not just about speakers. It envisions a social partnership between committed speakers and informed hearers, both of whom are entitled to be viewed as autonomous human beings vested with dignity, and both of whom are crucial to the proper functioning of choice-dependent institutions like democracy. A First Amendment jurisprudence that gave more than lip service to the dignitary and instrumental interests of autonomous hearers would move the needle closer to Madison's conception of a partnership between speakers and hearers, and away from the current master-servant relationship.

Let me be clear. I am not suggesting that we treat hearers as weak and malleable beings unable to defend themselves from rapacious speakers without help from a paternalistic state. That path empowers government speech regulators to overthrow the speaker and, in the name of protecting weak hearers, to substitute themselves as the dominant force in Mr. Madison's neighborhood. Both the FUCK THE DRAFT and flag-burning decisions were correct in refusing to go down that dangerous road.

I *am* suggesting, though, that First Amendment doctrine should recognize that hearers as well as speakers are entitled to be treated with dignity. As strong, autonomous beings, hearers do not require paternalistic protection against most offensive, distasteful, or even hostile speech. But when demonstrably false speech inhibits the proper functioning of choice-driven institutions or when speech is particularly corrosive of a hearer's dignity, is destructive of a hearers' right to equal treatment, and/or threatens to drown out alternatives, the definition of "the freedom of speech" should reflect proper concern for the hearer. For example, a politician consciously lying about receiving the Congressional Medal of Honor does not help our institutions of democratic choice work better. By vesting the liar with greater respect and persuasive power than he deserves, such a lie makes it harder for an autonomous hearer to make an informed choice about whether to support the liar's positions. Maybe the Court's decision in the Medal of Honor case is consistent with such a hearer-sensitive approach. Maybe that's what the Court meant by suggesting that the lie was not intended to induce specific behavior in reliance on it. But inducing specific behavior on the basis of a lie is not the only way a hearer's dignity can be violated. The undeserved deference and respect that the liar inevitably extracted from his immediate audience, to say nothing of the distress caused to actual winners of the medal for heroism when the lie was exposed, should have counted in the Court's legal calculus. Maybe the outcome would have been the same, but it should have been a much closer case. If we are concerned that the members of the motorcycle gang would use a ban on lying as a wedge to control speech they don't like, why not limit the penalties, rather than elevate the lie to protected status?

Likewise, a family burying a son lost in defense of the nation has earned a dignitary right to a moment's repose from the rantings of religious bigots, even when the rantings take place on a public sidewalk just out of earshot of the funeral. Once again, the Court seemed to nod in that direction when it stressed that the demonstration couldn't be seen or heard from the church. But actual disturbance at the church or grave site isn't the only way the speakers inflicted unnecessary pain on the grieving family. The family's contemporaneous knowledge that the funeral ceremony was being hijacked, just out of earshot, by demonstrators boisterously linking the young soldier's death to toleration of homosexuality at the very moment the young man was being interred imposed gratuitous pain on a family that deserved better. Perhaps even when the interest of the family as involuntary hearers is put into the balance, the case comes out the same way, but the Court's wholly speaker-centered opinion does not even acknowledge the dignity of the grieving family. If we are concerned that huge damage recoveries would risk deterring worthwhile speech, why not regulate the remedy by limiting damages, instead of insisting that speech so destructive of a hearer's dignity is fully protected by "the freedom of speech"? In short, why should the folks in Mr. Madison's neighborhood tolerate a steady diet of useless, potentially harmful speech just because they live in terror of the local motorcycle gang? Can't the gang be rehabilitated or disarmed?

REHABILITATING THE NEIGHBORHOOD MOTORCYCLE GANG

The modern First Amendment is shaped by an almost pathological mistrust of government's ability to regulate speech fairly. For many on the right, mistrust of government and hostility to regulation is a natural reflex, reflecting a worldview where government is always viewed with profound skepticism. For many on the left, more than a century of persecution of labor organizers, civil rights workers, and economic radicals has led to a belief that it is necessary to strip the government of virtually all power to regulate speech in order to prevent government officials from censoring speech that questions the political, social, and economic status quo.

The Supreme Court's pervasive mistrust of government speech regulation is reflected in the three elements of First Amendment strict scrutiny, which is triggered whenever the government seeks to regulate the flow of verbal speech ("pure speech" as opposed to "communicative conduct"). Once the Court unleashes strict scrutiny, the government must demonstrate: (1) a "compelling" governmental interest in regulating the speech immediately, (2) that the regulation will actually advance the government's compelling interest, and (3) that "less drastic alternatives" do not exist for dealing with the government's concern. It is a rare government regulation that survives strict scrutiny. Justice Kagan has perceptively suggested that the strict-scrutiny formula is really designed to police the government's good faith.[48] If the proffered government interest allegedly justifying censorship doesn't seem all that compelling or immediate, if the censorship program isn't likely to solve the problem or isn't the only way to cope with it, a whiff of suspicion is created that the government's real motive is to suppress the speech at issue. Under strict scrutiny, such a "whiff of suspicion" is fatal.

The Court's intense mistrust of government also underlies the five procedural hurdles that can derail an effort to regulate speech.

1. *Prior restraints on speech*, as opposed to subsequent sanctions, are deemed particularly dangerous because they tempt government censors to cover up wrongdoing and prevent unwelcome information from surfacing at all.[49] That's why the Supreme Court refused to let the government block publication of the Pentagon Papers, even though five justices indicated that anyone who leaked the documents might be subject to criminal prosecution.

2. *Overbroad speech regulations* that purport to ban both protected and unprotected speech can be a cover for improperly motivated or overzealous censorship and may frighten speakers away from gray areas.[50] That's why the poorly drafted ban on animal-torture videos was invalidated.
3. *Overly vague speech regulations* are invalidated because the Court fears that they provide local officials with too much discretion, tempting them to use their ill-defined power to advance their own views at the expense of a disliked speaker.[51] That's why so many poorly drafted statutes banning civil rights demonstrations were invalidated during the 1960s.[52]
4. *Unequal speech regulations* are invalid because when the government regulates one speaker but leaves a similarly situated speaker unregulated without a very good reason, the Court perceives a danger of hostility to the content of the speech or the identity of the speaker, and invalidates the statute prophylactically.[53] That's why the *Citizens United* Court reacted so negatively to a statute that allowed individuals, but not corporations, to speak. Unfortunately, the Court begged the question of whether natural persons and corporations are similarly situated speakers.
5. Finally, *First Amendment due process* requires a prompt opportunity for a speaker to protest—usually to a court—against government censorship.[54]

Regulation of communicative conduct, in which speech is closely bound up with action (such as picketing and demonstrating), does not trigger strict scrutiny. Accordingly, it is more vulnerable to improperly motivated censorship. Rather, the Court asks whether the regulation is a "narrowly tailored" good-faith effort at dealing with a "substantial" (as opposed to "compelling") government interest that is "unrelated to the suppression of speech." Unlike the pure-speech cases, the government usually wins communicative-conduct cases; a regulation's fate often depends on which category the Court invokes.

Unfortunately, the Court's formula for distinguishing pure speech from communicative conduct is, to put it charitably, a shambles. According to the Court, burning a flag is pure speech, but burning a draft card is communicative conduct. Spending millions to elect a candidate is pure speech, but casting a write-in protest ballot isn't even communicative conduct.

A third-class speech compartment exists solely for commercial speech (defined as speech that proposes an economic transaction), where fear of improperly motivated government censorship is at its lowest point. It's unlikely that the government cares much whether you buy a Ford or a Buick. Protection of commercial speech excludes false and misleading commercial messages and requires the government merely to prove a "legitimate" reason for regulating the flow of commercial speech.

Unlike the toothless equality standard of review currently used in equality-based voter-suppression cases, First Amendment strict scrutiny, reinforced by the five procedural corollaries, actually works. It's almost impossible to slip an improperly motivated censorship scheme involving "pure speech" past the courts. But such successful prevention has costs. The Supreme Court's most controversial exercise in prophylaxis was the enunciation of an exclusionary rule preventing the use of evidence obtained in violation of the Fourth and Fifth Amendments. The exclusionary rule succeeded in altering police behavior, but at a cost. Guilty persons were set free because the constable blundered. Once the rules were well established and police behavior had changed somewhat, the costs became more visible. The Court reacted by slowly loosening the screws in an effort to minimize unnecessary costs, while retaining the core deterrent effect of the exclusionary rule. First the Court limited federal judicial supervision (called habeas corpus) of state search-and-seizure cases, then it established a good-faith mistake exception, and finally it recognized a host of special settings where the rules would be suspended—most dramatically a public-safety exception that allowed Boston police and the FBI to question the surviving Boston marathon bomber for two days without counsel before falling under the prophylactic rule against using custodial incriminatory statements without telling the defendant he has a right to remain silent.

We are at a point in the evolution of First Amendment doctrine where similar cost-benefit questions may be asked. A powerful prophylactic First Amendment has achieved extraordinary success in deterring improperly motivated government censorship, but at the cost of exposing women to unwanted propaganda as they approach a health facility, exposing minority families to cross burnings, permitting conscious lies, invasions of privacy by bigots, desensitization of children to violence, and the sale of animal-torture videos. The time may be ripe for fine tuning on three levels. First, the deep mistrust of government that fuels First Amendment prophylaxis is based on a fear that officials will use censorship to advance their political or social views. When there are no political views to distort, perhaps the Court should ask whether full-scale protection is necessary. At a minimum, the five procedural corollaries could be loosened to give the regulators some breathing room.

Second, where the institutional value of speech turns on its accuracy and it's relatively easy to decide whether it is factually accurate—as in false advertising or false information about securities—the Court should ask whether the costs to hearers of tolerating consciously false speech clearly outweighs the risks of loosening the prophylactic screws to permit effective regulation of intentional lying.

Finally, when speech denigrates the hearer's dignity in ways that impede a hearer's ability to function as an equal, the Court should ask whether prophylactic protection really is best deployed up front to render the speech fully protected, as opposed to regulating at the back end by acknowledging the unprotected nature of the speech but imposing significant limits on the available sanctions. For example, in settings where speech denigrates the dignity of hearers or speech targets, it's possible to acknowledge the unprotected nature of the speech, while limiting relief to nominal damages or other symbolic remedies designed to restore lost dignity. In short, while keeping the neighborhood motorcycle gang on a very short leash is probably both necessary and wise in political speech settings, it may be neither necessary nor wise where government abuse of the censorship power is less likely. Maybe the best way to deal with the neighborhood motorcycle gang in those settings is just to take away their guns.

OUTING THE CONDUITS

As we've seen, conduits, the skilled artisans in Mr. Madison's neighborhood who are in the business of using technology to amplify the speech of others, have persuaded the Supreme Court to let them dress up as aristocratic speakers. When conduits are transmitting their own speech, as in newspaper editorials, it makes good sense to treat them as speakers. But when newspaper, broadband, or cable companies merely transmit the speech of others, they have their own First Amendment clause—"Congress shall make no law abridging . . . the freedom of the press." Under existing Supreme Court ground rules, though, the Free Press Clause has virtually no independent meaning. The Court reads it as a colony of an imperial Free Speech Clause that does all the heavy legal lifting. If the Free Press Clause is mentioned at all, it's usually to reject a separate role for it. It's as though Madison never bothered to add a provision protecting mass dissemination of speech.

In fact, the "freedom of the press," viewed as a Madisonian protection of the institution needed in a robust democracy to transmit individual speech to a mass of hearers, is not necessarily the same thing as speaker-centered "freedom of speech." Historically, government efforts at censorship initially centered on licensing or regulating the operation of the printing press, not the speaker. John Milton's *Areopagitica*, written in 1644, is rightly viewed as a crucial milestone in the evolution of the First Amendment. But it wasn't about speakers. It was about printers—a plea to parliament to end the practice of requiring the 1644 version of conduits to obtain a printing license from the Crown. Similarly, when in 1734 John

Peter Zenger, the publisher (and printer) of a New York newspaper, was charged with seditious libel for printing articles critical of the royal governor, Andrew Hamilton's celebrated successful defense to the jury was all about the rights of the printer, the conduit, not necessarily the rights of the authors who actually wrote the articles under assumed highfalutin Latin names.

If the Free Press Clause were decoupled from the Free Speech Clause and read as a protection designed for conduits, Madisonian press freedom might be both broader and narrower than the speech freedom currently enjoyed by the press. It could be broader because the institutional press might be viewed as enjoying privileged access to otherwise blocked speakers, such as prisoners, or having a duty to uncover information needed by hearers, such as improperly hidden government secrets. Viewed as a conduit, the press might even be treated more like the telephone company, having no legal culpability in merely transmitting the speech of others without knowing that the speech was false or otherwise unlawful. Such an institutionally protected press might also be subject to regulations seeking to broaden the ability of poor speakers to reach a mass audience or preventing any single press entity from becoming too powerful—a kind of First Amendment antitrust law. The Supreme Court has already opened the door a crack by ruling that when cable companies exercise a "gatekeeping function" that controls access by true speakers to critical speech-transmission technology, reasonable regulations ensuring fair access for vulnerable voices would not violate the cable company's First Amendment or property rights.[55] As we experience the increasing consolidation of the press into a few corporate entities exercising "gatekeeper" control over every form of technological amplification, mandated access for weak voices will become crucial to maintaining a genuine free market in ideas. How else can institutions such as Amazon or a merged Time Warner and Comcast be prevented from running the neighborhood?

FIRST AMENDMENT SWEAT EQUITY

Madison carefully placed a fifth clause protecting collective action immediately after the Free Press Clause had protected mass dissemination of an idea and immediately before the overtly political act of petitioning for a redress of grievances. Freedom of Assembly is perfectly positioned to protect the crucial evolution of an idea into a mass political movement, but you would never know it from current First Amendment doctrine, under which freedom of assembly is almost entirely subsumed under the imperial Free Speech Clause. The Supreme Court treats First Amendment assemblies as a disfavored form of free speech and calls them "communicative conduct." The resulting watered-down constitutional doctrine purporting to protect free assembly is toothless and incoherent. It recognizes that physical assembly is entitled to a degree of First Amendment protection but rapidly transfers broad discretionary authority to local law enforcement officials to regulate, even ban, assemblies in the name of public order.[56] The effect is to permit tightly controlled assemblies in designated places but to place them under intense police scrutiny and render them subject to dissolution virtually at will.

Witness the fate of Occupy Wall Street, an ambitious and chaotic effort to evoke sustained physical assembly in support of an amorphous vision of economic justice. Initial gatherings were tolerated in a number of cities, but the movement was eventually driven from the public square by hostile police forces.[57] It turns out that the right to assemble freely is awfully thin. The Free Assembly Clause's greatest supposed triumph, the protection of demonstrators during the civil rights and anti–Vietnam War era, was something of a mirage. In fact, the Supreme Court's civil-rights-demonstration cases of the 1960s do very little to clarify the law on when marchers or demonstrators are entitled to First Amendment protection. They read like a giant cat-and-mouse game: the Court almost always found a technical way to invoke prior restraint, overbreadth, vagueness, or unequal treatment as a procedural reason for reversing the convictions of demonstrators, without providing much in the way of prospective guidance about when free assembly is protected and when it is not.

Treating freedom of assembly as just a particularly intrusive form of free speech ignores its unique role in the Madisonian structure. Freedom of assembly differs from freedom of speech in at least two important ways. First, the very act of physically assembling generates by-products of the message, including noise, physical blockage, and the potential for conflict, violent and otherwise. Supreme Court doctrine reflects the physical impact of assembling by recognizing broad power to limit assemblies in the name of securing public order under the "time, place, or manner" doctrine, which grants substantial discretion to local police to regulate demonstrations intensively. But treating free assembly grudgingly, as a disfavored, potentially dangerous subsidiary of the Free Speech Clause, ignores the other important way that assembly differs from speech. Not only is free assembly the crucial point of transformation from abstract idea to collective political action, it is the only political component of the First Amendment that is actually free. Effective verbal speech requires mastery of language, inevitably privileging those with the resources to acquire an education and gain access to a mass public. Remember that as recently as 1959, the Supreme Court upheld literacy tests for voting. Freedom of the press is even more resource dependent. Access to expensive mass media capable of reaching and influencing mass audiences is a prerogative of the rich. Freedom of assembly, on the other hand, requires nothing more than physical commitment, a kind of First Amendment sweat equity that opens Madison's poem to the poor.

A jurisprudence of free assembly worthy of Madison's music would not have permitted suppression of Occupy Wall Street on the spurious grounds that it was a threat to public order. While reasonable regulations aimed at preventing violence and unacceptably severe interferences with public order are surely valid, the needle should be adjusted to prevent the police from invoking minor public inconvenience as a discretionary trump to efforts to assemble freely in support of a political ideal.

REMEMBERING THE SPEECH TARGETS

Speech targets are the lumpen proletariat of Mr. Madison's neighborhood. The modern Court almost invariably subordinates their interests to the interests of speakers, hearers, and conduits. The woods are full of Supreme Court decisions celebrating the Kantian dignity of heroic speakers, the importance of informed hearers, and value of hardworking conduits. But the Court rarely seems to notice that speech targets are also Kantian beings entitled to be treated with respect. That's why it was so easy to sacrifice the privacy interest of a deceased soldier's family to the speaker-centered interest of religious bigots eager to hijack the funeral as a way to enhance their audience. Once the Court made sure that no face-to-face hearer interest existed because the church was too far away for mourners to hear the chanting, the Court declined to recognize the family's dignitary interest in not being turned into an involuntary backdrop for hate speech. Perhaps in the end such a dignitary interest should not be enough to silence a speaker, but something seems wrong with the Court's refusal to acknowledge and grapple with the interest at all.

The modern Court's reluctance to acknowledge the dignitary interests of speech targets dates from its iconic 1964 decision in *New York Times v. Sullivan* constitutionalizing the law of libel.[58] The case arose in the context of the Southern civil rights movement, where national press coverage was crucial to the political success of Dr. Martin Luther King Jr.'s strategy of nonviolent moral confrontation. Beginning in the late 1950s, targets of critical Northern press coverage struck back with a series of libel actions before Southern juries, complaining of minor factual errors in the reporting. The speech targets succeeded in winning a series of massive damage awards. When *Times v. Sullivan* reached the Supreme

Court in 1964, the *New York Times* was facing five Southern libel judgments totaling more than $5 million (a huge sum in those days), jeopardizing its financial ability to continue aggressive coverage of the civil rights movement. The Supreme Court responded by developing a First Amendment law of libel making it impossible for a speech target in the public eye to win a damage award based on false defamatory speech unless she could prove that the speaker was on notice of the speech's falsity. The Court called it, confusingly, an "actual malice" standard of liability. Ironically, the *New York Times*, the principal defendant in *Times v. Sullivan*, wasn't functioning as a speaker at all. It was a paid conduit, being sued for printing a paid advertisement placed by a group of Southern clergy seeking to raise funds to defend Dr. King against a phony South Carolina tax prosecution. The advertisement described efforts by Southern college students inspired by Dr. King to fight Jim Crow, and recounted retaliatory actions against the students, including locking them out of their dining hall and subjecting them to police harassment. Claiming that the advertisement had harmed his reputation by exaggerating the level of police harassment, the local police chief won a $500,000 libel judgment against the *Times* from an all-white hometown jury.

Once it was clear that the *New York Times* had nothing to do with writing the advertising copy and had no reason to question the accuracy of the paid advertisement, *Times v. Sullivan* should have been an easy conduit case because the newspaper did nothing but carry a paid advertisement written by someone else. But the Supreme Court didn't treat the *Times* as a conduit. It treated the newspaper as a full-fledged speaker, and gave the *Times*-as-speaker the same First Amendment protection as the *Times*-as-conduit. Thus, under existing law, speakers as well as conduits are immune from damages for harms caused by false speech unless they knew the speech was false before they uttered it. That leaves a giant hole in the neighborhood safety net. Where is the dignitary protection for an innocent speech target harmed by false speech who can't prove that the speaker knew it was false? I believe that proper recognition of the dignitary interest of speech targets requires three tweaks in current libel doctrine.

First, the essentially subjective "actual malice" standard governing speakers should be modified to something resembling gross negligence. Some judges already do that by treating "reckless disregard of the truth" as the equivalent of "actual malice." But the idea should be expanded to impose a duty on both speakers and conduits to meet a reasonable standard of care in determining whether to utter harmful speech about a target. That's what good journalists do now. They should not have to compete with irresponsible or malicious speakers or conduits who don't care whether they are disseminating the truth, but who can hide behind the actual malice standard when their speech turns out to be false.

Second, the prospect of massive damage actions for libel should be minimized, if not eliminated. Elimination of the fear of massive damages would remove the principal reason for ignoring the speech target's interests. If damage actions designed to repair an unfairly damaged reputation were capped to take into account the restorative effect of judicial vindication, the proceedings would begin to resemble "honor courts," designed to restore reputation, not impose ruinous punishment on a speaker or conduit. If, instead of a massive $500,000 verdict in *Times v. Sullivan*, the paper had been faced with a $5, $500, or even a $5,000 verdict, the risk of ruinous deterrence would have been avoided, replaced by a modest incentive to eliminate mistakes, and a judicial finding that restores the speech target's reputation.

Finally, if speech targets are to receive more protection, they must be discouraged from using that protection to bluff speakers into silence. One way to achieve that goal is to limit damages. Another is to impose serious sanctions on baseless actions against speakers, including awards of attorney's fees and the imposition of damages. But whatever paths we take, it's time for a modest upgrade of the status of speech targets in the neighborhood.

8

Divine Madness

Hearing Madison's Music in the Religion Clauses

The Bill of Rights opens with a First Amendment structured as a narrative of a free people governing themselves. That story begins where it must begin, with freedom of conscience. More than a century before Freud, Madison understood that the mainspring of human behavior is found in our psyches. Ronald Reagan, living in twentieth-century fin de siècle California, thought the mainspring was greed. Sigmund Freud, living in nineteenth-century fin de siècle Vienna, thought the mainspring was sex. James Madison, living in eighteenth-century fin de siècle Virginia, was sure the mainspring was conscience. Madison understood that profound conscientious belief, especially religious belief, can be a form of "divine madness," a powerful psychological force that places a true believer in an impossible moral dilemma when forced by the state to choose between god and Caesar. Madison's two religion clauses are structurally designed to respond to that dilemma.

PRIVILEGING CONSCIENCE

As we'll see in a moment, the modern Free Exercise Clause, as tweaked by the Supreme Court, requires us to tolerate conscientiously driven private behavior to the outer limits of a free society's capacity for such tolerance. Conversely, Madison's Establishment Clause imposes strong preventive restrictions on the capacity of true believers wielding governmental power to use that power to impose their religious beliefs on others. What ties the two clauses together is Madison's understanding that the commands of conscience, especially religious conscience, can transcend the capacity for reasoned judgment.

If it had been up to Madison, the First Amendment would have opened with three different ways to protect conscience—non-establishment of religion, free exercise of religion, and freedom of conscience. Madison's original version of the First Amendment contained a separate clause for each.[1] Throughout the summer of 1789, the three clauses rotated in and out of the text. Sometimes the free-exercise clause was discarded in favor of the conscience clause. Sometimes the conscience clause was bumped in favor of free exercise. Sometimes establishment was dropped. The clauses were clearly seen by many to be overlapping, perhaps redundant. The version of the Bill of Rights that passed the House and went to the Senate contained all three clauses. The Senate deleted Madison's proposed conscience clause at the last minute, leaving the Establishment and Free Exercise Clauses to open the Bill of Rights. Because the Senate's deliberations were secret, we'll never know precisely why. I like to think it was because the senators believed that the Establishment, Free Exercise, and Free Speech Clauses already provided full protection to conscience, rendering a separate conscience clause redundant.

One hundred seventy-eight years later, in two cases arising out of the Vietnam War,[2] that's just what the Supreme Court ruled in granting conscientious objector status to two young pacifists who denied the existence of a Supreme Being but professed deeply held secular philosophical objections to wars of any kind. As a technical matter, the Court's plurality merely broadly construed a congressional statute granting conscientious-objector status to religious objectors to war in any form as applying to secular objectors, as well. The plurality's extremely broad reading of the statute was, however, explicitly designed to avoid the serious constitutional question that would have been raised if Congress had granted CO status on the basis of religious belief but denied it to an identical secular believer. Justice Harlan's influential concurrence makes it clear, moreover, that the commands of both religious and secular conscience enjoy equivalent First Amendment protection as long as secular conscience plays a comprehensive role in the believer's life analogous to religion.[3]

Justice Harlan's move from protecting religious conscience under the two religion clauses to protecting secular conscience in the white space between Free Exercise and Free Speech was pure Ninth Amendment equity of the statute in action. The commands of religious and secular conscience are closely analogous. Recognizing an implied protection of secular conscience is broadly harmonious with the First Amendment's text. Most important, as Madison had understood in 1789, protection of secular as well as religious conscience is vital to the First Amendment's story of the evolution of an idea in a well-functioning democracy. In fact, Justice Harlan simply made explicit in 1970 what had been implicit in Justice Jackson's magnificent 1943 rhetoric protecting the right of Jehovah's Witnesses schoolchildren to refuse to salute the flag. Justice Jackson chose not to rest his seminal flag-salute opinion on the Religion clauses. Instead, he recognized First Amendment protection of secular conscience.

Thus, although it took almost two centuries, the Supreme Court used Madison's Ninth Amendment equity of the statute to insert an implied right of secular conscience into the text of the First Amendment, finally correcting the Senate's erroneous rejection of Madison's proposed conscience clause in 1789.

Recognizing the primacy of freedom of conscience in the structure of the First Amendment has one important immediate payoff. It reveals the current Court's error in limiting full free-exercise protection to *intentional* government interferences with religious conscience. Under the Court's current narrow reading of the Free Exercise Clause, religious conscience receives virtually no constitutional protection unless the government is consciously targeting religion. For example, Justice Scalia, writing for a narrow majority, ruled in 1990 that Native Americans can be punished for using peyote in age-old religious ceremonies under general laws banning hallucinogenic drugs. The Court reasoned that since the drug ban was not intended to interfere with religion, the government had no duty to make an exception for a Native American caught between god and Caesar.[4]

Such a grudging view of the Free Exercise Clause cannot be squared with Madison's vision of the importance of a free conscience in a democracy. Intended or not, government prohibition of Native American religious practice forces the true believer to choose between god and Caesar—exactly the existential choice that Madison tried to avoid. Recognizing the primacy of conscience in the First Amendment should lead the Court to provide enhanced constitutional protection against all forms of government interference with individual behavior driven by sincerely held religious or secular beliefs, whether the interference is intentional, reckless, negligent, unthinking, or inadvertent. That's just what Congress did when it reacted to the peyote case by enacting the Religious Freedom Restoration Act (RFRA), providing enhanced protection for religious (and presumably secular) conscience against the federal government.

That is not to say that conscience always wins under Madison's First Amendment or Congress's new statute. Conscience is not a license to harm others. Freedom of conscience does not empower even a true believer to shift the costs of her belief to others.[5] For example, Christian Scientists may neither deny their children critical medical care nor enroll them in school without inoculation against communicable diseases.[6] A religious aversion to paying Social Security taxes doesn't license a true believer to avoid a general duty to help pay for the program.[7] Nor would a religious aversion to unions excuse an employer from complying with the collective bargaining rights in the National Labor Relations Act. In each of those settings, a true believer unfairly asks someone else to bear the costs of the believer's religious conduct. Thus efforts by family-owned corporations to carve a religious exemption from the duty to comply with the employee health insurance obligations of the Affordable

Care Act should have failed because, even if corporations may raise a religious freedom claim (itself a dubious proposition), granting the religious exemption would force the corporation's employees to bear the economic costs of their employer's religious conscience—a classic improper burden shift.

Justice Samuel Alito, writing for the U.S. Supreme Court's five Republican justices in *Burwell v. Hobby Lobby*, insisted that a religious exemption is mandated under RFRA because it carries "zero cost."[8] Read the Alito opinion carefully; it may be the only time in our nation's history that Republicans embrace the idea of a "free lunch." According to Justice Alito's voodoo economics, exempting religious employers from paying for insurance coverage for contraceptives carries no cost to their employees. They will continue to receive full health insurance coverage (including contraceptives), because the insurance company will willingly absorb the premium shortfall on the grounds that it's cheaper to provide contraceptive coverage for free than to pay for the ensuing pregnancy. If Justice Alito's free-lunch fairy tale is correct, the *Hobby Lobby* case is nothing more than an example of tolerating the free exercise of religion as long as there is no cost to anyone else. Who can argue with that? But the jury is out on whether health insurance companies will continue providing free contraceptive coverage to large numbers of employees who happen to work for profit-making corporations owned by religious shareholders. My prediction is that if the numbers get high, the insurance companies will demand a government subsidy that shifts the costs to the taxpayers. But, as we'll see in a moment, requiring taxpayers to subsidize the costs of someone else's religious beliefs is exactly what the Establishment Clause forbids. So we haven't heard the end of the Supreme Court's free-lunch story. Moreover, *Hobby Lobby* may be an example of being careful what you wish for. In order to allow a corporate employer to claim a religious exemption, Justice Alito had to dissolve the wall between shareholders in small family corporations and the corporation itself. A small, family-owned corporation is, Justice Alito ruled, just a group of closely related people gathered together to carry out an economic project. But if the shareholders can "pierce the corporate veil" from the inside in order to claim a corporate religious exemption, why can't creditors, government regulators, and the IRS pierce the veil from the outside to sue the shareholders, as well as the corporation? That's playing with fire because it endangers the bedrock principle of "limited liability" and "corporate separateness" on which our corporate culture rests. Maybe that's why the Chamber of Commerce didn't file a brief in *Hobby Lobby*.

Even when a conscientious exemption is not constitutionally required because it would impose an unfair burden on someone else, respect for the primacy of conscience in Madison's text should lead us to try hard to find a way to accommodate the belief or practice *without* harming others.[9] That's why we voluntarily provide for conscientious objection from compulsory military service, even in times of national crisis. Because exempting a true believer shifts the burden of military service to someone else, no free-exercise right exists, but, channeling Madison, we allow the believer to contribute to the nation in other ways through alternative service. That's probably what we should do in dealing with employers who have deep conscientious scruples about funding health plans providing for abortion or birth control. Perhaps a form of health care "alternative service" is possible that would ensure full benefits for employees while finding another way for the employer to satisfy the full duties of citizenship. Sure, that's formalistic. In the end, the economic consequences are virtually identical. But if it lets a true believer sleep better at night, Madison would be pleased and our democracy strengthened.

What happens when a particularly finicky believer says that her conscience won't even let her apply for the conscientious exemption? During the Vietnam War, we sent so-called noncooperators to jail in droves for refusing to apply for the CO status to which they were almost certainly entitled. Today, when nuns running a business or academics running a religiously affiliated college claim that they can't even fill out the government form that will exempt them from having to support employee health insurance for contraception, should the Supreme Court treat them as it treated Vietnam War noncooperators? I think the answer is no. We fell short of Madison's music when we jailed a generation of our most conscientious young men. We would fall short today if we can't find a way to exempt the nuns or academics without forcing them to violate their consciences. After all, everyone needs a *Shabbos goy* sometimes, even the Little Sisters of Mercy.[10] But whatever we do in an effort to tolerate religious conscience, it cannot shift a significant cost to nonbelievers. That's why religiously based claims to be free to discriminate against blacks or gays in employment or in the delivery of consumer services are such constitutional nonstarters. It would force members of the minority to bear the cost of the true believers' religious bigotry.

THE DARKER SIDE OF DIVINE MADNESS

The two religious conscience clauses function in tandem to ensure both freedom *from* and freedom *of* the most powerful psychological force known to Madison and the Founders: the commands of conscience, especially religious conscience. Madison understood that religion has a dark side capable of inciting true believers to inflict unspeakable cruelties on nonbelievers. Europe was a religious bloodbath; Catholics and Protestants took turns killing each other, uniting only to kill Jews. John Rawls, the leading American political philosopher of the twentieth century, reminded us that the West's vaunted commitment to religious tolerance is really an exhausted truce flowing from the mutual recognition by Europe's Catholics and Protestants that neither could wipe the other out. The Founders knew from personal experience that true believers often use the state to impose their beliefs on others and to persecute, harass, and even annihilate nonbelievers. Much of the New World had been settled by fugitives from government-enforced religious oppression in Europe. Ironically, many religious refugees were perfectly willing to use their newfound political power on this side of the Atlantic to oppress even weaker minorities, to say nothing of exterminating the "heathens" who were here first. That's why, even before there was a Bill of Rights, Article VI, clause 3 forbade the political majority from imposing religious tests for public office, one of the few protections of civil liberties in the text of the 1787 Constitution. Two years later, Madison opened the Bill of Rights with an Establishment Clause that takes the idea of separation of church and state one step further by forbidding public officials from using their government power to impose religious beliefs on others.

The tangled tale of Moscow's Church of Christ the Savior illustrates both sides of Madison's wisdom. Intended as an act of religious thanksgiving for Russia's defeat of Napoléon in 1812, the church's exterior was not completed until 1860 and was not formally consecrated until 1883, although Tchaikovsky's *1812 Overture* received its first public performance in the church a year earlier. Forty tons of electroplated gold embellished its enormous dome. The bejeweled and marbled interior, among the most lavish in Church history, propelled the Church of Christ the Savior to the center of Russian religious life, drawing Russian Orthodox believers for worship, baptism, and marriage from all parts of the realm. In 1930, Stalin, desperate for cash and in the midst of a purge of Russia's churches, ordered the Moscow church to be dynamited after the jewels and precious metals, especially the golden dome, had been confiscated by the state. Demolition was finally completed in 1937. In its place, Stalin ordered the construction of a secular Palace of the Soviets, a huge modernistic structure designed to celebrate the triumph of communism over superstition. Excavation for the enormous new building was interrupted by World War II and was only fitfully resumed during the postwar years of Stalin's waning power. After Stalin died in 1953, Khrushchev inherited an enormous hole in the ground, which he promptly turned into the immense Moscow municipal swimming pool.

In 1988, in my capacity as national legal director of the ACLU, I visited Moscow as a citizen member of an American government delegation discussing the rule of law with Soviet counterparts. It turned out that the two countries held very different ideas of what the rule of law means. We saw the idea as ensuring that those in power would be bound by law in dealing with the people. The Soviets saw it as ensuring that the people would be bound by law in obeying those in power. So it goes.

I noticed the enormous Moscow swimming pool on the bus ride from the airport. Although it was a very chilly day, I could see crowds of people in and around the pool, which stretched for what seemed like miles. I wryly commented to my Russian guide that her countrymen were much hardier than mine. "Americans," I laughed, "would never go swimming in such chilly weather." The guide looked around to make certain that no one was listening, smiled, and shook her head. "You don't understand," she said, "they're not swimming. They're baptizing their children. Stalin may have dynamited the Church of Christ the Savior," she whispered, "but people still come from all over Russia to be married and baptized in its ruins." Score one for Madison's prescient understanding of the unquenchable power of the religious spirit. That's what Free Exercise is all about.

In 1990, after the implosion of the Soviet Union, Boris Yeltsin built a more modest but still impressive cathedral over the Moscow municipal swimming pool. Completed in 1994, the church once again became a center of Russian Orthodox religious life. This time, though, there was an important difference. The clergy, especially the presiding metropolitan bishop, operated as close allies of the Russian state. When Vladimir Putin took power in 1999, he deployed the state-supported Russian Orthodox Church as an arm of the government, using religion as a form of state-imposed social control. The link between the church and Putin was particularly intense in the person of the metropolitan bishop, who vigorously condemned the demonstrations for greater freedom that were taking place in Moscow and urged from the pulpit Putin's reelection as president. In February 2012, three young women, politically active members of an all-girl punk group called Pussy Riot, staged an amateurish forty-second song-and-dance routine, "Virgin Mary, Chase Out Putin," in the nave of the church. The young women chanted opposition to Putin's use of the church as an arm of the state. No services were under way, and the church was almost deserted.

In an appalling overreaction by the state, the three young women were convicted not of the minor administrative offense of disorderly conduct punishable by a fine or a few days in jail but of the felony of "outraging religious sensibilities," and sentenced to two years in a Russian labor camp.

Score another one for Madison's all-to-accurate understanding of the state's capacity to harness the darker side of the religious impulse. The saga of Moscow's Church of Christ reminds us that Madison designed the Free Exercise Clause to protect true believers driven by conscience to baptize their children in a swimming pool where a church once stood, and the Establishment Clause to protect those very children from state-imposed religious and political conformity.

By the way, the fate of Pussy Riot illustrates why the Supreme Court is so nervous about punishing speakers for saying things that offend hearers. I suspect, though, that our disagreement with Putin's punitive reaction is not about whether Pussy Riot was engaged in protected speech. True believers should be entitled to rules banning unwelcome political activity in their church. But two years in prison for a minor transgression is indefensible. It's another reminder that the care and feeding of the First Amendment requires attention to the back-end issue of sanctions as well as the front-end issue of whether or not speech is protected.

HARMONIZING THE RELIGION CLAUSES

The two religion clauses display inconsistent attitudes toward religion. The ban on enacting laws "respecting an Establishment of religion" is deeply suspicious of religion, guarantying Americans the right to be free from state-imposed religious activity. The ban on laws denying the "free exercise of religion" is deeply supportive of religion, guarantying Americans the right to practice religion vigorously and openly. Many observers have noted the potentially discordant relationship between the two clauses. In fact, government efforts to assist the free exercise of religion may cross the line and become forbidden establishments of religion. Conversely, what appears to be a forbidden establishment of religion may also be defended as a government effort to make it easier for private citizens to exercise their religion freely. For example, should a law requiring private employers to grant employees paid time off on their holy days be viewed as improperly establishing religion or properly protecting its free exercise? For the Supreme Court, the answer lies on the Establishment side of the line, because such a law shifts a burden to other employees to work on the weekend.[11] The Court was right. Whenever government forces a nonbeliever to bear the costs of a believer's religious observance, it unconstitutionally "establishes" religion. But a rule merely requiring an employer to make a good-faith effort to respect the religious needs of employees without shifting an unfair burden to nonbelievers—perhaps by asking for volunteers and paying those volunteers overtime—would make Madison smile. We call that accommodating the free exercise of religion.

Consider the constitutionality of government-paid military or prison chaplains. Paying a clergyman a government salary to minister to soldiers or prisoners is unquestionably government assistance to religion that would ordinarily be barred by the Establishment Clause. Indeed, that is precisely how an "established" religion operates: the government uses general tax funds paid by nonbelievers to subsidize the operating expenses of a favored church. On the other hand, providing government-paid clergy in the military or in prisons may be necessary to permit believers confined to those institutions to exercise their religion freely. Indeed, failure to provide for military or prison chaplains might well be attacked as a violation of the Free Exercise Clause. Madison believed that government-paid military chaplains were unconstitutional, but even he could be wrong. No serious Establishment Clause objection has arisen to military or prison chaplains in modern times because the minor burden borne by the taxpayer is dramatically outweighed by the free-exercise benefits of the program. It's a clear net gain for conscience. It's much harder, though, to make the free-exercise argument for government-subsidized "legislative" chaplains who open legislative sessions with a prayer. Unlike prisoners or soldiers, legislators retain freedom of movement (at least until they're convicted), so it's unclear why they would need a government-paid, in-house chaplain to exercise their religious freely. Nevertheless, the Supreme Court has upheld the practice.[12] The Court relied on the fact that congressional chaplains had officiated during Washington's administration, and that Madison, as a congressman, had voted for one. The Court's majority overlooked the fact that an older and wiser James Madison profusely apologized for having voted for legislative chaplains, branding them flatly unconstitutional. The five Republican justices have now compounded the error by extending the idea to opening local town meetings with a so-called ceremonial prayer, even when the prayers are overwhelmingly Christian.[13] The Court simply ignored the question of why a nonbeliever should be forced to feel like an outsider when she attends her own town's zoning board deliberations. Stand by for Christian prayers before school board meetings and court sessions. How many nonbelieving parents and litigants will dare to refuse to stand and bow their heads for the ceremonial prayer? In upholding government-sponsored ceremonial Christian prayers, the five Republican justices appear to have imported the imperial Free Speech Clause idea of an aristocratic speaker whose interests almost always overwhelm those of a subordinate hearer into the Religion Clauses, where until now hearers were treated with far more respect and consideration. Until *Town of Greece*, the constitutional law regulating government-sponsored religious communications—whether prayers or religious displays on government land—was "hearer-centered." The Court always asked whether the nonbelieving hearer was made to feel like an outsider in her own land. After *Town of Greece*, nonbelieving hearers subjected to government-sponsored religious speech may well be told, "Get a thicker skin. After all, this is a Christian country. You're here as a tolerated guest." What the Court seems to have forgotten in *Town of Greece* is that, unlike private speech in most Free Speech Clause settings, a Christian prayer opening a town meeting is speech by the government, not a private person. It's bad enough to have corporations treated as aristocratic free speakers and sentient religious beings. But when the government starts praying, and we have no choice but to listen, it's time to look out!

However you decide the chaplaincy and public prayer cases, though, there is no escape from the paradox of two apparently discordant religion clauses pulling in different directions. Can such discord be harmonized?

DOUBLING DOWN ON DIVINE MADNESS

A narrow majority of the current Supreme Court seeks to tame the paradox by leveling both religion clauses down so that they don't clash. The levelers read both clauses as forbidding improperly motivated, irrational, or discriminatory government action dealing directly with religion, pro or con, but, as in the town meeting case, uphold just about everything else, even when the challenged government program has the effect of suppressing religious conscience or aiding religious institutions. The leveling-down approach turns the religion clauses into bland assurances that religion will be treated no better and no worse than comparable secular institutions. There is, of course, nothing wrong with such an assurance of equal treatment of religion. It is merely the flip side of Justice Harlan's insistence that secular conscience be treated as respectfully as religious conscience. But an exclusive focus on leveling down overlooks Madison's recognition of the immense psychological power of religious beliefs and experiences. The Court's current tendency to tamp down the two religious clauses decreases the tension between them, but at the cost of the structural role of freedom of conscience as the essential starting point for the entire Bill of Rights.

The current Supreme Court's leveling-down approach permits

the government to invoke ordinary drug laws to criminalize the use of peyote in Native American religious ceremonies. It lets the state drive a logging road through a Native American burial ground without considering readily available alternative routes. It condones denying convicted Muslim and Jewish prisoners access to pork-free diets and to religious services on their holy days, as well as a refusal to permit orthodox Jewish or Sikh members of the armed forces to wear religious headgear indoors.[14] Leveling down also permits financial aid or other forms of government support to religion through state scholarships to study for the ministry, financial aid to religious colleges, or tuition vouchers for parochial schools, even when the overwhelming effect of a particular program is to funnel aid disproportionately to religious institutions.[15] Justice Alito has suggested that he would even permit a taxpayer subsidy to cover the cost of allowing religious employers to opt out of paying for health insurance covering contraceptives, but the full Court has not yet faced the question. Stay tuned.

I believe that the key to harmonizing the two opening clauses in the Bill of Rights is not to level them down. Instead, we should *double down* on Madison's understanding of the extraordinary power of religious conscience for good or ill. Madison's vision calls for heightened not lessened protection in both Free Exercise and Establishment settings. Viewed as parallel responses to Madison's understanding of and respect for the enormous power of the religious impulse, the apparent paradox resolves into structural harmony. Ordinarily, we expect citizens to apply a rational cost/benefit analysis in deciding whether to comply with a government regulation or an official duty. When the cost of disobedience is high—such as criminal conviction or public obloquy—we assume that a rational citizen will choose to comply with the law. Madison understood, however, that rational analyses are useless when a true believer is forbidden by government to carry out the commands of god or is told by god to disobey the state. The true believer, by definition in the grip of divine madness for good or evil, has no moral choice but to obey god or conscience. In order to spare people from such a dilemma, Madison's poem provides heightened constitutional protection both *from* and *of* religion.

Of course, where government action is impermissibly motivated by hostility toward religion or an impermissible support of it, both the levelers and the divine-madness justices will strike it down, even if the challenged action advances a permissible government interest. For example, a local zoning ordinance forbidding the ritual slaughter of chickens that was intentionally designed to drive a minority religion out of town is unconstitutional under both a leveling-down and a divine-madness reading of the Free Exercise Clause.[16] Similarly, laws aimed at introducing religion into the public schools by requiring the reading of the Bible, the recitation of a prayer, the display of the Ten Commandments, or the teaching of creationism[17] are unconstitutional under both a leveling and a divine-madness reading of the Establishment Clause. But in the many settings where the government's purpose is opaque or unconnected with religion as the courts define it (as in the passage of drug laws), the leveling-down approach provides little or no constitutional protection for or against religious conscience, while the divine-madness reading is true to Madison's recognition of the power of the religious impulse.

As we've seen, even Madison's divine-madness reading of the Free Exercise Clause has limits. Madisonian respect for conscience does not include behavior that risks harm to others or shifts the burdens of citizenship to third persons. That's why subsidizing the cost of a religious employer's refusal to pay for health insurance covering contraception would violate the Establishment Clause. Nonbelieving taxpayers would be forced to bear the costs of someone else's religious observance. A harder question is whether the ban on voluntary plural marriage by adults is constitutional when it conflicts with the tenets of a religion. My guess is that the current Court would continue to uphold the nineteenth-century ban on plural marriage in order to protect vulnerable young women,[18] but I'm not sure that such a paternalistic approach would be consistent with Madison's intense preoccupation with freedom of conscience.

It may be that grown women know better than the state what kind of life (or marriage) to choose for themselves. Maybe the best answer is to set a minimum age of twenty-five for entry into plural marriage, and ensure an easy way out.

In the end, neither text nor history can fully resolve the paradox of two religion clauses pulling in different directions. But Madison's respect for the enormous power of religion, for good or ill, is the key to understanding them as powerful protections *from* and *of* the force of the religious impulse.

9

The Costs of Ignoring Madison's Music

The Enigma of Judicial Review

Our democratic scorecard leaves a good deal to be desired. The Electoral College, with a vote allocation formula that overrepresents rural states and constantly threatens to choose (and twice *has* chosen) the loser of the popular vote as president, is nobody's ideal of a distinguished way to elect a democratic chief executive. Nor can we be proud of our absurdly malapportioned Senate, where Montana, with 570,000 people, enjoys the same political representation as California, with 38 million, and where a filibuster rule enables senators representing 11 percent of the people to block laws desired by senators representing more than 89 percent. We certainly can't brag about the way we elect members of the House of Representatives when more than 80 percent of the elections are rigged by gerrymandering, or about House procedures where, under current rules, 118 Republicans can prevent the remaining 317 members from voting on legislation. Nor can we be proud of our appalling approach to election administration and voter registration. We have the lowest electoral turnouts in the democratic world, especially by the poor. If more than half the people vote in a presidential election, we consider it a triumph. We get positively giddy if all the votes actually get counted. Finally, if someone tried, he couldn't design a worse way to finance democracy than our judicially imposed campaign finance system, which guarantees the very rich, including large for-profit corporations, an absolute right to spend as much as they can in often successful efforts to manipulate voters and control elected officials.

Despite our less than stellar democracy report card, though, we can justly take credit for one of the most important contributions to the art of democratic governance. We pioneered the idea of giving unelected judges the power to trump the outcome of the democratic process in the name of enforcing the Constitution. We call it judicial review and celebrate it as the key to harmonizing democratic rule with individual rights. Most of the democratic world has now adopted a variant of the practice. But granting such power to a small group of black-robed bureaucrats carries real questions and risks. First, there is the troubling question of where American judges get their judicial review power from. Unlike European constitutions, the text of the U.S. Constitution doesn't contain a single word about it. Then there's the fact that the provisions of the Constitution that really matter, like the Bill of Rights, almost never have a single, objectively knowable meaning. Judges must decide what they actually mean, but more than two hundred years into our experiment with judicial review there is still no consensus about how judges should go about reading the Constitution's ambiguous text, often rendering the outcome of judicial review as unpredictable as the spin of a roulette wheel. Finally, history teaches that American judges have too often gotten the constitutional text terribly wrong, reading the Constitution in ways that reinforce the powerful and ignore the weak.

That's why recovering the ability to hear Madison's music is so important. Remembering how to read the Bill of Rights, especially the First Amendment, as a coherent narrative of democracy instead of a series of unconnected commands would immensely enrich a judge's interpretive tool kit, providing much needed guidance to intellectually honest judges and a firmer popular understanding of our most important political text. While recovering Madison's music will not turn judicial review into a mechanical process with a single right answer (the luminous abstractions in the Bill of Rights will always resist simplistic readings), it will lessen the arbitrariness of our current approach and should lower the odds that a judge will get a fragment of the text catastrophically wrong.

WHERE DOES JUDICIAL REVIEW COME FROM?

As an initial matter, though, why should we worry so much about how judges, as opposed to legislators, presidents, or the people, read the Bill of Rights? Why should an unelected Supreme Court justice's reading trump everybody else's reading? In short, exactly where does the power of judicial review come from?

Most Americans believe there is only one United States Constitution. Physically, of course, that's true. The signed originals of the 1787 Constitution, the 1791 Bill of Rights, and the subsequent seventeen amendments are locked up safe and sound behind plate glass in the Rotunda of Freedom at the National Archives. Most constitutional experts (including virtually all politicians and many judges) insist that there is only one legally correct meaning for each provision in the constitutional text. Expert after expert claims to have discovered the constitutional Rosetta stone that will instruct judges how to decipher the constitutional text's one true meaning. The problem, of course, is that the experts and judges disagree—often bitterly—about which Rosetta stone to use and what that one true meaning is. The problem is made worse by the failure of the Constitution to say anything about giving unelected judges the final power to read the Constitution. In 1803, Chief Justice John Marshall insisted in *Marbury v. Madison* (yes, our James Madison, making a cameo appearance as President Jefferson's secretary of state) that an American judge, confronted with a collision between the constitutional text and a congressional statute, has no choice but to give preference to the constitutional text, even if that means overturning an act of Congress.[1] Since then, whenever anyone asks where the awesome power of judicial review comes from, judges and law professors confidently answer, *Marbury v. Madison*. But my nose gets a little longer each time I use Marshall's reasoning to justify a judge's power to have the last word about the one true meaning of the Bill of Rights. If *Marbury* is really where judicial review comes from, we're in big trouble, because the case is a farce on just about every level. The facts read like the script of a Marx Brothers movie about life on the farcical island of Barataria, with politicians, office seekers, and judges scurrying about, behaving in antic ways. As for the law, Marshall's legal reasoning wouldn't pass muster in my first-year law class. In fact, the legendary chief justice cynically manipulated the facts and the law in an effort to score political points against President Jefferson, even if it meant sacrificing the rights of the litigants before the Court. When we take off the rosy self-congratulatory lenses through which we venerate *Marbury* as a bedrock of our political system, the case is revealed as a naked judicial power grab.

Judicial review is too important to our democracy and too valuable to our freedom to be left dangling from *Marbury v. Madison*. But don't take my word for it. Consider the case for yourself, without the hot air and self-justification that usually afflicts lawyers and judges when they try to explain where judicial review comes from. It's like trying to explain the origin of babies to your young kids. The product is sublime, but the process of creation is left to euphemisms like the stork. *Marbury* is the stork that brings us judicial review.

Those of you, dear readers, who do not enjoy the louche pleasures of American legal history can take my word that the facts of *Marbury* border on the farcical and the legal reasoning is seriously flawed. You may skip to page 171. But you'll be sorry.

MARBURY V. MADISON: A CONSTITUTIONAL FARCE IN THREE ACTS

Prelude to a Farce

Marbury v. Madison unfolds against the comic-opera backdrop of the election of 1800, the nation's first contested electoral transfer of presidential power from one political faction to another.[2] Before the adoption of the Twelfth Amendment in 1804, each presidential elector cast two votes in the Electoral College without designating which was for president and which for vice president. The candidate garnering the most Electoral College votes became president. The runner-up became vice president.[3] The only restriction on electors was that at least one of the two candidates for whom he voted had to be from a different state than the elector. That's how it worked during Washington's two terms. That's how it worked in 1796, the first contested presidential election, when Jefferson lost to Adams in the Electoral College by three votes and became Adams's vice president. Although the 1796 election featured slates for the first time—John Adams and Charles Pinckney for the Federalists versus Thomas Jefferson and Aaron Burr for the Democrats—the relatively large number of candidates receiving electoral votes (thirteen) acted to prevent ties between running mates. In the election of 1800, the voters were confronted with the same rival slates as in 1796, Adams/Pinckney versus Jefferson/Burr. Electors pledged to the Jefferson/Burr slate won a close but clear 73–65 victory in the Electoral College, but Jefferson almost blew the election by failing to ensure that at least one of his electors withheld his second vote from Aaron Burr to prevent a tie. The Federalists got it right. One Federalist elector from Rhode Island withheld his vote from Pinckney and cast it for John Jay, so that the Adams/Pinckney electoral vote was 65–64. Not only did the Jeffersonian electors fail to withhold a vote from Burr, but Anthony Lispenard, an elector from New York, actually sought to cast both of his votes for Burr. Lispenard eventually was persuaded that he couldn't cast both votes for someone from his own home state, so he cast his two votes for Jefferson and Burr. Ironically, while Lispensard was constitutionally disabled from casting two votes for Burr, he could have swung the election from Jefferson to Burr by merely casting his second vote for someone other than Jefferson, but he didn't seem to realize it. If he had done so, Burr would have been elected president by a vote of 73–72.

When the Electoral College ballots, including Lispenard's, were all counted in December 1800, Jefferson and Burr were tied at 73 votes each.[4] Once the 73–73 tie was announced, Burr infuriated Jefferson by failing to take affirmative steps to withdraw his candidacy for president, thereby throwing the formally tied presidential election into the House of Representatives, where, under Article II, section 1, clause 3, each of the then sixteen state congressional delegations was entitled to cast one vote. The votes of nine states were needed to elect the president.[5] Although the Jeffersonian Democrats had won a 68–38 majority in the new House of Representatives, under the Constitution as originally written, the newly elected Congress did not take office until March 4, 1801, leaving the Federalist-controlled lame-duck House of Representatives with the power to choose the next president. Although the Federalists controlled the lame-duck House by a popular vote plurality of 60 percent to 45 percent, they controlled only eight of the sixteen state delegations. Jeffersonian Democrats controlled seven. Vermont was evenly split.

In an effort to break the Electoral College tie, the House conducted thirty-five presidential ballots from February 11 to 17, 1801. The vote was always 8–6–2. Jefferson consistently carried eight states: the seven controlled by Jeffersonians—Kentucky, New Jersey, New York, North Carolina, Pennsylvania, Tennessee, and Virginia—plus Georgia, whose sole surviving Federalist congressman (Benjamin Taliaferro) voted for Jefferson as a matter of conscience.[6] Six Federalist states—Delaware, South Carolina, Connecticut, Massachusetts, New Hampshire, and Rhode Island—voted consistently for Burr. The Vermont delegation, evenly split, cast a blank ballot. The Maryland delegation, controlled by Federalists, also maneuvered to cast a blank ballot.

The deadlocked presidential voting revealed that more was at stake in 1800 than the transfer of power from one president to another. Jefferson was viewed by many as a dangerous egalitarian radical committed to the principles of the French Revolution. Burr, a successful New York lawyer, was considered a much safer bet by conservatives. Some Federalists actually hoped that a sustained deadlock would result in the reelection of John Adams as a compromise candidate. The irony of viewing Thomas Jefferson, a slaveholding Virginia planter with a voracious taste for luxury (he died more than $100,000 in debt), as a dangerous radical seemed lost on the eighteenth-century mind.

Barely two weeks before the scheduled March 4, 1801, inauguration, on the 36th ballot, James Bayard, the sole Federalist congressman from Delaware, persuaded Federalist allies in the evenly split Vermont and Maryland delegations to cast blank ballots, throwing both states to Jefferson. At the same time, Bayard shifted his Delaware vote from Burr to blank and persuaded the South Carolina Federalist delegation to similarly switch from Burr to blank. Although the final vote for Jefferson was 10–4–2, it was a close thing.

On February 17, 1801, when Jefferson's election was finally announced, the Supreme Court's prestige was at a low ebb, in large part because the six justices[7] decided only a small number of appellate cases (the Supreme Court decided only fifty cases in its first decade) and were routinely assigned to "ride circuit" throughout the country to serve as judges in the trial courts, a demanding task requiring arduous travel.[8] Washington's first chief justice, John Jay, had resigned in 1795 to become governor of New York, in part because the Supreme Court did so little and circuit riding was so exhausting.

Under the Judiciary Act of 1789, which had created the lower federal courts, federal courts were divided into three familiar tiers—district courts, circuit courts, and the Supreme Court. But the original circuit courts were not classic intermediate appeals courts. There were no permanent circuit judges. Initially, a circuit court consisted of two Supreme Court justices sitting twice a year with a local district judge. In 1793, the burden was lessened by requiring only one Supreme Court justice, although that created the possibility of a split two-judge circuit court. The two judges sat as multimember original trial courts for certain important cases and as an intermediate appeal forum for certain other cases.

After Jay's resignation in 1795, John Rutledge of South Carolina received a recess appointment in July 1795 as the second chief justice, only to have the Senate deny confirmation after he had presided for less than six months. Rutledge, who appears to have suffered a mental breakdown after the death of his wife, was said to have been so distraught at his rejection by the Senate that he attempted suicide by jumping into the St. James River. One of his slaves jumped in to fish him out.

Washington finally appointed Oliver Ellsworth in 1796. Ellsworth served as chief justice for four uneventful years.[9] He was in Europe negotiating a treaty with Napoléon when news of Jefferson's likely election victory reached him. Ellsworth wasted no time in immediately sending a resignation letter, dated September 30, 1800, to Adams to give the outgoing president time to nominate a successor.[10] Adams received Ellsworth's resignation on December 15, 1800, and immediately nominated John Jay, without bothering to ask him whether he would serve once again. Jay was quickly confirmed by the Senate on December 19, but declined the nomination on January 2, 1801. Adams didn't receive Jay's declination until January 19, 1801. The next day, Adams turned to his recently appointed secretary of state, forty-five-year-old John Marshall, who had been leader of the Federalists in the House of Representatives but had never served as a judge.[11] The Senate confirmed Marshall as chief justice on January 27, 1801, the one-week delay probably attributable to the unhappiness of certain conservative High Federalist senators from New England who viewed Marshall as too moderate.

Marshall took office on February 4, 1801, thirteen days before Jefferson was finally named president-elect. At Adams's request, Marshall agreed to continue serving as acting secretary of state as well as chief justice for another month until the close of Adams's term on March 4. In February 1801, the State Department was where the real power lay. It was Federalist patronage headquarters.

Building the Set: A Large Patronage Trough

The facts of *Marbury* unfold during the charged two weeks between Jefferson's delayed election as president on February 17, 1801, and his inauguration on March 4, as Federalists scrambled for patronage jobs before their party lost control of the national government it had dominated since 1789. The patronage bonanza was fueled by congressional passage of the District of Columbia Organic Act on February 27, 1801, just five days before the Federalists went out of power, giving the outgoing president the ability to appoint an entire government from scratch for the new District of Columbia. The D.C. Organic Act provided for a full complement of officials, ranging from an unlimited number of justices of the peace to marshals, notaries, surveyors, lawyers, and military officers. Well over a hundred new jobs were created.

On March 2, Adams nominated forty-two justices of the peace for the new District of Columbia, as well as a full complement of notaries, federal marshals, and other executive officials. The five-year low-level justice-of-the-peace posts were unsalaried. Compensation was based on charging fees for the issuance of legal writs. Jurisdiction was capped at $20. The judicial position appears to have been partly honorific but carried the general duty to maintain public order. The population of the District of Columbia in 1801 was approximately 10,000 whites and 4,000 blacks, including 800 freedmen, so 42 justices of the peace—one for every 240 residents—seems excessive. Jefferson eventually settled on 30.

The D.C. Organic Act also provided for a prestigious Article III three-judge circuit court with lifetime terms. Marshall's younger brother, James, received one of the plum circuit judgeships, as did Abigail Adams's nephew, William Cranch. But with only four days to perform the task, time ran out on Marshall's effort to find a chief judge for Adams to appoint. Adams's first choice, ex–Supreme Court justice Thomas Johnson, unexpectedly said no, leaving the coveted appointment to Jefferson. Jefferson promptly appointed a staunch supporter, William Kilty of Maryland.

The judicial patronage scramble didn't stop at the District of Columbia. On February 13, 1801, four days before Jefferson was named president-elect and just under three weeks before the Federalists went out of power, President Adams persuaded the lame-duck Congress to pass the so-called Midnight Judges Act, creating sixteen new lifetime Article III circuit judgeships throughout the country, in addition to the three for the newly created District of Columbia two weeks later. While they were at it, as part of the Midnight Judges Act, Congress prospectively reduced the number of Supreme Court justices to five (in an apparent effort to deny Jefferson an appointment), abolished circuit riding by the justices as no longer necessary (since there was now a permanent corps of nineteen new lifetime circuit judges), and granted power to the lower federal courts to decide questions of federal law (federal question jurisdiction), in addition to the already existing power to decide cases involving citizens of different states (diversity jurisdiction). The abolition of circuit riding, creation of permanent circuit intermediate appellate courts, and the grant of federal question jurisdiction were needed judicial reforms. Each was eventually adopted.[12] But the claimed justification for moving from six to five Supreme Court justices—a desire to avoid ties—seemed a transparent effort to deny Jefferson a Supreme Court nomination. It poisoned the entire bill, causing the legislation to be widely viewed as a partisan effort to perpetuate Federalist power through the judiciary after the party's defeat at the polls.

The entire Midnight Judges Act was repealed a year later on March 8, 1802, by the newly elected Jeffersonian Congress, returning the Supreme Court to six members, reinstating circuit riding, revoking the grant of federal question jurisdiction to the lower federal courts, and throwing sixteen of the new "lifetime" circuit judges out of work. No similar effort was made to repeal the 1801 Organic Law for the District of Columbia, leaving the forty-two low-level five-year justices of the peace and the three lifetime D.C. circuit judgeships unscathed.

Enter the Players

In 1801, John Marshall, wearing his secretary-of-state hat as chief of patronage for the outgoing Federalists, faced intense, ongoing pressure to produce patronage jobs. The pressure apparently affected

Marshall, who was also serving as chief justice. In late February 1801, Marshall botched the delivery of a federal district-court commission[13] to Federalist senator Ray Greene of Rhode Island, who had resigned from the Senate to accept Adams's judicial nomination. Greene had been named to the district court, but his commission incorrectly called it a circuit court. After he took office, Jefferson claimed that the transcription error voided Greene's appointment, and he named a new district judge for Rhode Island over howls of outrage from New England Federalists. Greene wound up losing both his Senate seat and the district-court judgeship. Adams paid a price as well. Greene's Rhode Island Senate vacancy was filled by Christopher Ellery, a Jeffersonian who voted in 1802 to repeal the Midnight Judges Act. Because repeal barely passed the Senate by a vote of 16–15 (with Vice President Burr in the chair in opposition), the botched Greene nomination probably cost Adams his sixteen midnight circuit judges.[14]

Most important for the case, Marshall also failed to deliver many of the District of Columbia patronage commissions. Because the office seekers did not even have offices to seek until passage of the D.C. Organic Act on February 27, 1801; hadn't been nominated by the president until March 2; and weren't confirmed by the Senate until March 3; it would have taken a Herculean effort in those pre-word-processing days to prepare, sign, seal (with wax), and deliver the numerous commissions of office before the expiration of Adams's term on March 4. Preparing and delivering the commissions was made even more difficult because Marshall had graciously lent Jacob Wagner, the chief clerk of the State Department, to Jefferson as a temporary secretary on February 17, as soon as Jefferson was named president-elect. When Jefferson became president on March 4, he discovered dozens of undelivered commissions on Marshall's desk at the State Department. Furious over the Federalists' patronage shenanigans, Jefferson instructed his acting secretary of state, Levi Lincoln, to withhold William Marbury's commission, along with the numerous others found undelivered in Marshall's office. Analogizing the commissions to deeds that don't pass title to real property until physical delivery, Jefferson argued that failure to deliver the commissions left the Adams patronage appointments incomplete and subject to revocation by a new president.

The Federalists accepted the argument for executive patronage appointments. For example, Adams's appointment of James Lingan as a federal marshal for the District of Columbia failed because the commission had not been delivered in time. Ironically, before learning that his appointment had failed, Lingan served as a marshal at Jefferson's inauguration, escorting him to the ceremony. But the Federalist legal brain trust (consisting largely of Charles Lee and John Marshall) rejected the analogy as applied to judicial appointments, insisting that even a low-level local judicial appointment like Marbury's, involving presidential nomination and Senate confirmation, became final after Senate confirmation, delivery of the commission being merely a formality.[15]

After being sworn in by Chief Justice Marshall on March 4, 1801, President Jefferson asked acting secretary of state John Marshall to serve for one more day until Levi Lincoln, Jefferson's choice for attorney general, could stand in for James Madison, delayed in Virginia on family business, as the new acting secretary of state. Marshall served the additional day but apparently made no effort to deliver the patronage commissions during the one-day reprieve.[16] The same cannot be said for his younger brother, James, newly appointed a lifetime D.C. Circuit judge. In a bizarre episode, James Marshall appeared at the State Department on March 4 and scooped up twelve undelivered JP commissions for Alexandria, Virginia, claiming that it was important to deliver them to ensure that a sufficient number of justices of the peace would be in office to maintain order in the face of anticipated rioting over Jefferson's inauguration. James Marshall does not appear to have signed a receipt for the commissions and seems to have returned most, if not all, undelivered by the end of the day. There was no rioting in connection with the inauguration.[17]

William Marbury, a Georgetown Federalist and protégé of Navy

Secretary Benjamin Stoddert, had snagged one of the forty-two justice-of-the-peace appointments.[18] He was a Jeffersonian nightmare.[19] The youngest son of a youngest son, Marbury was landless. He made his fortune, such as it was, as a banker, financial speculator, and Maryland government bureaucrat. He had served as Agent for the State of Maryland (the state's highest unelected office), where he functioned as a tax collector and dabbled in government procurement, most dramatically on behalf of Navy Secretary Stoddert. A hint of scandal dogged his work in connection with a Maryland shipbuilding contract. Marbury had also been active in Maryland Federalist politics, seeking unsuccessfully to alter the Maryland Electoral College voting scheme to prevent Jefferson from receiving any Maryland electoral votes in the 1800 election.

Although Jefferson granted recess appointments to twenty-five of Adams's forty-two nominees, leaving only five of his own choosing, Jefferson drew the line at Marbury and several other Federalist stalwarts. Nine months into Jefferson's first term, Marbury and three other disappointed nominees, Dennis Ramsay, Robert Townsend Hooe, and William Harper,[20] demanded their JP commissions from Madison, who shunted them off to his chief clerk, Jacob Wagner. Wagner claimed to know nothing about the matter and sent them to Levi Lincoln, who had been acting secretary of state from March 5 to May 7, when Madison finally took over. Lincoln was unhelpful. Rebuffed by Madison, Wagner, and Lincoln, the four office seekers, represented pro bono by Charles Lee (who had been the nation's third attorney general from 1795 to 1801 in both the Washington and Adams administrations), complained directly to the Supreme Court, seeking an order directing Madison, as secretary of state, to deliver the four commissions. The date *Marbury* was filed—December 16, 1801— is suspiciously close to Jefferson's first address to Congress on December 8, 1801, in which he had called for the repeal of the Midnight Judges Act. Filing *Marbury* was probably the Federalists' response to Jefferson's speech—a threat to challenge the constitutionality of any such repeal.

Lee sued directly in the Supreme Court, invoking its so-called original (as opposed to appellate) jurisdiction. Lee relied on a provision of the Judiciary Act of 1789 authorizing the Supreme Court to issue affirmative directions to federal officials, called writs of mandamus, to compel the officials to perform their duties. Marbury's petition claimed that he had been nominated by the president and confirmed by the Senate, that his commission had been duly signed by President Adams, and that the seal of the United States had been duly affixed by none other than John Marshall as acting secretary of state. Lee asked Marshall for an order directing Madison to carry out his clear legal duty to deliver the four duly signed and sealed justice-of-the-peace commissions.

Congress, the president, and the Supreme Court then staged a legal farce in three acts worthy of Monty Python.

Act I: The Disappearing Supreme Court Term

Act I begins with Jefferson's refusal even to acknowledge Marbury's petition. Although Jefferson's attorney general, Levi Lincoln, was physically present in the Supreme Court chamber on December 17, 1801, when the petition was presented to the Court, Jefferson directed him to ignore it. When Madison failed to respond, Marshall scheduled a hearing on the merits for the fourth day of the upcoming Supreme Court term scheduled to begin in February 1802. In an obvious effort to prevent Marbury's petition from being heard, Jefferson persuaded the newly elected Jeffersonian-controlled Congress to cancel the 1802 term of the Supreme Court, delaying the Court's next sitting for fourteen months. Instead of an 1802 appellate term, the six Supreme Court justices were bundled into stagecoaches and sent jolting all over the country as emergency trial judges.

In canceling the Supreme Court's 1802 term, Jefferson was probably more concerned over a potential challenge to Congress's decision to abolish the sixteen lifetime circuit judgeships created under the Midnight Judges Act and throw those new "permanent" judges out of work. Since no problem existed with their commissions, no deposed circuit judge brought a proceeding in the Supreme Court analogous to Marbury's, although twelve, led by Oliver Wolcott, unsuccessfully petitioned Congress for relief. Instead, Charles Lee, seeking a test case, questioned whether judgments issued by the deposed midnight judges while in office could be enforced by Supreme Court justices riding circuit as trial judges.[21] Lee argued that the repeal act of 1802 was invalid on two grounds—lack of power to throw the Article III circuit judges out of office and lack of power to make Supreme Court justices function as trial judges. Marshall could have accepted either of Lee's arguments and precipitated a showdown with Jefferson and Congress. In fact, Lee's second argument is the basis for Marshall's opinion in *Marbury*. Marshall appears to have tried to organize resistance to the repeal inside the Court by a series of letters to the justices but failed to obtain majority support. In the end, the Court blinked. Marshall, riding circuit as a trial judge, upheld his power to enforce a judgment issued by a deposed midnight circuit judge.[22] He then disqualified himself on appeal to the full Court. One week after the decision in *Marbury*, Justice William Patterson, writing for the remaining four members of the Court who were in Washington, affirmed. But that left the petition in *Marbury* to be decided.

Act II: How Not to Find Facts

Act II of *Marbury* opens in early February 1803, after the justices had limped back home in various stages of disrepair after a year of riding circuit. The Court was not able to scrape together a quorum until February 10. Justice William Cushing was so banged up that he never did make it to Washington for the 1803 term. Justice Alfred Moore's ailments delayed him in North Carolina until mid-February and caused him to miss the evidentiary hearing and oral argument. Justice Samuel Chase was so ill that the Supreme Court deliberations had to be adjourned from the Court's cramped and drafty chamber in the Capitol to the comparative comfort of the justices' residence at Stelle's Hotel.

As the moving parties, Marbury and his co-petitioners, who had alleged back in December 1801 that their commissions had been duly signed by President Adams and duly sealed by Secretary of State Marshall, had the burden of proving the truth of their allegations. The justice-of-the-peace nominations had not been made until March 2, 1801, and had not been confirmed by the Senate until March 3. Because Adams's term expired on March 4 (he left the White House for Boston at 4:00 A.M. on March 4 to avoid attending Jefferson's inauguration), and because Marshall was busy on the morning of March 4 swearing in the new president, there wasn't much time to prepare, sign, and seal the forty-two JP commissions and the numerous other commissions needed for the newly appointed notaries public, registers of wills, judges of the orphan's court, marshals, surveyors, military officers, and a D.C. attorney. Getting through all the paperwork was particularly difficult because Adams was working out of the unfinished White House, while Marshall was working out of rented rooms housing the Department of State about a quarter mile away, necessitating the shuttling of more than a hundred documents from the White House, where they were signed by the president, to the Department of State, where they were sealed by the secretary of state for delivery to the appointees. Although the weather on the night of March 3 appears to have been clear, the roads were unlit and unpaved. The operation appears to have run out of time, almost certainly leaving at least one or more of the justice-of-the-peace commissions in *Marbury* uncompleted when time ran out at midnight of March 3.[23]

As petitioner, it was Marbury's obligation to demonstrate that his commission had in fact been duly signed and sealed before time ran out. Otherwise there was no basis for claiming that Madison was avoiding his clear legal duty to deliver the completed commission. Because Jefferson was boycotting the proceedings, neither Marbury nor the justices ever got their hands on the disputed commissions, which had probably been destroyed long before Madison arrived in town on May 1, 1801.[24] Not only did Jefferson decline to produce the commissions, he also arranged for a friendly Senate to refuse to provide any information about whether Marbury and his co-petitioners had actually been confirmed. In order to allow Marbury's lawyer, Charles Lee, to prove the allegations in Marbury's petition, Chief Justice Marshall held a mini-trial in the Supreme Court chamber on February 10–11, 1803, before the four justices who were in town.[25] The hearing opened with compelled testimony from two State Department clerks. Jacob Wagner, the chief clerk, denied personal knowledge of the events because he had been temporarily assigned to president-elect Jefferson. Wagner stated that he believed that two commissions had been signed but that at least one remained unsigned. Daniel Brent, the ranking assistant clerk, testified that Marbury's commission had been on the list to be signed and that, while he lacked personal knowledge of the signing, he was "almost certain" it had been signed. Charles Lee then turned to Attorney General Levi Lincoln (who had been Jefferson's acting secretary of state from March 5 to May 7, 1801) and called him as a surprise witness. Lincoln declined to testify, claiming that he had no instructions from the president. Astonishingly, Lincoln also invoked the self-incrimination protections of the Fifth Amendment, perhaps because he had destroyed the commissions while acting as secretary of state. The commission has never been found. Lincoln also claimed a rudimentary form of executive privilege concerning facts learned by a cabinet officer in the course of his duties. It could've been a scene from the Nixon tapes case.[26]

Levi Lincoln finally agreed to consider written questions. The next day, he answered three of the four written questions propounded by Lee. Lincoln recalled seeing a large number of completed but undelivered commissions on the morning of March 4 but could not recall if Marbury's was among them. Lincoln then swore that he had not turned a commission for Marbury over to James Madison when Madison finally took office as secretary of state in early May 1801. Significantly, despite Lee's prodding, Marshall did not insist on learning what, if anything, Lincoln had actually done with Marbury's completed commission, assuming it ever existed. Either Marshall wanted to spare Lincoln from having to take the Fifth again, or he knew that Marbury's commission had never been completed because, as acting secretary of state, he was the person who would have completed it. Somehow, I doubt that Marshall was worried about Lincoln being forced to take the Fifth again.

In the end, the only evidence of Marbury's signed commission produced at the February 10 hearing was an affidavit from the fiercely partisan James Marshall, John Marshall's younger brother, describing his unauthorized March 4, 1801, foray into the State Department, where he claimed to have seen signed commissions for Hooe and Harper (but not Marbury) on a table. James Marshall's affidavit should have forced the disqualification of his older brother (especially because they had corresponded over John Marshall's failure to have delivered the commissions), and says nothing about a commission for Marbury. Charles Lee, Marbury's canny lawyer, aware of the hole in his proof, sought to supplement the record after the close of the February 11 hearing by submitting an affidavit from a third clerk, Hazen Kimball, who Lee claimed had returned to Washington without his knowledge immediately prior to the hearing.[27] Kimball, a partisan Federalist, was listed as one of President Adams's private secretaries and had left the State Department after Jefferson's election. Kimball swore that he had seen signed commissions for Marbury and Hooe on the evening of March 3. Kimball's affidavit, which is the only evidence that Marbury's commission was actually signed by President Adams, appears to have been treated as untimely. Because it had not been subjected to cross-examination or rebuttal, Marshall, an excellent trial lawyer, knew that it was inadmissible hearsay. Nor does it say anything about the commissions having been sealed. Only John Marshall could testify to that point. In the end, the untimely Kimball affidavit does not appear to have been accepted by the Court.[28]

The factual record supporting Marbury's petition, especially if one ignores the untimely Kimball affidavit, is very thin. The president did not appoint Marbury until March 2, 1801. The Senate, acting in executive session, did not confirm Marbury, his forty-one justice-of-the-peace colleagues, and the numerous other newly appointed D.C. officials until sometime on March 3. We know that Adams went to bed at nine P.M. on the evening of March 3 in order to catch the 4:00 A.M. coach out of town. We know that in the short period between Senate confirmation and Adams's bedtime, a river of commissions had to be signed by President Adams in the White House and shuttled to John Marshall at the State Department for signing, sealing, and delivery. We know that the paperwork was being prepared in the absence of the chief clerk, Jacob Wagner, who was then working for president-elect Jefferson, and in two locations a quarter mile apart linked by an unlit dirt road. We know that Marshall had no time to do anything with the paperwork on March 4 because, wearing his chief-justice hat, he was busy accompanying Jefferson to the swearing-in ceremony, where he administered the oath of office. The fact is that we will never know whether Marbury's commission was actually signed by President Adams before he retired for the night or, if signed, whether John Marshall affixed the seal of the United States before time ran out. What we do know is that the only two witnesses with personal knowledge of whether Marbury's commission was duly signed and sealed—John Adams and John Marshall—failed to represent that the document was timely signed and sealed.

Act II concludes when, after due consideration of the factual issues raised at the evidentiary hearing, Chief Justice John Marshall solemnly accepts the word of his younger brother, James, that Marbury's missing commission had indeed been duly signed and sealed by John Adams and John Marshall before the expiration of Adams's term,[29] even though James's affidavit says nothing about Marbury. Justice Moore joined the factual finding even though he was not present for the hearing. Can you say "banana republic"?

A Short Musical Hymn to the Rule of Law

Chief Justice John Marshall then leads the Court in a stirring, if somewhat partisan, hymn to the rule of law.[30] Marshall announces that, under the rule of law, the Supreme Court is duty-bound to pass on the legality of President Jefferson's and Secretary of State

Madison's failure to deliver the commission to Marbury. Because, intones Marshall, Madison is under a clear legal duty to deliver the commission, he and Jefferson should be ashamed of themselves for flouting the rule of law.

Act III: Find the Missing Court

Act III begins as poor Marbury, all but drunk on the rule of law, holds out his hands for his commission, only to have John Marshall wallop him with a rolled-up copy of the Constitution. Marshall tells the stunned Marbury that, despite his clear legal rights, the Supreme Court can do nothing for him because his fancy lawyer had mistakenly sought relief directly from the Supreme Court in reliance on an unconstitutional 1789 statute that mistakenly granted the Supreme Court power to hear Marbury's case immediately as part of its "original" jurisdiction. Since, rules Marshall, the 1789 statute gave the Supreme Court more power than the Constitution allows, the statute was unconstitutional. Marshall explains that Marbury's lawyer should have started in a lower court and then appealed to the Supreme Court, invoking its "appellate" jurisdiction.[31] The farce concludes with a bewildered Marbury on his hands and knees frantically searching for the lower court where he should have filed his case. Guess what? There was no lower court. The joke's on Marbury—and on us. Marbury had to be sacrificed to allow John Marshall to declare a law unconstitutional for the first time.

If Marbury had actually filed his case in the lower courts as Marshall's decision required, he would have faced a procedural double whammy. No lower federal court would have had power (federal question jurisdiction) to decide his claim that Madison was violating federal law by refusing to deliver the commission. And even if such power had existed, no lower federal court would have had power to issue an affirmative court order to Madison, because in 1803 lower-court federal judges were not authorized to issue a mandamus, a court order requiring an official to perform a specified official action.

Once Congress had repealed Adams's Midnight Judges Act on March 8, 1802, lower federal courts no longer had power to decide cases involving disputes over federal law (federal question jurisdiction). Believe it or not, after the Midnight Judges Act was repealed, only state courts could decide cases governed by federal law. Lower federal courts would not be given that power again until 1875. In the absence of some backup story about why a lower federal court was empowered to decide his case, it would have been futile for Marbury's lawyer to have filed his federal law case in a lower federal court just as Congress was getting ready to repeal the court's power to decide federal cases. The logical backup story for Marbury in 1801–2 would have been Congress's grant of power to the lower federal courts to decide cases when the opposing parties were from different states (diversity jurisdiction). But diversity jurisdiction was unavailable to Marbury in 1801 because the District of Columbia, where Marbury lived, was not treated as a state by Congress for the purposes of diversity jurisdiction until 1947. In 1801, Marbury would not have been deemed a citizen of any state for the purposes of invoking the power of a federal court under diversity jurisdiction.

Even if he could have figured out a way to get into lower federal court, Marbury would not have been able to get the affirmative court order he needed. In 1801, only the Supreme Court had clear power to issue an affirmative order of mandamus because the 1789 Congress had explicitly bestowed the power on the Supreme Court. Congress would not grant mandamus power to the lower federal courts until 1962.

Nor could Marbury have sought relief in state court. In 1801, state courts lacked power to give orders to a federal official. Indeed, they probably lack the power today. It might have been possible for Marbury, as a resident of the District of Columbia, to have sought relief in the new D.C. Circuit Court, which had survived repeal of the Midnight Judges Act. As a practical matter, though, the D.C. Circuit was off-limits, because one of the circuit judges was none other than James Marshall, John Marshall's younger brother, who had broken into the State Department in an effort to deliver the justice-of-the-peace commissions on the day of Jefferson's inauguration. I assume that even John Marshall wouldn't have had the chutzpah to decide an appeal from his brother involving factual findings about his own conduct in putatively placing the seal of the United States on Marbury's commission before Adams left office. Most important, though, William Kilty, chief judge of the D.C. Circuit Court, was a staunch Jeffersonian who got the job because Adams and Marshall ran out of time to fill it. Moreover, while the Supreme Court eventually upheld the D.C. Circuit's power to grant affirmative relief in 1838, that power was far from clear in 1801.[32]

The ACLU test-case lawyer in me says that in December 1801, Charles Lee was right in deciding that for Marbury it was the Supreme Court or nothing. It turned out to be nothing. In stating that an alternative forum existed, Marshall was just blowing smoke.

A Requiem for the Invention of Judicial Review

A solemn Chief Justice John Marshall then turns to the audience and seeks to justify judicial review. He insists that the Supreme Court was obliged to turn Marbury away out of respect for the rule of law despite his "clearly established" legal rights, because the 1789 statute that gave the Supreme Court power to decide cases like Marbury's violated the Constitution and was therefore unenforceable.[33] But hold the applause. First read Article III, which lays out the power of the Supreme Court, and judge for yourself whether the chief justice protests too much. The two relevant sentences of Article III provide:

> In all cases *affecting Ambassadors, other public Ministers and Consuls*, and those in which a State shall be a party, the Supreme Court shall have original Jurisdiction. In all the other Cases . . . the Supreme Court shall have appellate Jurisdiction, both as to Law and Fact, *with such Exceptions and under such Regulations as the Congress shall make.*

(paragraph)
The phrase omitted by the ellipsis is "before mentioned," which presumably refers to Constitutional III.2.1. Don't know why Neuborne thought that omission necessary.

Chief Justice John Marshall, the first constitutional literalist, argued that because Marbury was neither an ambassador, a public minister, nor a consul, his case could not be heard by the Supreme Court as an original matter, no matter what Congress said in 1789—although it still remains unclear to me why Marbury's case did not "affect" Madison in his capacity as a "public Minister."

Marbury responded that the concluding phrase, "with such Exceptions and under such Regulations as the Congress shall make," provided Congress with flexibility to move Supreme Court cases back and forth between appellate and original jurisdiction.

Marshall insisted, however, that the "Exceptions and Regulations" language applied only to the second quoted sentence dealing with appellate jurisdiction, which would give Congress the power to remove cases from the Supreme Court's appellate jurisdiction, but not to add them to the Court's original jurisdiction. In fairness, Marshall's reading has a slight grammatical edge because the use of a comma instead of a semicolon to introduce the exceptions-and-regulations language implies that it modifies only the sentence of which it is a part. But just as the use of capital letters in the Constitution is notoriously arbitrary, punctuation in 1787 was an art, not a science. The difference between a comma and semicolon is a thin reed on which to rest a reading of Article III that places the Supreme Court's appellate jurisdiction at the perpetual political mercy of Congress. Moreover, even if the exceptions-and-regulations language applies only to the second sentence of Article III, the first sentence describing the Court's mandatory original jurisdiction may be read as describing a jurisdictional minimum, not as imposing a jurisdictional maximum, which would mean that additional power could be granted to the Supreme Court above the enumerated constitutional minimum.

In the end, a fair reading of the literal text of Article III simply does not tell us for certain whether Congress may (or even must) remove a case from the Supreme Court's appellate jurisdiction by shifting it to original jurisdiction instead of just dropping it into a legal black hole. Structurally, Marshall's reading is a separation-of-powers disaster because it empowers Congress to eliminate the Supreme Court's crucial appellate jurisdiction without putting the appellate cases anywhere else. When President Bush and a complaisant Congress sought to strip the Supreme Court of appellate jurisdiction over appeals from detainees at the military prison at Guantánamo Bay, they were merely accepting the invitation issued by John Marshall in *Marbury*.

But wait, there's more. How could John Marshall, writing in 1803, have substituted his reading of an ambiguous Article III (drafted in 1787) for an equally plausible alternative reading that had obviously persuaded Congress in 1789 when it passed the law giving the Supreme Court power to hear cases such as Marbury's in the first place. Why would a Supreme Court justice in 1803 be in a better position to read Article III accurately than the 1789 Congress, many of whose members, including James Madison, were personally involved in the drafting, consideration, and ratification of Article III? And why adopt a reading of Article III that makes mincemeat of Congress's thoughtful policy decision in 1789 to trust the Supreme Court—and only the Supreme Court—with immediate affirmative judicial power over badly misbehaving federal officials? Most important, why adopt an interpretation of the Constitution leaving someone like Marbury with nowhere to enforce his "clearly established" legal rights? How does it advance the rule of law for Marshall to have adopted a reading of Article III that deprived a deserving litigant of any access to the courts and invited future Congresses to eviscerate judicial review by invoking Marshall's questionable reading of the "Exceptions and Regulations" Clause?

JUDICIAL REVIEW'S FIRST DIRTY LITTLE SECRET

That brings those of you, dear readers, who have survived the trek through the legal history wilds of *Marbury* to the first dirty little secret of judicial review. When a collision between a statute and the Constitution is clear and unavoidable, Chief Justice Marshall's opinion in *Marbury* makes a compelling logical case for a judge's duty to enforce the Constitution's text, not the statute's. But Marshall's reasoning in *Marbury* says next to nothing about settings, like *Marbury* itself, where reasonable people can differ over how to read the constitutional text. As a matter of logic, in settings where at least two plausible readings coexist, why should the judge's reading always trump Congress's equally plausible reading? In *Marbury*, it seems reasonably clear that, unlike a case where there's a clear collision between the constitutional text and a statute, Chief Justice Marshall had a choice—which he exercised poorly (or politically). He could have created a collision between the 1789 statute and Article III of the Constitution by reading the Exceptions and Regulations Clause very narrowly, or he could have avoided one by reading the Article III text more flexibly. Why shouldn't Marshall have been obliged to defer to James Madison's equally plausible reading of Article III as a member of the 1789 Congress that had adopted the statute in question?

So the first dirty little secret of judicial review is that in more than two hundred years of Supreme Court precedent glibly citing *Marbury* as the source of the Court's power to declare statutes unconstitutional the Court doesn't even try to distinguish between "train wreck" cases involving an unavoidable collision between the Constitution and a statute (where the reasoning of *Marbury* actually works) and cases where either the statute or the ambiguous constitutional text can be plausibly read to avoid the collision (where *Marbury* is no help at all). Invoking the iconic power of *Marbury* and relying on the fact that judicial protection of individual rights is one of our most admired contributions to the art of democratic governance,[34] the Supreme Court simply plows ahead, proclaiming its "responsibility" (and power) to "say what the law is."[35] Sometimes, as in Chief Justice Roberts's 2012 opinion upholding the Affordable Care Act,[36] the Court (or at least the chief justice) appears to maneuver to avoid a collision; sometimes, as in *Marbury* itself, the Court appears to labor to construct the collision. But in the absence of a constitutional train wreck, why should such a judicial power exist at all? More than two centuries after *Marbury*, we are in the uncomfortable position of being deeply committed to judicial review because it works so well in protecting the individual against majoritarian tyranny, while lacking an intellectually satisfying explanation of where such muscular judicial power comes from and how it should be exercised.

THE SECOND DIRTY LITTLE SECRET OF JUDICIAL REVIEW

Worse, once we get beyond train-wreck cases, in which Congress or the president has been caught violating *un*ambiguous parts of the Constitution's text, judges have absolutely no idea how to read the *ambiguous* provisions of either the Constitution or the challenged statute. Chief Justice Marshall's reasoning in *Marbury* invites us to think of the Bill of Rights as a self-propelled legal machine, automatically protecting our liberty by instructing judges to prevent a transient political majority from violating the rights of the individual. But history, logic, and common sense teach that the Bill of Rights does not operate on autopilot. Its real-world effectiveness depends on broad public understanding of and support for the values it catalogs, and on wise judicial readings of its necessarily abstract and ambiguous terms.

In recent years, waves of mostly right-handed repair specialists, inspired by Justice Antonin Scalia,[37] have tried to shore up the *Marbury* model by urging greater judicial respect for constitutional text as a source of objectively knowable commands to judges. These right-handed repair specialists promise us that fidelity to the text can provide a judge with a democratically legitimate, externally mandated way to decide constitutional cases without invoking the judge's own values.[38] My effort to mine the forty-five words of the First Amendment to recapture Madison's music is a tribute to the power of Justice Scalia's reminder that text matters. But it matters in different ways. My search for harmony and purpose in the whole text is a far cry from right-wing textualism. One group of right-wing textualists, calling themselves literalists, insist that the Constitution's single correct meaning can be found in each of its 4,543 words. All you need to decipher the Constitution's one true meaning, they claim, is a good 1789 dictionary and the courage to read the text literally.

Literalists have a minor point. When you want to know how many witnesses are needed to convict someone of treason (two), or how old the president must be (thirty-five), or the president's required citizenship status (native-born, not naturalized), or how many votes each state gets in the Electoral College (one for each of the state's two senators, plus one for each representative to the House), or how many electoral votes it takes to elect a president (currently, two hundred seventy), the Constitution's literal text delivers a single definitive answer. Even when the literal text seems ambiguous, the context often dictates that a word with more than one dictionary meaning must be read in only one plausible way. For example, when the Third Amendment states that "no soldiers shall in times of peace be *quartered* in any home," the clause can't be read as a ban on cutting up enlisted men for the stewpot. On the other hand, doubts can arise even when the text appears to have a single literal meaning. For example, while it's clear that the government needs two witnesses for a treason conviction, must both witnesses be physically present in court? Can one or both required "witnesses" be co-conspirators whose incriminating out-of-court statements in furtherance of the conspiracy currently satisfy the rules for evidentiary admission? There is no dictionary answer to that question. Someone has to decide what the word "witness" *should* mean in the constitutional text, not in the *Oxford Unabridged Dictionary*. Thus, useful as literalism can be in reading the Constitution in many relatively trivial settings, everyone agrees that the dictionary has its limits.

Many of the Constitution's words and phrases plausibly carry multiple dictionary meanings, especially the necessarily abstract words and phrases used in the Constitution's rights-bearing provisions. As we've seen, literalism is of absolutely no help in reading the First Amendment.[39] Like the term "witnesses" in the Treason Clause, the phrase "the freedom of speech" is a legal blank canvas that must be filled in by human readers of the text. There is no dictionary road map for the job.

It only gets harder to impose a single literal meaning on phrases such as the ban on "unreasonable searches and seizures" in the Fourth Amendment, the guaranty of "due process of law" in the Fifth Amendment, and the prohibition on "cruel and unusual punishment" or "excessive fines" in the Eighth Amendment. When you add "equal protection of the laws" in the Fourteenth Amendment, the nontextual implied guaranty of equality in the Fifth Amendment's Due Process Clause, and the nontextual addition of freedom of association to the First Amendment, the idea of a literal Constitution collapses.

A related group of repair specialists, the "originalists," led by Justice Antonin Scalia, argue that most constitutional ambiguities can be reduced to a single correct meaning, not necessarily by consulting a dictionary, but by asking what the Founders originally intended the words to mean. But figuring out the original meaning of an ambiguous constitutional phrase turns out to be much harder than Justice Scalia admits. For starters, it's unclear why we would want to adopt a method of reading the Constitution in the twenty-first century that locks us into the mind-set of an era in human history when slavery was legal, women couldn't participate in politics or most professions, only the rich could vote, and the idea of freedom of speech and political association was so weak that President John Adams locked up most newspaper editors who opposed him in the election of 1800. *Dred Scott v. Sandford*, a consensus choice for the worst decision in Supreme Court history, is a nightmare application of originalism, illustrating the moral and political price of looking backward to read our most precious legal text.

Chief Justice Roger Taney, writing in 1857, looked backward to the ethos of the 1787 Constitution and reasoned that the Founders had originally intended the Constitution to protect slavery and to ensure the continued subordination of an inferior black race.

Consequently, the Taney Court invalidated the Missouri Compromise of 1850 (banning slavery from much of the territories) as a deprivation of property without due process of law in violation of the Fifth Amendment. Not content with that exercise in historical racism, Taney also slammed the federal courthouse door to any future efforts by black people to find some rights, holding that as a matter of original intent, no black person could be a "citizen" within the meaning of Article III's grant of diversity jurisdiction. It took a bloody Civil War and the Thirteenth and Fourteenth Amendments to reverse Taney's toxic exercise in racist originalism.

Many originalists acknowledge the moral disaster of *Dred Scott* and recognize the danger of looking backward to read the constitutional text, but they claim we have no choice if we're to reconcile judicial review and democracy. The democratic legitimacy of the power of an unelected judge to invalidate a congressional or presidential act, they claim, depends under *Marbury* upon the existence of a clear constitutional command. In short, a train wreck. In the absence of such a train wreck, originalists argue that it is democratically illegitimate for an unelected judge to consult her own values in deciding whether an act of Congress or the president violates an ambiguous provision of the Constitution. They claim that originalism can deliver the train wreck.

It turns out, though, that an honest exercise in originalism almost never delivers on its promise to turn the Constitution into a document that can be read only one way. In the first place, originalists don't agree among themselves about whose original intent counts. Madison's? The delegates to the Philadelphia Constitutional Convention? The members of the various state ratifying conventions? The voters who elected the members of the state ratifying conventions? The 1789 Congress that adopted the Bill of Rights? The voters who elected the members of that Congress? An ill-defined fictive group that some originalists call the late-eighteenth-century "general public"? (Whatever that means! Does it include women? The poor? Native Americans? Free blacks?) Over the years, various schools of originalists have dallied with each category without settling on one. If you can't even agree on whose original intent you're looking for, how can you find a single "original" meaning?

Even more troubling, whichever category of Founders you choose to interrogate, careful historical research almost always reveals that they were as confused and divided over the meaning of the ambiguous provisions as we are today. You can't get a more privileged set of Founding insiders than Thomas Jefferson and Alexander Hamilton. Yet they spent most of their time in President Washington's first cabinet arguing over whether the Commerce Clause authorized the creation of the first bank of the United States. If Jefferson and Hamilton couldn't agree on the single correct original meaning of the Commerce Clause, even though they had just helped draft and ratify it,[40] how can we expect a definitive originalist interpretation today?

In fairness, no one else makes a more persuasive case for their recipe for discovering the single correct meaning of the constitutional text. Justice William J. Brennan Jr., the great liberal icon, called his interpretive approach the search for a "living constitution." Brennan, like Scalia, claimed to be able to talk to the Founders. Unlike Scalia, though, Brennan didn't pretend that he was talking to a real Founder. Instead, he summoned a "reasonable Founder," sat him (it was always *him*) down, and asked him what the living text should mean today. It's simply amazing how often the fictive Founder agreed with Justice Brennan.

While Justice Brennan's approach frees us from eighteenth-century prejudices and, in my opinion, delivered magnificent constitutional law, it hardly qualifies as a serious method of finding a single right answer to the meaning of the constitutional text. A ghostly Founder may have assured Justice Brennan that he wanted the Constitution to enshrine the "one person, one vote" principle in *Baker v. Carr*, the First Amendment "marketplace of ideas" in *New York Times v. Sullivan*, or money as pure speech in *Buckley v. Valeo*, but the rest of us were not in on the conversation.

A fourth approach to reading the Constitution is often called purposivism; it was championed by Justice David Souter during his nineteen underappreciated years on the Court and by his intellectual mentor Justice John Marshall Harlan. Purposivists don't pretend to talk to the Founders. Using the text, history, and structure of the Constitution as guides, they seek to ascertain the underlying "purpose" of a constitutional phrase and to construe doubtful phrases in a way that advances their purposes in the modern world. It's Brennan without the séances. Most American judges use it today as their preferred way of deciphering the text. But while purposivism is capable of producing excellent constitutional law, it fails to produce single right answers about the document's true meaning. The twin judicial tasks of ascertaining the dominant purpose of an ambiguous constitutional text and then deciding how best to advance that purpose in the modern era require repeated subjective, value-laden judgment calls that will almost certainly be contested by justices with a different value hierarchy. Remember how hard it is to ascribe a dominant purpose to the First Amendment.

Justice Steven Breyer's spin on purposivism takes it to a higher level of generality. He argues that the dominant purpose of the entire Constitution is to enhance participation in democratic self-governance.[41] Having identified such an overarching purpose, he professes to decide hard constitutional cases in ways that advance that laudable ideal. While it often leads to excellent outcomes, a general concern with advancing democracy that is not carefully rooted in the text hardly qualifies as a blueprint for a single right answer in a hard constitutional case. Why not, for example, treat protection of individual autonomy or economic efficiency as the overarching purpose of the Constitution? My effort to read all forty-five words of the First Amendment as a narrative of democracy is an effort to ground Justice Breyer's emerging intuition in the text itself.

A few intrepid souls acknowledge that the constitutional text is too ambiguous to generate single right answers in hard constitutional cases and that literalism, originalism, and purposivism all fail to deliver on their promise to produce a single objectively correct reading. They argue that the Founders' use of ambiguous phrases at a high level of generality acts as a delegation to future generations of the power and responsibility to interpret the Constitution in accordance with the felt necessities of the times. It's the way Justice Brennan actually decided hard cases. It's what the unanimous Supreme Court did in *Brown* when it rejected ninety years of contrary precedent to invalidate racial segregation in public schools.[42] But such a process, deeply dependent on a judge's value-laden personal assessment of what the times require, cannot possibly be thought of as generating a single objectively right answer. Ronald Dworkin tried to think himself out of that dilemma by analogizing constitutional interpretation to an extremely complex problem in mathematics for which all agree that a single solution exists but for which it is impossible under current conditions of knowledge to calculate the one right answer. All that mathematicians can do in such settings, Dworkin argued, is to work toward the solution using the best tools of the mathematical trade. Judges, Dworkin argued, also work toward a single but unknowable correct constitutional answer by consulting the best aspects of their culture to reach the fairest and most just results.

Whatever the attractions of Dworkin's approach to constitutional interpretation—and they are many—his approach also fails to deliver a single objectively right answer. Asserting that an unknowable constitutional meaning exists that judges can reason toward by using their understanding of the best elements of the culture simply asks judges to do what they think is best. Maybe that's the inevitable nature of constitutional judging, but it surely is not a formula for a single objectively correct reading of the constitutional text. Others, lacking Dworkin's intellectual firepower, just keep their heads down and say as little as possible about why aggressive judicial review is consistent with democratic theory. Much of the time, they camouflage their acts of creative interpretation in purposivist or originalist terms in order to shield their use of subjective values from the light of day.

So the second dirty little secret of judicial review is that, with the exception of literalism in a few trivial settings, none of the current approaches to reading the constitutional text delivers a single value-neutral indisputably correct constitutional meaning. Literalism fails. Originalism fails. Purposivism fails. Like it or not, judges must make value choices in deciding a hard constitutional case. That's where recovering the ability to listen to Madison's music could be of real help to an intellectually honest judge. Once we realize that values inevitably play a role in constitutional interpretation, Madison's music can provide significant assistance to a judge seeking coherent meaning in the ambiguous text of the Bill of Rights. Whatever your theory of constitutional interpretation, intellectually honest judges will almost certainly find useful guidance if they are able to read the Bill of Rights as an ordered, coherent narrative of liberty and democracy in which each idea is linked to another and all are linked to the overarching principle of fostering the First Amendment's democratic city on the hill.

THE THIRD DIRTY LITTLE SECRET OF JUDICIAL REVIEW (THE BIG SCARY ONE)

Marbury's apologia for judicial review is persuasive only in train-wreck cases where the collision between the constitution's clear text and a statute is unavoidable, and so far we haven't come up with a generally accepted way to read ambiguous provisions of the Constitution in non-train-wreck cases. That recognition leads us to the third secret of judicial review—the big scary one. The historical facts are indisputable: constitutional judging has too often reached appalling, politically driven results that have reinforced the strong at the expense of the weak. It turns out that vesting unelected judges with the enormous, essentially unconstrained power of judicial review is a huge gamble.

Gambling on Judges

During the nineteenth and most of the twentieth centuries, the United States was virtually the only democracy to place the power of judicial review in the hands of unelected judges. Sister democracies, such as Great Britain and France, were deeply suspicious of giving so much power to unelected judges because, frankly, judges, drawn from an elite segment of the population, don't always function terribly well when asked to protect the weak against the strong. The Warren Court may well have been an aberrational blip on the judicial radar. We've already looked at the partisan political fiasco of *Marbury v. Madison*, the Court's first judicial review of an act of Congress. The second was infinitely worse. *Dred Scott v. Sandford* invalidated Congress's effort to ban slavery from the territories and ruled that free blacks could never be recognized as citizens of a state. It's hard to read *Dred Scott* and retain faith in judges. Sadly, *Dred Scott* isn't alone. The first Supreme Court case to strike down a state statute as unconstitutional, *Prigg v. Pennsylvania*, was no better. The *Prigg* Court invalidated an effort by the Pennsylvania legislature to protect free blacks from being kidnapped from the streets of Philadelphia by bounty hunters allegedly searching for escaped slaves.[43] The Supreme Court struck down the Pennsylvania anti-kidnapping law, construing the Fugitive Slave Clause of the Constitution as guarantying slave owners the right to take the law into their own hands to recover their allegedly escaped property. Ugly as the Fugitive Slave Clause was, though, it says no such thing.[44] The majority justices in *Prigg* just made it up.

In the years following the Civil War, we turned to the federal courts and judicial review in an effort to protect the rights of newly freed slaves. Congress vested lower federal courts with broad federal-question power to enforce the Thirteenth, Fourteenth, and Fifteenth Amendments, hoping that judges actually would protect blacks. Instead, the Supreme Court upheld legally enforced racial segregation,[45] turned away desperate pleas to protect minority voting rights,[46] and allowed lynch law to flourish by striking down every nineteenth-century effort to enact federal legislation banning it.[47] Instead of protecting the weak, the Supreme Court invoked the federal judiciary's newly granted enforcement power to protect corporations[48] by severely restricting railroad rate regulation,[49] blocking unions,[50] and invalidating minimum-wage, maximum-hour, and child-labor laws.[51] Over the objections of Justice Oliver

Wendell Holmes Jr., who accused his Supreme Court colleagues of imposing economic Darwinism in the guise of constitutional interpretation, during the first third of the twentieth century a phalanx of deeply conservative federal judges invoked the Constitution to invalidate virtually every significant effort at regulating the economic and labor markets.

FDR's Wager

During the Great Depression of the 1930s, the Supreme Court's invalidation of critical aspects of the first New Deal[52] led to an effort by President Roosevelt in 1937 to pack the Supreme Court with justices more amenable to his views by appointing six new justices, one for every sitting justice over seventy, bringing the Court to fifteen members. Roosevelt's efforts at court packing had a surface constitutional plausibility. After all, in 1801, Adams had "unpacked" the Court by lowering its membership from six to five justices. In 1802, Jefferson had prevented the Court from sitting at all. In fact, the Constitution says nothing about the size of the Supreme Court. It began life in 1789 with six justices. In 1801, John Adams briefly shrank it to five to prevent president-elect Jefferson from having a vacancy to fill. The 1802 Congress restored the number to six. As the country grew, Supreme Court membership was increased to seven in 1807, nine in 1837, and ten in 1863. It shrank to nine in 1866 and eight in 1867. In 1869, membership was returned to nine, where it has remained ever since.

FDR was rebuffed by Congress, but at least one sitting justice—Owen Roberts—got the message and switched his position on several important constitutional issues, voting to uphold crucial aspects of Roosevelt's program, especially the National Labor Relations Act.[53] Roberts's conversion has been known ever since as "the switch in time that saved nine." The crisis passed with the death or retirement of four justices, giving FDR the ability to build a comfortable Democratic majority on the Court, but the message that judicial review is a subjective and intensely political process was reinforced again.

Post–New Deal exercises of judicial review by the Supreme Court continued to generate fierce political controversy, this time about social rather than economic issues. During World War II, the historic flag salute decision in *West Virginia v. Barnette* reversed a 1940 decision and ruled that schoolchildren could not be forced to salute the flag. A year later, though, the Court sustained the constitutionality of the Japanese internment camps in the infamous *Korematsu* decision.[54] The postwar Court's attention then shifted to the linked problems of racial discrimination and the regional failure of Southern political and judicial institutions to confront Jim Crow. *Brown v. Board of Education* invalidated racial segregation in public schools and ushered in the era of the Warren Court, named for Chief Justice Earl Warren, a Republican governor of California who had been elected three times with broad bipartisan support but had supported the Japanese internment camps. Warren was appointed chief justice in 1953 by President Eisenhower and presided over a controversial egalitarian surge that reinterpreted much of the Constitution and laid bare the politics of judicial review.

The Warren years ended in 1969, when President Lyndon B. Johnson and Justice Abe Fortas botched the process of appointing Warren's successor. Fortas, tapped by his crony LBJ as the new chief justice, was eventually forced to resign from the Court over financial conflicts of interest, leaving the power to fill that vacancy and the power to appoint Warren's successor to Richard Nixon. Like Roosevelt (and Harding) before him, Nixon parlayed four Supreme Court appointments into operational control of the Court, although Nixon's justices, confronted with a bewildering array of social issues, turned out to be more unpredictable than Roosevelt's economic phalanx.

In the ensuing years, a closely divided Supreme Court careened unpredictably from one social issue to the next, often by 5–4 votes:

- protecting a woman's right to choose whether to bear a child[55] and then taking back much of the right,[56]
- approving affirmative action[57] and then turning on it,[58]

- expanding freedom of religion[59] and then contracting it,[60]
- enforcing freedom from religion[61] and then not so much,[62]
- powerfully reinforcing free speech[63] but not at the bottom of a hierarchy,[64]
- revolutionizing criminal procedure[65] and then undoing much of the revolution,[66]
- building a dysfunctional law of democracy[67] and then refusing to budge from it,[68]
- gutting efforts at gun control while[69] decrying violent crime,
- recognizing broad national power to regulate the economy[70] and then chipping away at it.[71]

The only constant over time has been the Court's fierce determination to preserve its own power, rooted solely in *Marbury v. Madison*, to impose the definitive reading of the Constitution's ambiguous text.[72]

The only clear message that emerges from over two centuries of experience with judicial review is that it's a game of chance—unpredictable and deeply dependent on the political beliefs of the justices who read the open-ended provisions of the Constitution against the backdrop of their personal values. Every presidential election is a rolling constitutional convention empowering the winner, with the advice and consent of the Senate, to populate the Supreme Court with justices who will, in hard cases, bend the arc of the Constitution to reflect the values of the president who appointed them. That's not to say there is no difference between judges and legislators. In most cases (especially in the lower courts), a combination of clear text and binding precedent provides real guidance to a principled judge, overriding political preferences. Even in the Supreme Court, where cases are chosen primarily because lower courts disagree over the right answer, most cases can be decided as a matter of text and precedent. But in genuinely hard cases, where text and precedent run out, there is no escape from value-laden judging. Would recovering Madison's music provide a complete antidote to the huge gamble that is judicial review?

Would it eliminate value-driven disagreement over constitutional meaning? Of course not. The Constitution's abstract and ambiguous text will always resist efforts to domesticate it fully and can never be divorced entirely from the values of the judges doing the reading. But rediscovering the music in Madison's lost poetry would improve the odds by vesting the Bill of Rights with a coherent theme. Over time, the magnetic field of that theme should lead to a reading of the text that is closer to both its brilliantly structured organization and its timeless story of the intimate relationship between democracy and individual freedom.

THE CONSTITUTION ON RAINY DAYS

Despite the blip of the Warren Court, many believe that the Bill of Rights seeks to do the impossible. The rights of the weak, critics argue, can never be effectively protected against the tyranny of the strong by something as ephemeral as ambiguous "parchment barriers" construed and enforced by human beings dressed in judicial robes. Judges, critics argue, will inevitably vote their politics and their fears and call it law.

Unfortunately, the critics have a point. The "parchment barriers" in the First Amendment have too often failed to protect vulnerable people, especially in times of fear and crisis. We've already seen the collapse of the First Amendment in the frenzy of censorship unleashed by President John Adams during the run-up to the election of 1800. A year after Benjamin Franklin's nephew died in jail after being arrested for criticizing Adams too severely, his successor at the *Philadelphia Aurora*, William Duane, was arrested for printing a confidential letter from Adams discussing pro-British sentiment in his administration. Freed temporarily to consult with counsel at the urging of Vice President Thomas Jefferson, Duane went into hiding until the end of Adams's term.

After the Alien and Sedition Acts had expired on December 31, 1801, John Marshall's fiercely partisan younger brother, James, a D.C. Circuit judge, ordered a common-law seditious libel prosecution of newspapers in the District of Columbia for criticizing the Federalist judiciary. Jefferson simply ignored the younger Marshall's order. Yet even Jefferson tried to lock up his critics. In 1806, he instigated a common-law seditious libel prosecution against the publisher of a Connecticut newspaper for claiming that Congress and the president had bribed Napoléon in order to facilitate a treaty with Spain. The criminal prosecution was not dismissed until 1812, when the Supreme Court finally put an end to judge-initiated federal criminal libel prosecutions, ruling that only Congress could create a federal crime.[73] Occasional state seditious libel prosecutions continued for another 150 years until the Supreme Court finally outlawed them in 1964 as a violation of the First Amendment.[74]

First Amendment parchment barriers did not prevent one of our iconic presidents, Abraham Lincoln, from imposing unilateral military rule, imprisoning critics of the Emancipation Proclamation, jailing opponents of military action against the South, and closing hostile newspapers. Lincoln began in 1861 by imposing de facto military rule in the area surrounding Washington, D.C., unilaterally suspending the writ of habeas corpus in apparent violation of Article I, section 9, clause 3, which vests the suspension power in Congress. In Lincoln's defense, because Congress wasn't in session when the Civil War broke out, the president probably had no choice but to act alone in order to safeguard railway approaches to the capital enabling troops from Pennsylvania to reinforce those at Washington. When John Merryman, a captain in the Maryland Horse Guards and a well-known Confederate sympathizer, was arrested by federal military authorities and charged with treason on suspicion of seeking to cut the railroad line, Lincoln ignored the opinion of Chief Justice Roger Taney directing the president to release Merryman for trial in a civilian court.[75] Because it was the same Roger Taney who had written the racist *Dred Scott* decision three years earlier and because Merryman was little more than an armed terrorist, it's hard to be too upset with Lincoln's high-handed behavior during a genuine emergency. Indeed, faced in

1862 with Congress's refusal to exercise the suspension power and with several lower-court decisions agreeing with Taney's *Merryman* opinion, Lincoln finally ordered the release of almost all political prisoners in military custody, including Merryman.[76]

Whatever the extraconstitutional justification for Lincoln's unilateral resort to military rule in the early days of the Civil War, his treatment of Clement Vallandingham is hard to swallow. Vallandingham was a two-term Democratic member of Congress from Dayton, Ohio, who vigorously opposed the use of military force to preserve the Union. After his defeat for reelection in 1862, Vallandingham continued to lead the opposition to the war in Ohio. In 1863, he delivered a fiery address attacking "King Lincoln's" "cruel and unjust war." In response to the speech, the military governor of Ohio, General Ambrose Burnside, ordered Vallandingham's arrest and trial by military court martial. Vallandingham was convicted and sentenced to two years in a military prison. The Supreme Court declined to intervene.[77] Lincoln personally approved Vallandingham's arrest and military trial but commuted his sentence to banishment to Confederate territory. Once behind Confederate lines, Vallandingham promptly ran the Union blockade to Bermuda and continued to Canada, where he accepted the Democratic nomination for governor of Ohio. Vallandingham ran a defiant gubernatorial campaign from his Canadian headquarters in Windsor, Ontario, but lost in a landslide to the Union candidate.[78] After the war, Vallandingham returned to the practice of law. In 1877, while showing colleagues how an alleged murder weapon could have accidentally discharged, he shot himself fatally. His client was acquitted. Now that's vigorous advocacy!

Lincoln's treatment of Lambdin P. Milligan was a replay of his treatment of John Merryman. Milligan was an Indiana lawyer (he had been in the same law class as Lincoln's secretary of war, Edwin Stanton) who vocally opposed the war. By 1864, Milligan was suspected by military authorities of plotting to free Confederate soldiers from Northern prisoner-of-war camps by force and arm them to lead insurrections. Milligan and five colleagues were arrested in Indiana, tried before a military commission, and sentenced to death. Two days before the scheduled hangings, President Andrew Johnson commuted the sentences to life. In 1866, the Supreme Court, emboldened by the end of the war, echoed Taney's decision in John Merryman's case, holding that Milligan should not have been tried by a military commission because the civilian courts were open and capable of conducting a traditional criminal trial.[79] Five justices based their opinion on lack of explicit congressional authorization of the military tribunals. Four ruled that Congress lacked power to force a civilian to stand trial in a military tribunal when the civilian courts are open. Milligan was released and promptly sued General Alvin P. Hovey, the general who had ordered his arrest and military trial, for false imprisonment. Milligan won, but the jury returned a verdict of only $5 against General Hovey, reflecting its disgust with Milligan's efforts to extend the war. General Hovey was brilliantly defended by Benjamin Harrison, who would go on to become the twenty-third president.

After Lincoln's assassination, the military government in the Reconstruction South continued to use force to crack down on dissent.[80] William H. McCardle, a newspaper editor from Vicksburg, Mississippi, wrote an inflammatory editorial challenging the legality of Reconstruction. He was promptly jailed by the local military commander. McCardle appealed directly to the Supreme Court, questioning the constitutionality of continued military occupation of the South. After the Supreme Court had heard four days of oral argument, Congress, nervous about what the Court might say about the constitutionality of Reconstruction and citing Marshall's disastrous reading of the Exceptions and Regulations Clause in *Marbury*, retroactively eliminated the Supreme Court's appellate power to hear cases like McCardle's. President Johnson vetoed the court-stripping bill, but Congress overrode the veto. The *McCardle* case ended with a whimper when the Supreme Court caved in and dismissed McCardle's appeal for lack of jurisdiction.[81] The Supreme Court never did consider the constitutionality of military occupation of the South, which continued until 1876, when

Rutherford B. Hayes won the presidency by a vote of 185–184 in the Electoral College despite losing the popular vote. Hayes secured the votes of 20 contested presidential electors needed to put him over the top by promising to withdraw troops from the South, ushering in an era of intense racial discrimination throughout the states of the old Confederacy. The "safe-harbor" provision at issue in *Bush v. Gore* was intended to prevent replays of the 1876 fiasco.[82]

Nor did the First Amendment's parchment barrier provide much shelter to war resisters jailed for opposing World War I. Eugene Debs, who had been imprisoned for four months in 1895 for urging Pullman workers to strike in the teeth of a no-strike injunction, was arrested in 1917 for expressing opposition to World War I. Debs, who had run for president on the Socialist ticket in 1904, 1908, and 1912 (polling almost 10 percent of the popular vote in 1912), was convicted and sentenced to ten years in prison. The great Oliver Wendell Holmes Jr. affirmed Debs's conviction and draconian sentence in 1919, ruling for a unanimous Supreme Court that Debs's public speeches praising draft resisters and criticizing the war demonstrated a seditious intent to obstruct the war effort.[83] From his prison cell in the Atlanta Federal Penitentiary, Debs polled almost one million votes for president in 1920. The great Woodrow Wilson rejected repeated pleas for clemency on Debs's behalf from his attorney general, A. Mitchell Palmer, hardly a supporter of radical causes.[84] It wasn't until President Warren G. Harding (perhaps our most reviled president) took office in 1921 that Debs, by then a very sick man, had his sentence commuted to time served. Debs left the Atlanta Penitentiary to the cheers of the prisoners, visited President Harding at the White House briefly to say "thank you," and returned home to a crowd of fifty thousand well-wishers in Terre Haute, Indiana. Banned under his sentence from ever voting or running for office again, Debs died in 1926.

Charles Schenck, the general secretary of the Socialist Party, and his colleague Dr. Elizabeth Baer shared Debs's legal fate, although not his excessive sentence. Schenck and Baer arranged for the printing and mailing of leaflets opposing the war, arguing that the military draft was a form of slavery in violation of the Thirteenth Amendment. The leaflets, which urged citizens to assert their rights and to refuse to be intimidated, called the draft a "monstrous injustice" calculated to help Wall Street, but the writers carefully refrained from advocating disobedience, instead urging recipients to petition for redress of grievances. Despite the relatively restrained nature of the leaflets, Schenck and Baer were convicted in federal court in Philadelphia. Schenck was sentenced to six months in jail; Baer, ninety days. In 1919, Oliver Wendell Holmes Jr., writing for a unanimous Supreme Court (including the great Louis Brandeis), affirmed the convictions because, in the Court's view, the leaflets posed an unacceptable danger to the war effort.[85]

At least Debs, Schenck, and Baer knew what they were getting into. Some opponents of World War I never knew what hit them. Jacob Frohwerk and Carl Gleeser, editors of the *Staats Zeitung* (National News), a German-language newspaper in Kansas City, Missouri, wrote a series of editorials in German aimed at the German-speaking community of Missouri, charging that the prosecution of the war was corrupt and was designed to favor moneyed interests. The articles never mentioned the draft. Gleeser pled guilty to unlawfully obstructing the war effort in the hope of receiving a lenient sentence. He got five years. Frohwerk, who was the president of the Kansas branch of the National German-American Alliance, went to trial, was convicted, and got ten years. The court noted that his editorials might have found their way into the hands of draft-eligible German American youth and exerted a "bad tendency" to foster resistance to the draft. Oliver Wendell Holmes Jr. once again spoke for a unanimous court in affirming Frohwerk's conviction and harsh sentence.[86]

What happened to Jacob Abrams and his co-defendants, Mollie Steimer, Hyman Lachowsky, and Samuel Lipman, was even worse. Abrams and his three confederates were charged with tossing copies of two leaflets from a tenement window to a street on the Lower East Side of Manhattan. One leaflet, written in English, opposed the use of American troops in Russia. The second, in

Yiddish, called for a general strike and the cessation of munitions production. The four young radicals were arrested and convicted. A fifth, Jacob Schwartz, died in police custody under suspicious circumstances. The federal trial judge ruled that the leaflets had a "bad tendency" to lead readers to engage in unlawful acts. The three men were each sentenced to twenty years in prison. Mollie Steimer, twenty years old, four feet nine inches tall and weighing all of ninety pounds, was sentenced to fifteen years.

This time, Holmes and Brandeis finally voted to reverse the convictions, but seven members of the Supreme Court voted to affirm.[87] After Woodrow Wilson refused to consider a postwar amnesty for political prisoners, Warren Harding ordered the four released, but only if they agreed to be deported to Russia.[88] Samuel Lipman died in Stalin's purges. Hyman Lachowsky perished under the Nazis. Mollie Steimer was arrested by the Bolsheviks in 1922 and deported from Russia to Germany the following year. When Hitler assumed power, she fled from Germany, only to be arrested in France and placed in a concentration camp. After World War II, Mollie settled in Mexico City, where Jacob Abrams was editing a Yiddish-language newspaper. She died in Mexico in 1980 at the age of eighty-three.

"Parchment barriers" had a decidedly mixed record during World War II. Things started badly in 1940 when the Supreme Court, picking up just about where it had left off with Mollie Steimer in 1919, voted 8–1 (with justices Black and Douglas joining the majority) to uphold the expulsion of young Jehovah's Witnesses from public school for refusing to salute the flag.[89] Three years later, though, the Court reversed itself and issued one of its most celebrated free speech opinions, ruling 6–3 that compulsory flag salutes violate the First Amendment. Felix Frankfurter dissented.[90] Seventy years after it was written, Justice Jackson's magnificent First Amendment rhetoric in *Barnette* retains the power to inspire.[91] In 1944, however, the parchment barriers collapsed once again. In *Korematsu v. United States*, the Supreme Court upheld the constitutionality of military orders forcing more than 130,000 innocent Japanese Americans, citizens and lawful permanent residents alike, into internment camps during World War II.[92] Not one of the internees was or has ever been charged with unlawful action. No similar wartime programs were even considered for the nation's German or Italian communities.

We feign astonishment today that we could have been so racist, but the infamous *Korematsu* opinion was supported by FDR and Earl Warren (as governor of California), written by Hugo Black, and joined by William O. Douglas. In fact, Black and Douglas were the swing votes in a 6–3 decision.

Things didn't get much better in the 1950s, during the Cold War. During the McCarthy years, despite the First Amendment, ninety-three leaders of the American Communist Party went to jail, not for anything they actually did, but simply for leading a lawful political party pledged to the violent overthrow of capitalism at some point in the indefinite future.[93] Thousands of Americans were fired, harassed, and blacklisted solely because of suspected sympathy with communism or socialism. Consider the fate of one of the nation's original defenders of free speech, Elizabeth Gurly Flynn. Flynn's life was the stuff of legend. Born in Concord, Massachusetts in 1890, Flynn and her family moved to New York City in 1900. In 1906, Elizabeth celebrated her sixteenth birthday, gave her first speech (at the Harlem Socialist Club), was arrested for the first time (along with her father) for speaking on Broadway without a permit, and was expelled from high school for political activities. By her seventeenth birthday in 1907, Flynn was a full-time organizer for the International Workers of the World, touring Western mining camps as a charismatic platform speaker. She worked with Big Bill Haywood, visited Joe Hill in jail in 1914 (he wrote a song for her called "Rebel Girl"), and played prominent roles in strikes and IWW free-speech movements in Spokane, Missoula, Philadelphia, Lawrence, Paterson, Duluth, Chicago, and the Mesabi Range. Theodore Dreiser called her a young Joan of Arc. Along with Roger Baldwin (and Felix Frankfurter), she was a charter member of the ACLU in 1919. Her membership was not surprising, for in its early days, one of the ACLU's reasons for being was protection of IWW organizers, both from prosecution for opposing World War I and from arrest for union-organizing activities. Beginning in 1921, Flynn worked tirelessly in an unsuccessful effort to spare Sacco and Vanzetti from the death penalty. In 1927, she collapsed on a speaking tour of the West. Medical diagnoses included an obscure heart ailment, an impacted wisdom tooth, and a strep infection, but the root cause of Flynn's collapse was almost certainly emotional. The execution of Sacco and Vanzetti literally broke her heart. Flynn remained in Portland, Oregon, for almost ten years. In 1936, she returned to New York and was welcomed home as a prodigal daughter. The ACLU unanimously elected her to its board of directors. The American Communist Party welcomed her as a new member in 1937, elected her to the Central Committee in 1938, and to the Political Bureau in 1941. In 1942, Flynn ran for Congress at-large from New York State on the Communist Party ticket and received more than fifty thousand votes. In 1951, she led the mass movement in support of the Communist Party defendants in the first wave of Smith Act prosecutions and was swept up in the second round of indictments. Convicted of holding a leadership position in the American Communist Party, Flynn served two years in federal prison. In 1961, she became chair of the American Communist Party. Flynn died unexpectedly in Moscow in 1964. Her posthumous papers revealed that one of her great regrets was not defending the principle of free speech within the American Communist Party. Perhaps it was just deserts, but the free-speech principle that Flynn ignored as a Communist Party official not only failed to protect her from criminal prosecution for her beliefs, but it couldn't even protect her from being expelled from the ACLU board in 1938 for her association with communists.

During the Vietnam era, although the Court provided significant First Amendment protection to anti–Vietnam War demonstrators, protection did not extend to young men who burned their draft cards in public to express opposition to a war that Congress had never explicitly authorized. They went to prison as convicted felons.[94] A unanimous Supreme Court that included Earl Warren, William O. Douglas,[95] and William Brennan Jr. held that because burning a draft card to make a political point was communicative conduct, not pure speech, it was not entitled to first-class speech protection. Of course, that didn't stop the justices eight years later from ruling that spending unlimited amounts of money to influence an election is pure speech, not communicative conduct.[96] Nor did it stop five members of the Court in *Citizens United* from ruling that large for-profit corporations are engaged in pure speech when they pour unlimited treasury funds into an election campaign. Five members of the Supreme Court have even held that providing matching subsidies to underfunded candidates, enabling them to respond to privately funded campaign speech, unconstitutionally "burdens" the free-speech rights of rich candidates.[97]

Today despite the First Amendment's parchment barriers, we still can't buy Cuban magazines and newspapers or visit Havana without special permission from the government. Idealistic Americans are forbidden, on pain of prison, from teaching peaceful methods of resolving grievances to foreign groups labeled by the executive as terrorists.[98] Students have virtually no free-speech rights to publish uncensored high school newspapers or express unwelcome opinions about drugs or their teachers. The free-speech rights of public employees and labor unions are under siege. And despite the First Amendment right to political anonymity and the Fourth Amendment's protection of personal privacy, the promise of constitutional protection against universal government surveillance is in shambles.

So much for parchment barriers.

THE DECK CHAIR THEORY OF THE FIRST AMENDMENT

Sometimes, usually just after I've lost a case, I succumb to what I call the deck-chair theory of the First Amendment. I grumble that when the weather is sunny, we unfold an elegant deck chair that we call the First Amendment. As we lounge in our chair, we extol its comfort and sophisticated design, congratulating ourselves for owning such a useful and stylish piece of furniture. At the first sign of rain, though, we fold up our beautiful deck chair and put it away until the sun comes out again. Could it be, I ask myself, that the real reason the First Amendment has flourished for more than two hundred years is that it's never gotten wet? When I emerge from my funk, though, I remember that the historical record is much more complex. I remember that the story of our past is not just a cynical tale. Courageous popular support for freedom can—and has—made a difference. I remember that in each period of crisis, brave voices have rallied to the Bill of Rights. John Adams jailed his critics, but the people rejected the Alien and Sedition Acts in the election of 1800. Congress declined to renew the Acts in 1802, and President Jefferson pardoned the victims. I remember that President Lincoln tolerated a huge amount of dissent and criticism during the Civil War, presiding fairly over a hard-fought 1864 presidential election in which he was vigorously challenged by George McClellan, one of his ex-generals. Clement Vallandingham came out of hiding and actually served as McClellan's shadow secretary of war during the election. I remember that, responding to public concern, Lincoln tempered his initial resort to military rule by granting an amnesty to all political prisoners in 1862. And I remember that once the Civil War was over, the Supreme Court repudiated Lincoln's effort at unilateral military rule, establishing important precedents that protect us today. I remember that the World War I prosecutions of war resisters, including Schenck and Debs, eventually impelled justices Holmes and Brandeis to issue the dissent in *Abrams* and the concurrence in *Whitney* that lit the way to the modern First Amendment. I remember that on the very day the Supreme Court upheld the Japanese internment camps in *Korematsu*, it ruled that every detainee must be given a prompt individual hearing on dangerousness,[99] dooming the camps as a practical matter and leading to their closing three months later. I remember that in 1968, Congress apologized to the surviving Japanese detainees and awarded them $10,000 each—too little too late, but something. I remember that the Supreme Court eventually blunted some of the worst excesses of the McCarthy years and that it was Joe McCarthy who was eventually censured by the Senate. I remember that it was the Supreme Court that kept the civil rights movement in the South from being smothered by hostile police. I remember that the Supreme Court refused to permit the president to block publication of the Pentagon Papers, and that popular opposition to the Vietnam War drove a sitting president from office, hastening the end of the carnage. I remember that despite occasional slipups, the scope and intensity of our current First Amendment freedoms are remarkably broad.

Finally, I remember that the real lesson of our First Amendment history is that a Bill of Rights without popular support really is a toothless parchment barrier but that a rights-bearing document backed by popular support can move mountains.

That's where the loss of Madison's music hurts most deeply. The aesthetic force of Madison's lost poetry could be of incalculable value in rallying the level of public support needed to sustain the practical vitality of the Bill of Rights, especially the First Amendment, in storm-tossed times. It's possible, of course, to attempt to rally popular support for fragments of the Bill of Rights displayed as isolated slogans. But if the isolated slogans were understood by the people as threads in a harmonious tapestry, interacting with and reinforcing each other as the elements of a magnificent poem to human freedom and political democracy, it would be much easier to rally "We the People" to defend the Bill of Rights, for it would speak to them in the coherent voice of poetry. Would that prevent us from giving in to fear in time of crisis? Of course it wouldn't. Human beings are not machines. Fear and emotion will always be part of the equation. But precisely because fear and emotion can erode the protections of the Constitution and Bill of Rights, it is doubly important to couch First Amendment protections in their strongest, most persuasive form—as an integrated, lapidary poem to democracy and freedom with not a word or idea out of place.

10

Madison, the Reluctant Poet

How the Great Poem Almost Didn't Get Written

The story of the textual evolution of the Bill of Rights during that febrile summer of 1789 makes it difficult, if not impossible, to claim that the structure and organization of the Bill of Rights was driven by a single person's vision.[1] Madison didn't even want to produce a single, coherent Bill of Rights. The Senate's role remains delphic. Too many other important players, including Roger Sherman and Elbridge Gerry, were involved to claim that Madison's intentions controlled everything. What should matter today, though, is not what a group of long-dead, slave-owning white men of substantial property may have been thinking about in 1789. Their world is long gone, and a good thing, too. Their evanescent intentions have little or no relevance to a contemporary world that they could not have imagined. It's the enduring text that matters. As I've noted earlier, great poems aren't beautiful because poets have willed them so. The unique beauty of great poetry is found in the text itself, in the imagery, emotions, and meaning produced by the order, cadence, structure, and content of the words. Madison and his friends, whatever they may have been thinking as summer turned into autumn in that remarkable year, transmitted a text to us that turns out to be a great poem about freedom and democracy, if only we will take the time and effort to read it closely. There is the music of poetry in the order, cadence, structure, and content of the text of the Bill of Rights, especially the First Amendment, if we are wise enough to hear it.

We almost didn't have a Bill of Rights, though, much less a coherent poetic celebration of democracy and freedom. It's not as though bills of rights were rare in 1787. Starting in 1215 with the Magna Carta and running through the burst of Revolutionary rights-bearing documents produced from 1765 to 1783, I count at least four English declarations of rights, three major colonial compilations of rights, and eighteen Revolutionary efforts to describe individual rights. In fact, Madison had at least forty-two source documents to choose from, to say nothing of dozens and dozens of proposed amendments suggested by the states. But it all almost came to nothing.

Our first effort at a national charter, the 1781 Articles of Confederation, did not contain a Bill of Rights, perhaps because the national government under the Articles was so weak—it lacked an executive, a judiciary, and the power to tax—that it was deemed unnecessary to list protected rights. When the fifty-five Founders gathered in Philadelphia on May 25, 1787, to discuss amending the Articles of Confederation to strengthen the national government, sentiment quickly turned to scrapping the Articles entirely in favor of a brand-new Constitution, even if that appeared to exceed the delegates' original mandate. The consensus among the delegates was that it would be a mistake to include a bill of rights in the new Constitution. Some, such as Alexander Hamilton, believed that the proposed new national government was already too weak and should not be further hobbled by declarations of rights. Others, such as James Wilson, feared that a formal enumeration of rights would be dangerous because it would imply a strong central government with power to violate them. Madison himself, accurately predicting a future Antonin Scalia, feared that any written enumeration of rights might accidentally leave some important rights out, making it difficult or impossible for new rights to evolve and be recognized. While several halfhearted efforts were made late in the game to insert provisions protecting rights into the new constitution, they got nowhere. After a formal proposal to add a bill of rights was unanimously rejected, the Constitution was finally signed on September 17, 1787, without a bill of rights.

The closest thing to rights in the original constitutional text was the promise in Article VI that "no religious Test shall ever be required as a Qualification to any Office or public Trust under the United States." Article 1, section 9 contains a promise that Congress would not suspend habeas corpus except in times of war or rebellion, and a promise that bills of attainder and retroactive criminal laws would be prohibited. But those two essentially procedural guaranties, while important, are separation of powers–based protections of the rule of law generally, not protections of particular rights. A potential equality provision in Article IV, section 1 promised that "[t]he Citizens of each State shall be entitled to all Privileges and Immunities of Citizens in the several states," but any hint of serious protection of equality was immediately erased by the notorious clause providing for the apprehension and return of fugitive slaves, and the nonamendable guaranty of the right to import slaves for twenty-one more years, until 1808. Four prominent delegates, Elbridge Gerry (Mass.), George Mason (Va.), Luther Martin (Md.), and Edmund Randolph (Va.), refused to sign the proposed new constitution because it lacked a bill of rights. John Lansing and Robert Gates, the delegates from New York, actually walked out of the Constitutional Convention after six weeks in order to begin organizing opposition to the document.

Ratification was far from a sure thing. Unlike the Articles of Confederation, which had required unanimous consent, the 1787 Constitution required ratification by only nine states to become effective, at least within the territory of the ratifying states. Because two states, Rhode Island and North Carolina, openly opposed the new constitution (Rhode Island refused to call a ratifying convention; North Carolina held a convention and overwhelmingly rejected it), the ratification math was harder than it first appeared; approval by nine of the eleven states in play was needed. The Founders didn't trust either an up-or-down popular vote on ratification in each state or ratification by the state legislatures. Instead, they insisted on state ratifying conventions with delegates often elected from malapportioned districts. The slice of the population that elected the delegates excluded women, members of racial minorities, and white men who didn't have enough money to meet each state's property qualifications for voting. While a few states relaxed property qualifications somewhat to permit broader white male participation in the ratification process, there was no thought of permitting women, African Americans, or Native Americans to vote. The closest thing to a feminist consciousness was Abigail Adams's plaintive plea to her husband, John, "not to forget the ladies."

When the proposed new constitution was presented to the Confederation Congress (which served under the Articles of Confederation from 1781 to 1789 and had issued the call for amendments to the Articles in the first place), the Confederation Congress declined to endorse it, in part because many members believed that the delegates had exceeded their authority by drafting an entirely new constitution instead of amending the Articles of Confederation. The best the Founders could do was to obtain unanimous consent from the Congress to submit the new draft constitution to the states for possible ratification, without an endorsement. Opponents of ratification, calling themselves Anti-Federalists, viewed the new constitution as a threat to individual freedom. A strong national government, they feared, would be controlled by men like Alexander Hamilton, who favored industry and manufacture over an Arcadian vision of citizen farmers. The failure to provide for a bill of rights became a rallying point for the Anti-Federalists, who argued that the powers granted to the national government by the new constitution were too dangerous unless they were constrained by a written list of rights.

The new constitution's supporters, calling themselves Federalists, led by Hamilton, Madison, and John Jay, answered that the twin structural protections of federalism and separation of powers would be much more effective in preserving freedom than any "parchment barriers." In the end, facing likely defeat in the ratification process, the Federalists promised to amend the new constitution by adding a Bill of Rights as soon as it was ratified.

Even with the promise, it was a close thing. Five states, Delaware (December 7, 1787), Pennsylvania (December 12), New Jersey (December 18), Georgia (January 2, 1788), and Connecticut (January 8), quickly ratified by comfortable margins, although the debate in Pennsylvania, which ratified by a vote of 46–23, was fierce and was marred by resort to mob violence aimed at compelling dissenting members of the state legislature to attend the legislative session calling for a ratifying convention. The dissenters had stayed away hoping to prevent a quorum. The next state up, Massachusetts, was a battleground, eventually ratifying by a vote of 187–168 on February 5, 1788, but only after the Federalists promised to enact a Bill of Rights and submit a series of proposed amendments. On February 13, facing almost certain defeat in New Hampshire, the Federalists engineered a vote of 56–51 to adjourn the ratifying convention to allow the delegates to seek guidance from their constituents. It was a brilliant tactical move that probably saved the Constitution. Ratification by comfortable margins in Maryland (April 28, 1788) and South Carolina (May 23) brought the number of ratifying states to eight. When New Hampshire reconvened and ratified on June 21, 1788, by a vote of 57–47, the new Constitution officially became law in the nine ratifying states.

Without Virginia and New York, though, it would've been stillborn. After bitterly contested elections in each state, Virginia ratified on June 26, 1788, by a vote of 89–79, and New York followed suit on July 26 with a razor-thin ratification margin of 30–27. The New York vote was something of a surprise, for the Anti-Federalists appeared to control the convention by a wide margin. Once again, the tactical brilliance of the Federalists in delaying New York's vote until ten other states had ratified probably snatched victory from almost certain defeat. Virginia narrowly rejected a conditional ratification, expressly contingent on the adoption of a bill of rights. New York's ratification came with twenty-five proposed rights amendments and thirty-one other assorted suggested changes. North Carolina and Rhode Island refused to ratify until a bill of rights was adopted. North Carolina finally ratified on November 21, 1789, a year after Washington was elected president. Rhode Island held out until May 29, 1790, and ratified by a vote of 34–32, but not until the Rhode Island delegates adamantly demanded a bill of rights, despite the fact one had already been adopted by Congress eight months earlier.

The first United States Congress elected under the new Constitution was scheduled to convene on March 4, 1789, but didn't assemble a quorum until April 1. Actually, it was the nation's fourth Congress. The first Continental Congress met briefly in 1774 to coordinate economic resistance to Great Britain. The second Continental Congress reconvened in 1775 after Lexington and Concord, issued the Declaration of Independence in 1776, appointed George Washington as commander in chief, and remained in session until 1781 to manage (or mismanage) the Revolutionary War. The third congress, the Confederation Congress, was a unicameral legislature established under the Articles of Confederation. The Confederation Congress was in session from 1781 to 1789. It negotiated the Treaty of Paris, ending the Revolutionary War, enacted the Northwest Ordinance in 1787, set in motion the process of drafting a new constitution, and organized the first elections for president and Congress under the new Constitution in November 1788.

When it finally got to work on April 1, 1789, the first United States Congress had a lot on its plate. The executive and judicial branches had to be created and organized from scratch. Given the press of urgent business, Congress was in no hurry to consider a bill of rights. Only after Virginia and New York had submitted formal demands on May 5 and 6 for a new constitutional convention capable of rewriting the entire document was Madison able to focus his colleagues' attention on a declaration of rights. On June 8, 1789, Madison, who had won a hard-fought congressional election victory against James Monroe, finally took the floor of the House of Representatives and proposed a draft declaration of rights in the form of a series of freestanding constitutional amendments to be interpolated into the existing text. Madison's House colleagues complained long and loud about being diverted from really important work but reluctantly agreed to hear him out.

Madison was a political genius but a very reluctant poet. As of June 8, 1789, he had no intention of drafting a bill of rights at all, much less a coherent poem to human freedom. Instead, he proposed that a series of rights-declaring clauses be interpolated into the body of the Constitution at the point where the potentially dangerous government power the clauses were designed to limit was found. Instead of a poem, Madison was thinking about a good-government cookbook, in which spicy, potentially indigestible helpings of government power could be made palatable by immediate immersion in a soothing rights-protective sauce. Given the debates over a bill of rights during the ratification process, there was a careful method to Madison's original structural madness. By avoiding a coherent and comprehensive listing of rights, Madison was attempting to avoid an inadvertent freezing of rights to only those described by the literal text. Moreover, by structurally placing the right at the point where the power was created, Madison hoped to avoid any implication that a written catalog of rights implied the existence of power not explicitly granted in the text.

Madison began his recipe for good government with an elegant proposed new preface to the Constitution drawn from George Mason's preface to the 1776 Virginia Declaration of Rights, which had formed the basis for Thomas Jefferson's Declaration of Independence. Madison's preface asserted that government exists solely to protect the people's enjoyment of life and liberty, the right of acquiring and using property, and the pursuit of happiness and safety. He even inserted a right of rebellion if government failed to fulfill its purpose. The newly elected members of the fledgling national government did not take kindly to Madison's suggestion that they were sitting uneasily atop a revolutionary volcano of popular rejection. The elegant preface with its right of rebellion never made it out of Congress.

Madison then proposed two structural fixes designed to correct perceived flaws in the Constitution's original text having nothing to do with rights. He urged, first, that the provisions of Article I, section 2, clause 3 setting out the structure of the House of Representatives be amended to set a maximum on the size of the House and the number of constituents each member could represent. A modified apportionment formula raising the ceiling to 50,000 constituents was eventually adopted by Congress but was ratified by only nine of the needed eleven states. If Madison's original June 8 apportionment proposal had been ratified by the necessary eleven states, the current House of Representatives would consist of 20,000 members, a terrifying thought. Today, each of the 435 members of the House represents approximately 670,000 people.

Madison's second proposed structural fix urged that Article I, section 6, clause 1, dealing with Congress's compensation, be amended to ensure that a sitting Congress could not increase its own salary. The proposal made it through Congress but was initially ratified by only five states. The proponents never gave up. In 1992, when Michigan became the thirty-eighth state to ratify Madison's proposal, the idea of limiting Congress's power to vote itself a pay raise finally achieved acceptance by three quarters of the states and became the Twenty-Seventh Amendment only 74,003 days after Congress had first recommended its adoption by the states. Better late than never.

With the preface and structural fixes out of the way, Madison got down to the real business of rights. The story of the Bill of Rights begins with Madison's June 8 proposals for amending Article I, section 9, inserting a series of separate clauses protecting religious freedom, free speech, free press, free assembly, the right to petition, the right to bear arms, limiting the quartering of troops, banning double jeopardy, guarantying due process of law, prohibiting unlawful search and seizure, banning cruel and unusual punishment, protecting jury trial and the right to counsel, and recognizing the possibility of additional unenumerated rights. Madison's proposed text was often wordy, and the poetic structure was not yet evident to the naked eye—although Madison had already grasped much of it, especially the structure and content of what became the First

Amendment. In fact, the order of the six rights textually protected in what became the First Amendment was fixed on June 8, even though each was treated as a separate interpolation. Madison's June 8 provisions eventually evolved into the First, Second, Third, Fifth, Eighth, Fourth, Sixth, and Ninth Amendments, in that order. As of June 8, though, no one could accuse Madison of poetry.

Madison also urged that a new clause be placed into Article I, section 10, forbidding states from violating the rights of conscience, freedom of the press, and jury trial in criminal cases. The 1789 Senate, consisting of twenty-one white men of substantial property elected by the state legislatures, erased this effort to impose rights-based limitations on state governments. It took the Civil War, the enactment of the Fourteenth Amendment in 1868, and years of legal wrangling before Madison's vision of a Bill of Rights limiting state as well as federal government finally became a reality through the "incorporation" of most of the Bill of Rights into the Fourteenth Amendment's Due Process Clause, an act of genuine semantic daring.

Madison continued by suggesting a new clause in Article III, section 2, limiting the power of the Supreme Court by imposing a minimum jurisdictional amount on appeals and forbidding Supreme Court review of jury verdicts except in accordance with existing common law principles. This was a very big deal in a legal world where juries often decided what the law was. The second half of Madison's proposed jury material eventually became the "reexamination clause" of the Sixth Amendment. In addition, the third clause of Article III, section 2 was to be replaced by a guaranty of a unanimous and impartial jury in all criminal cases, grand jury presentment in capital cases, and jury trial in civil cases, protections that eventually found their way into the Sixth, Fifth, and Seventh Amendments. Madison concluded his June 8 speech with a recommendation that a clause protecting separation of powers be placed in Article VI, forbidding the three branches of government from poaching on each other's turf, together with a federalism clause, ensuring that powers not given to the federal government or forbidden to the states be reserved to the states. Although the federalism clause became the Tenth Amendment, Madison's separation-of-powers clause, like his elegant preface and his clauses protecting religious freedom, free speech, and jury trial against the states, was rejected by the Senate. Eventually, though, all of Madison's "lost clauses" but one became law through the magic of aggressive judicial review. Separation of powers is enforced nontextually; state governments are bound under the incorporation doctrine; but the Seventh Amendment right to jury trial in federal civil cases has not yet been applied to the states.

When Madison finally sat down on June 8, many of his colleagues were less than enthusiastic about the substance of his handiwork, and about taking time away from genuinely important things to debate the abstractions of a declaration of rights. Several sought to table the discussion indefinitely. Several others sought to refer the matter to a committee, where it might die a quiet death. Yet others doubted the necessity and wisdom of the entire enterprise. Finally the House was persuaded to continue considering the adoption of a bill of rights as a committee of the whole whenever time permitted. It took Madison more than a month to get the Bill of Rights onto the House's agenda again. On July 21, he asked the House to consider his proposed June 8 amendments as a committee of the whole. The response was more griping about taking time away from pressing matters, especially because many members feared that each amendment recommended by a state ratifying convention would be discussed at length on the House floor. Instead, Madison's colleagues voted to refer the matter to a select committee of eleven members (the Committee of Eleven), one from each ratifying state (North Carolina and Rhode Island had refused to ratify the Constitution without a bill of rights and were, therefore, not members of the union in 1789). The committee would review Madison's proposed draft, canvass the large number of amendments recommended by the state ratifying conventions, and report back to the full House with a formal proposal. To his discomfort, Madison had his first set of congressional editors.

The Committee of Eleven met from July 21 to July 28, 1789, but kept no written records. By and large, they were an unimpressive group. It's hard to imagine them editing James Madison's work. The two leading members were Madison himself, representing Virginia, and Roger Sherman from Connecticut. Sherman, who had been a member of the Committee of Five that had drafted the Declaration of Independence, was the Founders' version of Leonard Zelig. He was the only person to sign all four of our foundational documents—the Continental Association (1774), the Declaration of Independence (1776), the Articles of Confederation (1781), and the United States Constitution (1787). The ubiquitous Sherman is also the only person to serve on the three editorial committees that produced the Bill of Rights—the Committee of Eleven, the three-person Committee on Style, and the three-person House delegation to the House/Senate conference committee. Madison served on the Committee of Eleven and the House/Senate conference committee, but was not a member of the Committee on Style.

But that's getting ahead of the story. The other nine earnest back-benchers on the Committee of Eleven were John Vining (Del.), Egbert Benson (N.Y.), Abraham Baldwin (Ga.), Aedanus Burke (S.C.), Nicholas Gilman (N.H.), George Clymer (Pa.), Benjamin Goodhue (Mass.), Elias Boudinot (N.J.), and George Gale (Md.). Boudinot had served in the ceremonial post of president of the Continental Congress from 1782 to 1783. As president, he had signed the Treaty of Paris formally ending the Revolutionary War. He went on to head the United States Mint. Egbert Benson became one of John Adams's short-lived Article III "midnight judges," appointed to the Second Circuit in 1801 and serving until his post as chief judge was abolished by the Jeffersonian Congress in 1802. George Gale went on to become superintendent of distilled spirits for Maryland.

Roger Sherman turned out to be Madison's editor in chief, not because he was much help in conceiving or drafting the rights-bearing provisions, but because he was so committed to listing them in a single coherent document. During the Committee of Eleven's deliberations, Sherman actually drafted a handwritten version of a proposed bill of rights, but Madison, acting like any stubborn author, would have none of it. Madison insisted on his original June 8 model of interpolating freestanding protections into the Constitution's text, and persuaded the Committee of Eleven to go along over Sherman's objections. No signs of poetry yet.

The Committee of Eleven's first task was to sift through the blizzard of proposed amendments that had accompanied many of the state ratification documents. The editors made short work of them. In fairness, Madison had already carefully reviewed the existing state bills of rights, the old colonial charters, and the four historic English bills of rights, beginning with the Magna Carta, as well as the state ratifying materials, and in his June 8 proposals he had included a proposed rights-bearing amendment on any issue raised by at least three of the source documents. Although Elbridge Gerry (immortalized as the inventor of the gerrymander) would later demand that every amendment proposed by the state ratifying conventions be debated on the floor of the House, the obvious care with which Madison had responded to the issues raised by the conventions made that task unnecessary. Gerry's motion was soundly defeated. Freed from the necessity of considering each proposed amendment, the editors turned to Madison's June 8 text. They quickly scrapped the elegant preface, including its right of revolution. In its place, the committee recommended a single introductory phrase:

> Government being intended for the benefit of the people, and the rightful establishment thereof being derived from their authority alone, We the People . . .

Even that scaled-down snippet of Enlightenment political science failed to make it into the final version submitted to the states. The committee then modified Madison's structural apportionment clause to place a ceiling of 175 on House membership. The ban on

Congress raising its own salary survived unscathed. As we've seen, both of Madison's structural fixes survived the congressional editing process (Congress eventually eliminated the 175 House member ceiling in place of a ceiling of 50,000 people per representative), but neither was ratified by the necessary three quarters of the states, a number that had grown from ten to eleven with the delayed ratification by North Carolina and Rhode Island and the admission of Vermont into the Union as the fourteenth state.

The real editing work began with the provisions of Madison's June 8 draft that would become the First Amendment. The committee cut Madison's one hundred seven words to fifty-two. Madison had opened with a protection of religious freedom to be inserted in Article I, section 9, between clauses 3 and 4:

> The civil rights of none shall be abridged on account of religious belief or worship, nor shall any national religion be established, nor shall the full and equal rights of conscience be in any manner, or on any pretext, infringed.

The Committee of Eleven penciled in a shorter version that eliminated Madison's protection of religious belief or worship but kept the ban on establishing religion (without the word *national)* and the protection of equal rights of conscience but flipped the order. The committee put the ban on establishing religion first and dropped the language about religious belief or worship, relying on the protection of equal rights of conscience. We're still arguing about why the editors put the ban on establishment of religion ahead of protection of its free exercise. The edited version read:

> No religion shall be established by law, nor shall the equal rights of conscience be infringed.

The committee apparently viewed Madison's separate clauses protecting "religious belief and worship" and "equal rights of conscience" as redundant. Subsequent editors in the Senate would also view the two clauses as overlapping but would elect to reinstate an explicit protection of religious worship and eliminate the provision on equal rights of conscience. It would take almost two hundred years for the Supreme Court to undo Congress's editorial mischief and reinstate Madison's brilliant perception that while conscience and religion are deeply intertwined, the two ideas are not necessarily coterminous. Centuries ahead of his time, Madison understood, though his colleagues on the Committee of Eleven and in the Senate did not, that deeply felt secular conscience is entitled to the same degree of constitutional respect as religious belief.

Madison's first crack at protecting free speech in his June 8 draft inserted two clauses into Article 1, section 9, providing:

> The people shall not be deprived or abridged of their right to speak, to write, or to publish their sentiments; and the freedom of the press, as one of the great bulwarks of liberty, shall be inviolable.
>
> The people shall not be restrained from peaceably assembling and consulting for the common good; nor from applying to the Legislature by petitions, or remonstrances, for redress of their grievances.

The committee shortened Madison's wordy version into a single clause about half as long:

> The freedom of speech, and of the press, and the right of the people peaceably to assemble and consult for the common good, and to apply to the government for redress of grievances, shall not be infringed.

Score one for the editors. But note that Madison had already settled on the order of the six rights in what came to be the First Amendment.

The committee's other editing coup was organizational: the transfer of Madison's material guarantying fair criminal procedure—

public trial, notice of the charges, confrontation of witnesses, compulsory process, and right to counsel—from Article 1, section 9 (dealing with legislative power) to Article III, section 2 (dealing with the judiciary), where it was united with the provisions guarantying jury trial, local venue, and grand jury indictment. The editorial decision to link criminal trial rights, including notice, confrontation, and right to counsel, with the jury trial provision is the first sign of an effort to attain structural coherence. It was the first tentative hint of the poetry to come. Curiously, the editors left Madison's other criminal procedure guaranties, including double jeopardy, self-incrimination, and due process provisions, back in Article I, section 9. That link would be made later.

The rest of the committee's editorial efforts were the kind of minor changes that drive authors—and subsequent readers—crazy. Madison's original version of what would become the Second Amendment's right to keep and bear arms had three clauses:

> The right of the people to keep and bear arms shall not be infringed; a well-armed and well regulated militia being the best security of a free country: but no person religiously scrupulous of bearing arms shall be compelled to render military service in person.

The committee rearranged and shortened the clauses:

> A well regulated militia, composed of the body of the people, being the best security of a free State, the right of the people to keep and bear arms shall not be infringed, but no person religiously scrupulous shall be compelled to bear arms.

While Madison's operational phrase "the right of the people to keep and bear arms" was left intact by the editors, the editors flipped the order of the militia clause and the keep-and-bear-arms clause. Folks have argued for years about what legal effect, if any, should flow from the flipping of the order of the first two clauses, and whether the short-lived addition (and subsequent disappearance) of the phrase "composed of the people" was intended to mean anything. The right to religiously based conscientious objection to military service was eventually eliminated by the Senate. But the power of Madison's vision has triumphed, persuading Congress to provide for conscientious objection from the draft.

The editors made only trivial changes to Madison's quartering-of-troops clause, which eventually became the Third Amendment. Madison had proposed:

> No soldier shall in time of peace be quartered in any house without the consent of the owner; nor at any time, but in a manner warranted by law.

The committee's version read:

> No soldier shall in time of peace be quartered in any house without the consent of the owner; nor in time of war but in a manner to be prescribed by law.

The committee's version is marginally better, but I wouldn't pay much for the improvement.

The editors' emerging concern with structure also appears in the minor change to Madison's double-jeopardy draft. Madison had written, "no person shall be subject . . . to more than one punishment or one trial for the same offence . . ." The editors put "trial" before "punishment" to reflect the chronology of the two events. The more significant editorial change to Madison's proposed clauses protecting against double jeopardy, self-incrimination, deprivation of due process of law, and unlawful taking of private property, which eventually became the Fifth Amendment, involved a rewrite of the takings clause. Madison had originally written:

> . . . nor be obliged to relinquish his property, where it may be necessary for public use, without a just compensation.

The editors substituted:

> . . . nor shall private property be taken for public use without just compensation.

Score another minor point for the editors.

On the other hand, the editors just couldn't keep their hands off Madison's prototype of the Fourth Amendment. Madison wrote:

> The rights of the people to be secured in their persons, their houses, their papers, and their other property, from all unreasonable searches and seizures, shall not be violated by warrants issued without probable cause, supported by oath or affirmation, or not particularly describing the places to be searched, or the persons or things to be seized.

The committee removed the *d* from "secured," deleted the word *their* from "their houses" and "their papers," and substituted the term *effects* for "their other property." The editors also removed the reference to "all unreasonable searches and seizures," and changed the last two *ors* to *ands*. Because protection from "unreasonable searches and seizures" is the heart of the clause, it's hard to imagine what the editors had in mind when they took that language out. The phrase was promptly reinstated during congressional debate, with the suggestion that its omission had been inadvertent.

Madison had ended his proposed interpolations into Article I, section 9 with a clause designed to respond to critics who had argued that a bill of rights was dangerous because it would preclude the recognition of additional unwritten rights, and imply the existence of a muscular government with implied powers capable of violating rights. Madison's clause, which eventually evolved into the Ninth Amendment, provided:

> The exceptions here or elsewhere in the Constitution, made in favor of particular rights, shall not be construed as to diminish

> the just importance of other rights retained by the people, or as to enlarge the powers delegated by the Constitution; but either as actual limitations of such powers, or as inserted merely for greater caution.

The editors shrank Madison's text from fifty-seven to twenty-one words, entirely eliminating the clause designed to prevent the implied growth of government power.

> The enumeration in this Constitution of certain rights shall not be construed to deny or disparage others retained by the people.

The proposed limits on the power of the states in Article I, section 10 survived with minor editorial tinkering. Madison's *violate* was changed to "abridge," and the *or*s became *nor*s. Madison's clause limiting appeals from civil jury verdicts—which eventually became the Reexamination Clause of the Sixth Amendment—remained virtually intact, with a $1,000 jurisdictional amount imposed on Supreme Court appeals, and one minor editorial change. Madison had written:

> nor shall any fact, triable by jury, according to the course of the common law, be otherwise re-examinable than may consist with the principles of common law.

The editors improved the diction:

> Nor shall any fact, triable by a Jury according to the course of the common law, be otherwise re-examinable than according to the rules of the common law.

In addition to moving the criminal procedure trial rights from Article I to Article III, the editors tinkered with the text. Madison had provided for notice of "the cause and nature of the accusation." The editors flipped the order of *nature* and *cause*. Madison had provided that an accused be "confronted by his accusers and the witnesses against him. . . ." The editors removed *accusers* but left *witnesses*. Presumably, they believed the two categories were interchangeable, but who knows for sure? Madison's catchall jury trial clause that eventually fragmented into parts of the Fifth, Sixth, and Seventh Amendments was substantially edited for the better. Madison's June 8 draft included a guaranty of grand jury indictment "in all crimes punishable by loss of life or member." The editors provided:

> no person shall be held to answer for a capital, or otherwise infamous crime, unless on presentment or indictment by a Grand Jury.

Madison originally included a rambling provision on the location of criminal trials. The editors provided that trial should take place where the crime occurs, but that if a crime occurs in a place in possession of an enemy or where an insurrection was taking place, a trial could be moved to a new location. Madison's June 8 civil-jury-trial language provided:

> In suits at common law, between man and man, the trial by jury, as one of the best securities to the rights of the people, ought to remain inviolate.

This was shortened by the editors and placed in a separate clause to read:

> In suits at common law the right of trial by jury shall be preserved.

Finally the editors tinkered slightly with Madison's proposed closing clause, designed to preserve separation of powers and federalism. Madison had written:

> The powers delegated by this Constitution are appropriated to the departments to which they are respectively distributed: so that

> the Legislative Department shall never exercise powers vested in the Executive or Judicial, nor the Executive exercise the powers vested in the Legislative or Judicial, nor the Judicial exercise powers vested in the Legislative or Executive Departments.
>
> . . .
>
> The powers not delegated by this Constitution, nor prohibited by it to the States, are reserved to the States respectively.

The committee cleaned up the text, providing:

> The powers delegated by this Constitution to the government of the United States, shall be exercised as therein appropriated, so that the Legislative Department shall never exercise the powers vested in the Executive or Judicial, nor the Executive exercise the powers vested in the Legislative or Judicial, nor the Judicial exercise powers vested in the Legislative or Executive Departments.
>
> . . .
>
> The powers not delegated by this Constitution, nor prohibited by it to the States, are reserved to the States respectively.

In the end, the first round of editing by the Committee of Eleven made few substantive changes to Madison's June 8 draft but did carry out some useful reorganization. It also occasionally condensed Madison's discursive language into sharper prose. Given the committee's makeup, I suspect that the minor structural reorganizations came from Roger Sherman, but I'll bet that the felicitous line editing was Madison editing himself.

On July 28, when John Vining sought to present the report of the Committee of Eleven recommending adoption of seventeen clauses, he was met by the House's usual unwillingness to take time from important matters to discuss something as abstract as a declaration of rights. The report was promptly tabled for future consideration. It wasn't until August 3 that Madison could get the floor. The best he could do was to obtain a commitment by the House to consider the report as a committee of the whole as soon as time was available. On August 13, the House, sitting as a committee of the whole, finally began debate on the report of the Committee of Eleven.

The discussion began with the by now ritual grumblings about taking time away from more important matters. In fairness, the House was simultaneously debating the structure of the judicial department and voting on what became the Judiciary Act of 1789. John Vining didn't make matters easier by apologizing profusely for interfering with the scheduled debate over a bill to appoint land agents for Western lands, which he acknowledged was much more important than the Bill of Rights. Theodore Sedgwick, who would later play an important editorial role on the Committee on Style, grumbled that the House had "much other and more important business requiring attention." Elbridge Gerry, who had refused to sign the Constitution because it lacked a bill of rights and who had demanded that every amendment proposed by a state ratifying convention be discussed on the floor of Congress, continued to play his complex game by urging Madison to withdraw his proposals entirely. Gerry hoped that failure to adopt a bill of rights would require the calling of a new constitutional convention with power to rewrite the 1787 document. Madison didn't take offense. In fact, Gerry eventually served as Madison's vice president from 1813 until Gerry's death in 1814.

Debate began on August 13. Roger Sherman, who had lost the argument in the Committee of Eleven, urged once again that the seventeen pending clauses be consolidated in a single coherent bill of rights. Once again, Madison, the reluctant poet, disagreed, insisting on interpolating the clauses into the body of the Constitution at five different places. Elbridge Gerry then piped up, ridiculing the idea of a single coherent bill of rights. Sherman's motion for a single bill of rights was once again roundly defeated.

On August 14, the House finally began considering Madison's handiwork. His stripped-down addition to the preamble was adopted by a vote of 27–23, although it was eventually rejected by the Senate. His apportionment fix, linking House representation to thirty thousand constituents and fixing the maximum size of the House at 275, carried 27–22. His structural limit on Congress raising its own salary carried easily. None of it made its way into the final Bill of Rights. On August 15, a Saturday, the House finally began debating the committee's edited version of Madison's effort to protect religious freedom. The committee's version read:

> No religion shall be established by law, nor shall the equal rights of conscience be infringed.

Roger Sherman moved to strike the amendment entirely, arguing that it was unnecessary because Article I, section 8 did not give Congress the power to establish a religion in the first place, so no need existed for an antidote. After Madison reminded his colleagues that some feared that the Constitution's "necessary and proper" clause would expand Congress's power beyond the literal text of the Constitution, Sherman's motion was overwhelmingly defeated. Attention then turned to the text. Madison explained that the clause was intended to prevent Congress from establishing a national religion and requiring people to observe it by law. Samuel Livermore (N.H.), an opponent of strong national government who had opposed the creation of lower federal courts, moved to amend the text to read:

> Congress shall make no laws touching religion, or infringing the rights of conscience.

While the House adopted the Livermore version by a vote of 31–20, subsequent editing would veer back toward Madison's "establishment" language. Theodore Sedgwick then ridiculed Madison's insistence on protecting the right of assembly as well as speech. His effort to excise "assembly" was roundly defeated. A sustained effort to augment Madison's protection of the freedom to apply to the government for redress of grievances by adding a right of the people "to instruct their representatives" was defeated by a vote of 41–10, but not before it triggered a discussion of Edmund Burke and the nature of representative democracy. The day ended with Fisher Ames unsuccessfully seeking to derail all further discussion of the committee's work.

Madison had a good day on Monday, August 17. The House voted to approve Madison's "right to keep and bear arms" clause, including a narrow 24–22 vote to retain a provision guarantying religious conscientious objection to military service. Madison's "cruel and unusual punishment" clause was upheld over objections that it was too vague, and his ban on "unreasonable search and seizures" was reinstated. The text of what would become the Fourth Amendment was strengthened by Egbert Benson's motion adding the language "no warrants shall issue [without probable cause etc.]." Madison's recognition of unenumerated rights that eventually evolved into the Ninth Amendment was adopted verbatim. Gerry couldn't even get a second for his effort to substitute *impair* for *disparage*. Finally, Madison's effort to limit the states from interfering with religious freedom, speech, or the press, which he described as the most important element of his work, was overwhelmingly accepted with a minor edit that shifted it into a positive statement:

> . . . the equal rights of conscience, the freedom of speech, or the press, and the right to trial by jury in criminal cases, shall not be infringed by any State.

On Tuesday, August 18, the House ended its consideration of the Committee of Eleven's edit of Madison's June 8 proposals by approving his separation-of-powers clause and slightly modifying his federalism clause, which had read:

> The powers not delegated by the Constitution, nor prohibited by it to the States, are reserved to the States respectively.

The House added "or to the people" at its close. So, after a week of debate, the only significant change imposed by the committee of the whole on the Committee of Eleven's proposals was a minor redraft of Madison's religious-freedom amendment. But surviving the committee of the whole was just the beginning. Madison had to do it all over again before the same House of Representatives in its formal parliamentary dress.

Poetry struck late on August 19. After the House rejected what was left of Madison's effort to amend the preamble, the indefatigable Roger Sherman moved for a third time to reorganize Madison's separate clauses into a single coherent Bill of Rights. This time, after an unreported debate, Sherman won. Madison was less than pleased. He did not serve on the three-person Committee on Style charged with rearranging the clauses into a single document. In fact, Sherman did Madison—and us—a huge service by insisting that Madison's music be displayed in a manner that reveals its majestic harmonies. If Madison ever receives royalties from his poetry, he should split them with Roger Sherman.

In fairness to Madison the poet, though, he had already developed the content, order, and structure of the rights sprinkled throughout the larger text. All Sherman did was to lift the rights out one by one in the order that Madison had placed them and list them all in a single place. It took a day. If they do split the royalties, Madison is entitled to the lion's share.

On August 20, Fisher Ames successfully urged yet another rewrite of the religious-freedom clause, reinstating an explicit protection for free exercise, retaining the right of conscience, and continuing to place establishment before free exercise:

> The Congress shall make no law establishing religion, or to prevent the free exercise thereof, or to infringe the rights of conscience.

The "keep and bear arms" clause was also slightly amended to reinstate Madison's original use of the words "in person" at the close of the conscientious-objection provision, presumably to signal that conscientious objectors could be required to perform alternative service. Because the conscientious-objection clause did not make it through the Senate, we'll never know exactly what the House had in mind. The rest of the material that became the Bill of Rights sailed through with little debate. Fittingly, on August 21, Roger Sherman had a redundant last word by editing Madison's federalism clause to read:

> . . . the powers not delegated to the United States by the Constitution nor prohibited by it to the States, are reserved to the States respectively, or to the people.

That was the way it already read except for the one comma after the word *States*.

August 22 was devoted to unsuccessful efforts by House members to place pet amendments into the text, and to the adoption of the final version of Madison's doomed apportionment clause setting a ceiling of fifty thousand on the number of constituents a House member could represent. The big news on August 22 was the appointment of a three-person Committee on Style, consisting of Roger Sherman, Egbert Benson, and Theodore Sedgwick, to rearrange Madison's separate clauses into a single Bill of Rights. Madison, having lost the argument over whether to interpolate the rights into the body of the Constitution or to list them separately, was sulking in his tent, but he had already done most of the heavy organizational lifting. The order of his June 8 proposals meticulously prefigures the organization of the First, Second, and Third Amendments and closes with material tracking the Ninth and Tenth. The material that evolved into the Fourth through Eighth Amendments was somewhat less meticulously organized. But that left something for Roger Sherman to do. The three members of the Committee on Style closeted themselves for a day or so and quickly presented the House with a document containing seventeen proposed articles on August 24, 1789. The first two articles were the ill-fated apportionment and congressional pay raise provisions, having nothing to do with rights. With the exception of Madison's separation-of-powers clause, which didn't get through the Senate, the remaining fifteen articles prefigure the remarkable order and structure of the Bill of Rights. The three editors didn't tinker with Madison's placement of the order of the rights that became the First, Second, and Third Amendments, although the First Amendment material is still divided into separate religious and secular clauses. They did, however, bring organizational order to much of the material that became the Fourth, Fifth, Sixth, and Eighth Amendments. The three editors put together a pretty good draft for the Senate's consideration. It was adopted by the House without debate on August 24.

The House Resolution was transmitted to the Senate on August 25 and taken up for debate on September 2. Unfortunately, the Senate met in closed session in those days, so we have even less of a record than in the House. The Senate rejected several important pieces of Madison's handiwork, including the guaranty of conscientious objection to bearing arms and the presence of separate clauses protecting both religious exercise and the rights of secular conscience. The Senate also refused to restrict state efforts to interfere with the crucial rights of religious freedom, free speech, free press, and criminal jury trial and also rejected an explicit separation-of-powers clause. Ironically, every single item that the Senate stripped from the bill of rights ultimately became the law of the land. The Supreme Court has not hesitated to enforce the separation of powers without an explicit textual clause. The right of secular conscience is now constitutionally protected. The states are now bound by the provisions of the Bill of Rights. And Congress has provided for conscientious objection to the military draft.

A blizzard of efforts at other substantive changes failed in the Senate, but the twenty-one senators took their editorial responsibilities very seriously. They carefully edited the language of virtually every House provision, producing the final textual versions of almost everything in the Bill of Rights, except for the final version of the First Amendment and a minor tweak of the Fifth that were hammered out on September 24 in a House-Senate conference committee that included Sherman, Benson, and Madison.

The twelve proposed amendments were submitted to the states on October 2, 1789. Acting through the state legislatures, the people were the final editors of the great poem, excising the two structural provisions dealing with the maximum size of a congressional district and regulating congressional pay raises. Only the ten rights-bearing amendments were ratified. Between November 20, 1789, and December 15, 1791, eleven states—New Jersey, Maryland, North Carolina, South Carolina, New Hampshire, Delaware, New York, Pennsylvania, Rhode Island, Vermont, and Virginia—ratified the Bill of Rights. Georgia and Connecticut—Roger Sherman's Connecticut—never got around to voting on the Bill of Rights, perhaps because once eleven states had ratified, additional ratifications had no legal effect. In a spate of delayed patriotism, though, both states symbolically ratified the first ten amendments in 1939. Both houses of the Massachusetts legislature apparently ratified the Bill of Rights in early 1790, but never got around to enacting a formal ratification bill. To make sure, Massachusetts also symbolically reratified in 1939.

I don't suppose that Wallace Stevens or Robert Frost wrote poetry this way. But the result is the remarkable poem to democracy and individual freedom unlike anything the world has ever seen. Thanks to Madison and his friends, where the Bill of Rights is concerned, the house is quiet. The world is calm. And the reader can become the book, if only you'll try.

NOTES

I have sought to keep notes to a minimum. Cases are cited only when necessary to provide an example of the Supreme Court's actions. Historical citations are designed to enrich the narrative, not to document it. For those of you seeking more complete notes, many of the themes in this book have been foreshadowed in my recent academic writings, which include: "The House Was Quiet and the World Was Calm," *Vanderbilt Law Review* 57 (2004); "Democracy and the Poor," in *Law and Class in America*, ed. Paul Carrington and Trina Jones (2006); "The Gravitational Pull of Race on the Warren Court," *Supreme Court Review* 2010, no. 1: 59–102; "Felix Frankfurter's Revenge: An Accidental Democracy Built by Judges," *NYU Review of Law & Social Change* 35 (2011): 602; "Serving the Syllogism Machine," *Texas Tech Law Review* 44 (2011): 1; "Of Singles without Baseball: Corporations as Frozen Transactional Moments," *Rutgers Law Review* 65 (2012): 745; and "One State/ Two Votes: Do Supermajority Voting Rules Violate the Article V Guaranty of Equal State Suffrage?" *Stanford Journal of Civil Rights and Civil Liberties* 10 (2014): 27. If you can't find the note you seek in those sources, I'll be glad to visit you at home and deliver it.

I owe a debt to two academics whose writing has stimulated my thinking about reading the Constitution's text. Charles Black's pioneering efforts to read the Constitution functionally opened my eyes to the possibility of viewing the Constitution as a coherent narrative, and Akhil Amar's imaginative approach to constitutional text stimulated me to look for poetry in the Bill of Rights. I also owe a debt to Justice Antonin Scalia, whose passionate engagement with the Constitution's text challenged me to attempt to find a more coherent way of reading our most cherished political document.

2. Why Reading the First Amendment Isn't Easy

1. The drama surrounding the election of 1800 is described in John Fering, *Adams v. Jefferson: The Tumultuous Election of 1800* (New York: Oxford University Press, 2004). The best summary of President John Adams's use of the Alien and Sedition Acts to stifle his opponents is Geoffrey Stone, *Perilous Times: Free Speech in Wartime, from the Sedition Act of 1798 to the War on Terror* (New York: Norton, 2004).

2. The widespread imposition of censorship of criticism of slavery throughout the South is described in Michael T. Gilmore, *The War on Words: Slavery, Race, and Free Speech in America* (Chicago: University of Chicago Press, 2010).

3. *Vegelhan v. Guntner*, 167 Mass. 92 (1896).

4. *Abrams v. United States*, 250 U.S. 616 (1919).

5. *Debs v. United States*, 249 U.S. 211 (1919).

6. *Dennis v. United States*, 341 U.S. 494 (1951).

7. The classic statement of Justice Holmes's justification for a robust free-speech clause occurs in his dissent in *Abrams* 250 U.S at 624–31 (Holmes and Brandeis dissenting). Both Holmes and Brandeis were a little late to the First Amendment party, voting to uphold the convictions and sentences in *Schenck* and *Debs*.

8. The classic statement of Justice Brandeis's justification for a robust free-speech clause occurs in *Whitney v. California*, 274 U.S. 357, 372–80 (1927) (Brandeis and Holmes concurring).

9. See Frederick Schauer, *Free Speech: A Philosophical Enquiry* (New York: Cambridge University Press, 1982).

10. *Texas v. Johnson*, 491 U.S. 397 (1989); *United States v. Eichman*, 496 U.S. 310 (1990): flag burning is protected speech. The voting breakdown was Justices Brennan and Marshall, joined by Justices Scalia, Blackmun, and Kennedy. Chief Justice Rehnquist and Justices White, O'Connor, and Stevens dissented.

11. E.g., *Citizens United v. FEC*, 558 U.S. 310 (2010): corporations may spend unlimited funds from their treasuries in support of candidates; *Arizona Free Enterprise Club v. Bennett*, 131 S. Ct. 2806 (2011), invalidating matching subsidies.

12. Stephen Breyer, *Active Liberty: Interpreting Our Democratic Constitution* (New York: Oxford University Press, 2006).

3. Madison's Music: Lost and Found

1. It is true, of course, that what we call the First Amendment was originally in third place, preceded by proposed structural amendments setting a limit of fifty thousand on the number of constituents a House member could represent and prohibiting Congress from raising its pay until the next Congress. While both the

A10: The powers not delegated to the United States by the Constitution, nor prohibited by it to the States, are reserved to the States respectively, or to the people.

constituent limit and pay raise amendments preceded the First Amendment, they were both viewed as structural fixes for errors or omissions in the original text. Neither purported to recognize or protect a fundamental human right. I discuss the two structural provisions in Chapter 10.

2. The Fourth through Eighth Amendments provide:

AMENDMENT IV

The right of the people to be secure in their persons, houses, papers, and effects against unreasonable searches and seizures, shall not be violated, and no Warrants shall issue, but upon probable cause, supported by Oath or affirmation, and particularly describing the place to be searched or things to be seized.

AMENDMENT V

No person shall be held to answer for a capital, or otherwise infamous crime, unless on presentment or indictment of a Grand Jury, except in cases arising in the land and naval forces, or in the Militia, when in actual service in time of War or public danger; nor shall any person be subject for the same offence to be twice put in jeopardy of life and limb; nor shall he be compelled in any criminal case to be a witness against himself, nor be deprived of life, liberty, or property, without due process of law; nor shall private property be taken for public use without just compensation.

AMENDMENT VI

In all criminal prosecutions, the accused shall enjoy the right to a speedy and public trial, by an impartial jury of the State and district wherein the crime shall have been committed, which district shall have been previously ascertained by law, and to be informed of the nature and cause of the accusation; to be confronted with the witnesses against him; to have compulsory process for obtaining Witnesses in his favor, and to have the Assistance of Counsel for his defence.

AMENDMENT VII

In Suits at common law, where the value in controversy shall exceed twenty dollars, the right of trial by jury shall be preserved, and no fact tried by a jury shall be otherwise re-examined in any Court in the United States, than according to the rules of the common law.

AMENDMENT VIII

Excessive bail shall not be required, nor excessive fines imposed, nor cruel and unusual punishments inflicted.

4. The First Amendment as a Narrative of Democracy

1. The phrase "city on a hill" is derived from Massachusetts Bay Colony governor John Winthrop's 1630 sermon "A Model of Christian Charity," delivered aboard the *Arabella* immediately before disembarking in the New World. In describing the ideal commonwealth that he hoped to found as a "city on a hill,"

A9: The enumeration in the Constitution, of certain rights, shall not be construed to deny or disparage others retained by the people.

Winthrop was echoing language in the parable of salt and light from the Sermon on the Mount, Matthew 5:14.

2. The forty-two rights-bearing antecedents to the Bill of Rights, were:

(1) four British documents: the Magna Carta (1215), the English Petition of Rights (1628), Cromwell's Agreement of the People (1628), and the English Bill of Rights (1689);

(2) three detailed colonial charters: the Massachusetts Body of Liberties (1641), the Pennsylvania Charter of Government (1682), and the New York Charter of Liberties and Privileges (1683), together with less detailed colonial charters for Maryland (1639), Rhode Island (1663), Carolina (1669—drafted by John Locke, no less), New Jersey (1677), and Pennsylvania (1701);

(3) nineteen Revolutionary-era Constitutions and Declarations: Virginia (1765), Massachusetts (1772), the First Continental Congress (1774), the Address to the Inhabitants of Quebec (1774), the Declaration of Independence (1776), Virginia (1776), Thomas Jefferson's Draft Virginia Constitution (1776), New Jersey (1776), Pennsylvania (1776), North Carolina (1776), Connecticut (1776), Delaware (1776), Maryland (1776), Georgia (1777), New York (1777), Vermont (1777), South Carolina (1778), Massachusetts (1780), and New Hampshire (1783); and

(4) eleven documents dating from the Founders' era: the Northwest Ordinance (1787), the United States Constitution (1787), the French Declaration of the Rights of Man (1789), six documents prepared during the ratification debate proposing amendments to the United States Constitution submitted by Massachusetts, South Carolina, New Hampshire, Virginia (North Carolina submitted a verbatim copy of Virginia's proposed amendments), and New York, and three minority reports seeking amendments from Delaware, Pennsylvania, and Maryland.

3. Madison initially resisted listing our rights in a single poetic document, preferring to intersperse them throughout the constitutional text. It was Roger Sherman who kept insisting on a single, integrated Bill of Rights. I describe the textual evolution of the Bill of Rights in Chapter 10.

4. I discuss the fate of Madison's conscience clause in Chapter 10.

5. *United States v. Seeger*, 380 U.S. 163 (1965); *Welsh v. United States*, 398 U.S. 333 (1970).

6. *Buckley v. Valeo*, 424 U.S. 1 (1976), invalidating limits on campaign spending and forbidding efforts to limit campaign spending in an effort to equalize political power.

7. *Arizona Free Enterprise Club v. Bennett*, 131 S. Ct. 2806 (2011), invalidating Arizona matching-funds campaign subsidy plan.

8. *Citizens United v. FEC*, 558 U.S. 310 (2010), invalidating a ban on corporate campaign spending.

9. *California Democratic Party v. Jones*, 530 U.S. 567 (2000), invalidating California's "blanket primary."

10. *Shaw v. Reno*, 509 U.S. 630 (1993), invalidating legislative lines designed to benefit a racial minority.

11. *Shelby County v. Holder*, 133 S. Ct. 2612 (2013), invalidating pre-clearance provisions requiring advance certification by the Department of Justice that a proposed change in a covered state's election procedures would not adversely affect black voters.

12. *Crawford v. Marion County*, 553 U.S. 181 (2008), upholding requirement of voter ID.

13. *Vieth v. Jubelirer*, 541 U.S. 267 (2004), upholding Republican gerrymander of Pennsylvania.

14. *LULAC v. Perry*, 548 U.S. 399 (2006), upholding Republican gerrymander of Texas.

15. See Curtis Gans, *Voter Turnout in the United States, 1788–2009* (Washington, DC: CQ Press, 2010).

16. *Bush v. Gore*, 531 U.S. 98 (2000), terminating Florida recount and ensuring election of George W. Bush.

17. In *McCutcheon v. Federal Election Commission*, 134 S. Ct. 1434 (2014), the justices debated the Supreme Court's responsibility for the quality of the democracy their decisions have built. Chief Justice Roberts, writing for the Court's Republican majority, argued that the quality of the resulting democracy was not the Court's problem. Justice Breyer, writing for the four Democratic dissenters, argued that ensuring the quality of the democracy is an important aspect of the Court's work.

18. The Third Amendment seeks to protect robust democracy against suffocation by military occupation, as opposed to armed overthrow. Fortunately, we have had no occasion to invoke it.

> AMENDMENT III
>
> No soldier shall, in time of peace be quartered in any house, without the consent of the Owner, nor in time of war, but in a manner to be prescribed by law.

19. The body of the 1787 Constitution sought to minimize the danger of armed subversion by limiting military appropriations to two years, forbidding military officers from serving in the government, appointing a civilian, the president, as commander in chief of the armed forces, and eliminating the executive's unilateral power to declare war.

20. *District of Columbia v. Heller*, 554 U.S. 570 (2008).

21. *Mapp v. Ohio*, 367 U.S. 643 (1961).

22. *Miranda v. Arizona*, 384 U.S. 436 (1966).

23. *In re Winship*, 397 U.S. 358 (1970); *Gideon v. Wainwright*, 372 U.S. 335 (1963).

24. The nineteenth-century Supreme Court took a more holistic view of the criminal procedure amendments, e.g., in *Boyd v. United States*, 116 U.S. 616 (1886). Alas, *Boyd* has been abandoned by the modern Court. *Fisher v. United States*, 425 U.S. 391 (1976).

25. The history of "equity of the statute" is recounted in James M. Landis, "Statutes and the Sources of the Law," *Harvard Legal Essays* (1934); Ivor Jennings,

"Courts and Administrative Law: The Experience of English Housing Legislation," *Harvard Law Review* 49 (1936): 426. For a more skeptical modern view, see John F. Manning, "Textualism and the Equity of the Statute," *Columbia Law Review* 101, no. 1 (2001): 1.

26. *NAACP v. Alabama*, 357 U.S. 449 (1958).

27. *Mapp v. Ohio*, 367 U.S. 643 (1961); *Miranda v. Arizona*, 384 U.S. 436 (1966).

28. *In re Winship*, 397 U.S. 358 (1970).

29. *Gideon v. Wainwright*, 372 U.S. 335 (1963).

30. *United States v. Seeger*, 380 U.S. 163 (1965); *Welsh v. United States*, 398 U.S. 333 (1970).

5. Madison's Music Restored

1. *Baker v. Carr*, 369 U.S. 186 (1962).

2. *Baker*, 369 U.S. at 266–330, Frankfurter, J., dissenting. See also *Colegrove v. Green*, 328 U.S. 549 (1946).

3. Article IV, section 4 provides: "The United States shall guaranty to every state in this Union a Republican Form of Government."

4. The Equal Protection Clause of the Fourteenth Amendment provides: "No state . . . shall . . . deny to any person within its jurisdiction the equal protection of the laws."

5. *Baker v. Carr*, 369 U.S. at 368, Harlan, J., dissenting.

6. The Supreme Court ruled in 1844 that it lacked power under the Republican Form of Government Clause to decide which of two competing factions constituted the legitimate republican government of Rhode Island. Ever since, the Court has treated the clause as a judicial dead letter.

7. The origins of the Twelfth Amendment are discussed in Chapter 10.

8. See *Minor v. Happersett* , 88 U.S. 162 (1874), denying the vote to women; *Giles v. Harris*, 189 U.S. 475 (1903) (Holmes, J.), denying the vote to blacks.

9. *Ex parte Yarbrough*, 110 U.S. 651 (1884), conspiring to use force to prevent blacks from voting punishable as a federal crime; *Guinn v. United States*, 238 U.S. 347 (1915), invalidating racially discriminatory literacy tests; *Nixon v. Herndon*, 273 U.S. 536 (1927), striking down a Texas statute forbidding blacks from voting in primary elections.

10. *Carrington v. Rash*, 380 U.S. 89 (1965).

11. *Harper v. Board of Elections*, 383 U.S. 663 (1966).

12. *Williams v. Rhodes*, 393 U.S. 23 (1968).

13. *Kramer v. Union Free School District*, 395 U.S. 621 (1969).

14. *Dunn v. Blumstein*, 405 U.S. 330 (1972).

15. *Lassiter v. Northampton Bd. of Elections*, 360 U.S. 45, 51–53 (1959).

16. *Richardson v. Ramirez*, 418 U.S. 24 (1974).

17. A third area where Justice Brennan's equality-based approach fell short of protecting the franchise was in so-called special-purpose elections, which often limit the franchise to persons directly affected by the election. *Salyer Land Company v. Tulare Lake Basin Water Storage District*, 410 U.S. 719 (1973), limiting

water allocation votes to landowners, allocating vote by acreage; *Ball v. James*, 451 U.S. 335 (1981), limiting vote for directors of state water conservation district to local landowners. But see *Hill v. Stone*, 421 U.S. 289 (1975), striking down property ownership requirement in city bond elections.

18. *Gomillion v. Lightfoot*, 364 U.S. 339 (1960).

19. *Lane v. Wilson*, 307 U.S. 268 (1939).

20. *Washington v. Davis*, 426 U.S. 229 (1976).

21. *City of Mobile v. Bolden*, 446 U.S. 55 (1980).

22. After the Voting Rights Act of 1982 forbade election regulations with the "effect" of denying blacks a fair chance to elect candidates of their choice, and after the Supreme Court ruled that the Voting Rights Act applied to judicial elections, New Orleans was finally divided into two districts. Justice Bernette J. Johnson was elected from the new district in 1994 and sits today as Louisiana's first black chief justice.

23. *Hunter v. Underwood*, 471 U.S. 222 (1985).

24. *Johnson v. Bush*, 214 F. Supp.2d 1333 (S.D. Fla. 2002), granting summary judgment for Florida on issue of improper purpose.

25. *Johnson v. Governor*, 377 F.3d 1163 (11th Cir. 2004), reversing grant of summary judgment, remanding for further fact-finding.

26. *Johnson v. Governor*, 405 F.3d 1214 (11th Cir. 2005), en banc, reinstating district court dismissal, cert. denied, *Johnson v. Bush*, 564 U.S. 1015 (2005).

27. *United Jewish Organizations of Williamsburg v. Carey*, 430 U.S. 144 (1977).

28. *Shaw v. Reno*, 509 U.S. 630 (1993); *Shaw v. Hunt*, 517 U.S. 899 (1996).

29. Lest you think such a 10:1 disparity is unrealistic, the United States Senate functions under a 72:1 disparity between senators from California, who represent more than 38 million voters, and senators from Montana, who represent about 570,000 voters.

30. *Davis v. Bandemer*, 478 U.S. 109 (1986).

31. *Vieth v. Jubilirer*, 541 U.S. 267 (2004); *LULAC v. Perry*, 548 U.S. 399 (2006).

32. *Terry v. Adams*, 345 U.S. 461 (1953).

33. *Tashjian v. Republican Party*, 479 U.S. 208 (1986).

34. *Rosario v. Rockefeller*, 410 U.S. 752 (1973).

35. *Kusper v. Pontikes*, 414 U.S. 51 (1973).

36. *American Party of Texas v. White*, 415 U.S. 767 (1974).

37. *California Democratic Party v. Jones*, 530 U.S. 567 (2000).

38. *Washington State Grange v. Washington State Republican Party*, 552 U.S. 442 (2008).

39. *New York State Board of Elections v. Lopez-Torres*, 552 U.S. 196 (2008).

40. *Clingman v. Beaver*, 544 U.S. 581 (2005).

41. *Williams v. Rhodes*, 393 U.S. 23 (1968).

42. *Munro v. Socialist Worker Party*, 479 U.S. 189 (1986); *Storer v. Brown*, 415 U.S. 724 (1974); *Jessess v. Fortson*, 403 U.S. 431 (1971).

43. *Timmons v. Twin Cities Area New Party*, 520 U.S. 351 (1997).

44. *Burdick v. Takushi*, 504 U.S. 428 (1992).

45. *McCutcheon v. FEC*, 134 S. Ct. 1434 (2014).

46. Finally, *Buckley* upheld disclosure rules requiring most campaign contributions to be made public, although Congress has left huge loopholes in the disclosure process, and state disclosure rules are often either nonexistent or toothless.

47. *Buckley v. Valeo*, 424 U.S. 1 (1976).

48. *United States v. O'Brien*, 391 U.S. 367 (1968).

49. *Caperton v. A. T. Massey Coal Co.*, 556 U.S. 868 (2009).

50. *Citizens United v. FEC*, 558 U.S. 310 (2010).

51. 531 U.S. 98 (2000), per curiam. The safe-harbor provision emerged from the turbulent Hayes-Tilden presidential election of 1876, in which Tilden won an absolute majority of the popular vote, but lost by 185–184 in the Electoral College after a series of fiercely partisan congressional challenges favored 20 contested Hayes electors from Florida, Louisiana, South Carolina, and Oregon.

52. *Crawford v. Marion County*, 553 U.S. 181 (2008).

53. *Hale v. Henkel*, 201 U.S. 43, 74–75 (1906).

54. *Braswell v. United States*, 487 U.S. 99 (1988).

55. In fairness, Justice Kennedy argues that hearers would be benefited by granting First Amendment protection to for-profit corporations, while no such third-party benefit is available in the self-incrimination cases. But if *Citizens United* rests on the alleged benefits of unlimited corporate electioneering, surely Justice Kennedy was obliged to confront the fact that the voter/hearers had overwhelmingly voted to be free from corporate political speech.

56. *Virginia Pharmacy Board v. Virginia Citizens Consumer Council*, 425 U.S. 748 (1976); *Central Hudson Gas v. Public Service Comm'n*, 447 U.S. 557 (1980).

57. *FEC v. Massachusetts Citizens for Life*, 479 U.S. 238 (1986).

6. The Democracy-Friendly First Amendment in Action

1. *Anderson v. Cellebreze*, 460 U.S. 780 (1983).

2. *Poe v. Ullman*, 367 U.S. 497, 523 (1961), J. Harlan dissenting; *Griswold v. Connecticut*, 381 U.S. 479 (1965).

3. *Roe v. Wade*, 410 U.S. 113 (1973).

4. *Moore v. East Cleveland*, 431 U.S. 494 (1977).

5. *Lawrence v. Texas*, 539 U.S. 558 (2003).

6. *Loving v. Virginia*, 388 U.S. 1 (1967); *Zablocki v. Redhail*, 434 U.S. 374 (1978).

7. The American Political Science Association deems a district contestable if the gap in pre-election party voter registration is less than 55 percent to 45 percent. Districts with a pre-election gap greater than 60 percent to 40 percent are designated landslide districts.

8. *Borough of Duryea v. Guarnieri*, 131 S. Ct. 2488 (2011).

9. The debate over "instruction" is described briefly in Chapter 10.

7. Mr. Madison's Neighborhood

1. *West Virginia State Bd. of Education v. Barnette*, 319 U.S. 624 (1943) (banning compulsory flag salutes); *Cohen v. California*, 403 U.S. 15 (1971) ("Fuck the

draft" protected speech); *Texas v. Johnson*, 491 U.S. 397 (1989); *United States v. Eichman*, 496 U.S. 310 (1990) (burning flags protected).

2. Galileo was excommunicated and placed under house arrest for challenging the Church's commitment to Ptolemaic astronomy, which viewed the earth as the center of the universe. See Maurice A. Finnochiario, *The Galileo Affair: A Documentary History* (Berkeley: University of California Press, 1989). John Milton's *Areopagitica: A Plea for Unlicensed Printing* (1644), one of the landmarks in the evolution of free-speech theory, was almost certainly influenced by the young Milton's visit to Galileo during Galileo's house arrest. See William Riley Parker, *Milton: A Biography* (Oxford: Clarendon, 1996).

3. *RAV v. City of St. Paul*, 505 U.S. 377 (1992); *Wisconsin v. Mitchell*, 508 U.S. 476 (1993).

4. *Virginia v. Black*, 538 U.S. 343 (2003).

5. *National Socialist Party v. Skokie*, 432 U.S. 43 (1977).

6. *Chaplinsky v. New Hampshire*, 315 U.S. 568 (1942). In the years since *Chaplinsky*, the Supreme Court has never sustained a conviction for using "fighting words." The case may well be a dead precedent.

7. *Kovacs v. Cooper*, 336 U.S. 77 (1949); *Ward v. Rock Against Racism*, 491 U.S. 781 (1989).

8. *Burson v. Freeman*, 504 U.S. 191 (1992). *Burson* is a rare example of the government winning a strict-scrutiny case.

9. *Florida Bar v. Went for It, Inc.*, 515 U.S. 618 (1995).

10. *Rowan v. United States Post Office*, 397 U.S. 728 (1970).

11. *Frisby v. Schultz*, 487 U.S. 474 (1988).

12. *Hill v. Colorado*, 530 U.S. 703 (2000).

13. *McCullen v. Coakley*, 12-1168, transcript of oral argument, 29, 32, 44.

14. *Lamont v. Postmaster General*, 381 U.S. 301 (1965).

15. See *Pell v. Procunier*, 417 U.S. 817 (1974) and *Saxbe v. Washington Post*, 417 U.S. 843 (1974), rejecting an investigatory role for the press.

16. *Turner Broadcasting System, Inc. v. FCC*, 512 U.S. 622 (1994); *Turner Broadcasting System, Inc. v. FCC*, 520 U.S. 180 (1997).

17. *New York Times v. Sullivan*, 376 U.S. 254 (1964).

18. Frederick Schauer is one of the leading proponents of the cautionary approach to government censorship. Frederick Schauer, *Free Speech: A Philosophical Enquiry* (New York: Cambridge University Press, 1982).

19. *United States v. Alvarez*, 132 S. Ct. 2537 (2012).

20. *Snyder v. Phelps*, 131 S. Ct. 1207 (2011).

21. *Brown v. Entertainment Merchants' Ass'n*, 131 S. Ct. 2729 (2011).

22. *United States v. Stevens*, 559 U.S. 460 (2010).

23. Geoffrey R. Stone, *Perilous Times: Free Speech in Wartime from the Sedition Act of 1798 to the War on Terror* (New York: W.W. Norton, 2004).

24. See *Dennis v. United States*, 341 U.S. 494 (1951), upholding criminal convictions of Communist Party leaders. See generally, Ellen Schrecker, *The Age of McCarthyism: A Brief History with Documents* (Boston: Bedford/St. Martin's, 2002); Ellen Schrecker, *Many Are the Crimes: McCarthyism in America* (Boston: Little, Brown, 1998).

25. For the bad-tendency test in action, see *Whitney v. California*, 274 U.S. 357 (1927); *Gitlow v. New York*, 268 U.S. 652 (1925); *Abrams v. New York*, 250 U.S. 616 (1919); *Debs v. United States*, 249 U.S. 211 (1919); *Frohwerk v. New York*, 249 U.S. 204 (1919); *Schenck v. United States*, 249 U.S. 47 (1919). The most notorious use of the bad-tendency test in modern times took place in *Dennis v. United States*, 341 U.S. 494 (1951), when the Court upheld the conviction of the leaders of the American Communist Party for the crime of being leaders of the American Communist Party. Although the Supreme Court used the language of clear and present danger, it deferred to Congress's assessment of the imminence of the danger posed by a political party pledged to violent revolution at some indefinite time in the future, reducing the judicial role to that of a bystander. Many read *Brandenburg v. Ohio*, 395 U.S. 444 (1969), per curiam, as overruling *Dennis*.

26. See e.g., *Tinker v. Des Moines School Board*, 393 U.S. 503 (1969), cannot punish student for wearing black armband to class to protest Vietnam War in absence of showing strong likelihood that would disrupt class; *Edwards v. South Carolina*, 372 U.S. 229 (1963); *Cox v. Louisiana*, 379 U.S. 536 (1965) (*Cox* I); *Cox v. Louisiana*, 379 U.S 559 (1965) (*Cox* II), reversing convictions of civil rights marchers.

27. *Brandenburg v. Ohio*, 395 U.S. 444 (1969), per curiam.

28. *Cohen v. California*, 403 U.S. 15 (1971).

29. For a description of the conservative intellectual renaissance, see George H. Nash, *The Conservative Intellectual Movement in America Since 1945*, 2d ed. (Wilmington, DE: ISI Books, 2006); Jeffrey Hart, *The Making of the American Conservative Mind: The* National Review *and Its Times* (Wilmington, DE: ISI Books, 2007).

30. See, for example, Robert Nozik, *Anarchy, State, and Utopia* (New York: Basic Books, 1974).

31. I am, of course, referring to the short period of virtually unanimous political support for President James Monroe from 1816 to 1820.

32. *Texas v. Johnson*, 491 U.S. 397 (1989); *United States v. Eichman*, 496 U.S. 310 (1990). Justice Brennan wrote for the Court in both cases. The dissenters were Chief Justice Rehnquist and Justices White, Stevens, and O'Connor. Justice Scalia was the swing vote.

33. *Buckley v. Valeo*, 424 U.S. 1 (1976), per curiam. The fragmented series of per curiam and individual opinions in *Buckley* usually shake out to 7–1, with Chief Justice Burger dissenting and Justice Stevens not participating.

34. *Virginia Pharmacy Board v. Virginia Citizens Consumer Council*, 425 U.S. 748 (1976). Justice Blackmun wrote for seven justices, including Brennan and Marshall. Chief Justice Burger wrote a concurrence. Justice Rehnquist was the lone dissenter. Justice Stevens did not participate. The commercial-speech doctrine received its fullest articulation several years later in *Central Hudson Gas & Elec. Corp. v. Public Service Commission of New York*, 447 U.S. 557 (1980). The eight justices who voted to invalidate a ban on promotional messages by electric companies found it very difficult to identify exactly what falls under commercial speech, proffering four different tests. Chief Justice Rehnquist continued to dissent from the grant of broad First Amendment power to corporations.

35. *First National Bank of Boston v. Bellotti*, 435 U.S. 765 (1978).

36. Although the Court rejected a right to reply to press attacks in *Miami Herald Publishing Company v. Tornillo*, 418 U.S. 241 (1974), the Court was initially receptive to government efforts to provide dissenting voices with access to the broadcast media. *Red Lion Broadcasting Co. v. FCC*, 395 U.S. 367 (1969), upholding "fairness doctrine"; *FCC v. National Citizens Committee for Broadcasting*, 436 U.S. 775 (1978), upholding ban on cross-ownership of newspaper and TV station in same market. See generally *Associated Press v. United States*, 326 U.S. 1 (1945), applying antitrust laws to media settings. After repeal of the fairness doctrine by the FCC, the Court rejected a First Amendment right of access to broadcast media. *CBS v. Democratic National Committee*, 412 U. S. 94 (1973). The autonomy of broadcasters was upheld in *FCC v. League of Women Voters*, 468 U.S. 364 (1984), invalidating ban on editorials by public TV stations; *Arkansas Educational Television Comm'n v. Forbes*, 523 U.S. 666 (1998), upholding exclusion of candidate from debate on public TV; *Turner Broadcasting v. FCC*, 512 U.S. 622 (1994) (*Turner* I), rejecting application of *Red Lion* to cable broadcasting. The chaotic state of current law on media diversity is reflected in *Prometheus Radio Project v. FCC*, 373 F.3d 372 (3d Cir. 2004); *Sinclair Broadcasting, Inc. v. FCC*, 284 F.3d 148 (D.C. Cir. 2002); and *Fox Television Stations, Inc. v. FCC*, 280 F.3d 1027 (D.C. Cir. 2002). Each case rejects an FCC rule on media ownership.

37. *RAV v. City of St. Paul*, 505 U.S. 377 (1992), invalidating conviction for cross burning because statute overbroad; *Virginia v. Black*, 538 U.S. 343 (2003), invalidating convictions for cross burning in absence of proof beyond reasonable doubt of intent to intimidate.

38. *Connick v. Myers*, 461 U.S. 138 (1983), limiting freedom to circulate internal criticism at work; *Waters v. Churchill*, 511 U.S. 661 (1994), upholding dismissal based on employer assessment of disruptive nature; *Garcetti v. Ceballos*, 543 U.S. 1186 (2005), upholding dismissal of assistant DA for internal criticism of failure to respond to misrepresentations in search warrant.

39. *Bethel School District v. Fraser*, 478 U.S. 675 (1986), upholding discipline for student nominating speech with sexual innuendos; *Hazelwood School District v. Kuhlmeier*, 484 U.S. 260 (1988), upholding principal's editorial control over official student newspaper; *Morse v. Frederick*, 551 U.S. 393 (2007), upholding discipline for displaying banner with drug connotations.

40. *Hazelwood v. Kuhlmeier*, 484 U.S. 260 (1988); *Morse v. Frederick*, 551 U.S. 393 (2007).

41. *Knox v. SEIU*, 132 S. Ct. 2277 (2012), five members of Court *in dicta* suggest that employees must opt in to public union decision to use mandatory dues for political purposes; four justices disagree.

42. *Holder v. Humanitarian Law Project*, 561 U.S. 1 (2010).

43. *Citizens United v. FEC*, 558 U.S. 50, (2010), Stevens, J., dissenting, joined by Justices Ginsburg, Breyer, and Kagan.

44. *Arizona Free Enterprise Freedom Club PAC v. Bennett*, 131 S. Ct. 2806 (2011), invalidating Arizona matching-fund law 5–4.

45. *McCutcheon v. FEC*, 134 S. Ct. 1434 (2014).

46. Article I, section 10 forbids any state from passing a "Law impairing the Obligation of Contracts." The Fifth and Fourteenth Amendments forbid both federal

and state governments from depriving a "person" of "life, liberty, or property without due process of law." The Fifth Amendment also provides that "private property [shall not] be taken for public use, without just compensation."

47. *Virginia Pharmacy Board v. Virginia Citizens Consumer Council*, 425 U.S. 748 (1976) (protecting advertising about drug pricing); *Central Hudson Gas v. Public Services Comm'n*, 447 U.S. 557 (1980) (declining to protect advertising promoting unlawful activities).

48. Elena Kagan, "Private Speech, Public Purpose: The Role of Government Motive in Free Speech Doctrine," *University of Chicago Law Review* 63 (1996): 413.

49. *New York Times v. United States*, 403 U.S. 713 (1971).

50. *Gooding v. Wilson*, 405 U.S. 518 (1972); *Coates v. City of Cincinnati*, 402 U.S. 611 (1971).

51. *Smith v. Goguen*, 415 U.S. 566 (1974).

52. Burt Neuborne, "The Gravitational Pull of Race on the Warren Court," *Supreme Court Review* 2010, no. 1 (2010): 59, 77.

53. *Minneapolis Star & Tribune Co. v. Minnesota Comm'r of Revenue*, 460 U.S. 575 (1983).

54. *Freedman v. Maryland*, 380 U.S. 51 (1965).

55. *Turner Broadcasting System v. FCC*, 520 U.S. 180 (1997) (Turner II).

56. *Cox v. New Hampshire*, 312 U.S. 569 (1941).

57. For a useful summary of academic articles on the Occupy Wall Street movement, see the forum established by the *Berkeley Journal of Sociology*, "Understanding the Occupy Movement: Perspectives from the Social Sciences," bjsonline.org/2011/12/understanding-the-occupy-movement-perspectives-from-the-social-sciences. No summary of the legal confrontations appears to exist, although New York City settled several cases arising out of violent confrontations between the police and the demonstrators.

58. *New York Times v. Sullivan*, 376 U.S. 254 (1964).

8. Divine Madness

1. The textual evolution of the First Amendment is discussed in Chapter 10.

2. *United States v. Seeger*, 380 U.S. 163 (1965); *Welsh v. United States*, 398 U.S. 333 (1970).

3. Justice Harlan had joined the majority in *Seeger* in merely construing the statute to provide the defendant with conscientious-objector status despite his failure to believe in a Supreme Being. In his influential concurrence in *Welsh*, however, Justice Harlan repudiated his reading of the statute in *Seeger* and ruled that the Constitution required recognition of claims of secular conscience in both cases. It is Justice Harlan's concurring opinion that we remember.

4. *Employment Division v. Smith* , 494 U.S. 872 (1990).

5. *Prince v. Massachusetts*, 321 U.S. 158 (1944), child labor laws.

6. *Gillette v. United States*, 401 U.S. 437 (1971), military conscription.

7. *Jimmy Swaggert Ministries v. Board of Equalization*, 493 U.S. 378 (1990), sales tax; *United States v. Lee*, 455 U.S. 252 (1982), Social Security taxes.

8. *Burwell v. Hobby Lobby*, 2014 WL 2921709.

9. *Corporation of the Presiding Bishop v. Amos*, 483 U.S. 327 (1987).

10. In observant Judaism, the *Shabbos goy* is the good Samaritan who comes into your home and lights the furnace on the Sabbath, when observant Jews are prohibited from doing so. When I was growing up in Queens, several wonderful non-Jewish neighbors (who happened to be black) made sure that nearby elderly observant Jews stayed warm on cold Saturday afternoons. I loved them for it, and tutored their kids.

11. *Thornton v. Caldor, Inc.*, 472 U.S. 703 (1985).

12. *Marsh v. Chambers*, 463 U.S. 783 (1983).

13. *Town of Greece v. Galloway*, 134 S. Ct. 1811 (2014).

14. *Lyng v. Northwest Indian Cemetery Protective Ass'n*, 485 U.S. 439 (1988) (allowing road through Indian burial ground); *O'Lone v. Estate of Shabazz*, 482 U.S. 342 (1987) (rejecting prisoner's petition); *Goldman v. Weinberger*, 475 U.S. 503 (1983) (enforcing military headgear rule).

15. *Witters v. Department of Services for the Blind*, 474 U.S. 481 (1986); *Zobrest v. Catalina Foothills School District*, 509 U.S. 1 (1993); *Agostini v. Felton*, 521 U.S. 203 (1997); *Mitchell v. Helms*, 530 U.S. 793 (2000); *Zelman v. Simmons-Harris*, 536 U.S. 639 (2002).

16. *Church of the Lukumi Babalu Aye, Inc. v. City of Hialeah*, 508 U.S. 520 (1993).

17. *Engel v. Vitale*, 370 U.S. 421 (1962); *Abington School District v. Schempp*, 374 U.S. 203 (1963); *Wallace v. Jaffree*, 472 U.S. 38 (1985); *Lee v. Weisman*, 505 U.S. 577 (1992); *Stone v. Graham*, 449 U.S. 39 (1980); *Epperson v. Arkansas*, 393 U.S. 97 (1968); *Edwards v. Aguillard*, 482 U.S. 578 (1987).

18. *Reynolds v. United States*, 98 U.S. 145 (1878).

9. The Costs of Ignoring Madison's Music

1. *Marbury v. Madison*, 5 U.S. 137 (1803).

2. The three earlier presidential elections had been won by Federalists. The presidency passed to the Jeffersonian Republicans in 1800, and stayed there until the election of John Quincy Adams by the House of Representatives in 1824.

3. Article II, section 3, clause 2 originally provided: "In every Case, after the Choice of the President, the Person having the greatest number of Votes of the Electors shall be Vice President."

4. There was a problem with Georgia's four electoral votes. While there is no doubt that the Georgia electors actually voted for Jefferson and Burr, the votes were recorded in a technically defective certificate that failed to follow the prescribed formula. Jefferson, presiding over the electoral count as vice president, ignored the procedural defect and counted the Georgia electoral votes for himself. If the four Georgia votes had been disqualified on a technicality, the electoral vote would have been 69–65 in favor of Jefferson, throwing the election into the House of Representatives because no candidate would have obtained the necessary majority of 70. Because Jefferson eventually won election in the House anyway, the counting of the Georgia votes probably did not affect the outcome of the presidential election.

5. The admission of Tennessee in 1796 had brought the number of states in 1800 to sixteen.

6. Georgia's other Federalist member of Congress, James Jones, had died on January 11, 1801.

7. The first section of the Judiciary Act of 1789 (Act of September 24, 1789, 1 Stat. 73) set the number of Supreme Court justices at six—a chief justice and five associate justices.

8. The practice of Supreme Court circuit riding is discussed in Joshua Glick, "Comment: On the Road: The Supreme Court and the History of Circuit Riding," *Cardozo Law Review* 24, no. 4 (2003): 1753.

9. Ibid.

10. It is possible that Ellsworth's resignation letter dated September 30, 1801, was occasioned by ill health, not by a desire to give Adams the chance to appoint a successor. If I were cross-examining, though, I'd want to know why a letter dated September 30 was not received by Adams until December 15. Backdating is always a possibility. Moreover, although the formal electoral balloting was not decided until December 1801, when South Carolina gave its eight electoral votes to Jefferson, it was clear as early as April 1801 that New York would support Jefferson, making him the likely winner.

11. Despite never having served as a judge, Marshall enjoyed a reputation as an excellent lawyer. In 1789, Washington had offered him the post of U.S. attorney for Virginia. Marshall declined. In 1795 Washington had asked him, at the age of thirty-nine, to serve as attorney general. When Marshall declined for financial reasons, the job went to Charles Lee, who served as counsel in *Marbury*. In 1797, Marshall accepted Adams's nomination as one of three commissioners to France. He was expelled from France as part of the XYZ Affair, burnishing his political reputation in the United States. See William Stinchcombe, *The XYZ Affair* (1980), describing Talleyrand's unsuccessful effort to extort a bribe from the United States commissioners and their expulsion from France upon refusing to pay. In 1798, Marshall, again moved by financial considerations, declined an offer by Adams of a nomination as an associate justice of the Supreme Court, recommending Bushrod Washington instead. In 1799, Marshall reluctantly agreed to run for the House, winning a close election largely on the basis of his popularity as a result of the XYZ Affair. Marshall served as Federalist leader in the House until Adams nominated him as secretary of war in early May 1800. When Marshall refused the post because of financial considerations, Adams renominated him as secretary of state one week later, with a salary large enough to permit Marshall to give up his law practice. Nine months later, Adams nominated Marshall as the fourth chief justice.

12. Circuit riding was limited in 1869 and abolished in 1891. Act of April 10, 1869, 16 Stat. 44; Act of March 3, 1891, 26 Stat. 826. The appellate courts were restructured in 1887–88, 1891, 1911, and 1925. Act of March 3, 1887, 24 Stat. 552, corrected by Act of Aug. 13, 1888, 25 Stat. 433; Act of March 3, 1911, 36 Stat. 1087 (formally abolishing mixed circuit courts); Act of February 13, 1925, 43 Stat. 936 (providing for discretionary review by Supreme Court). Federal question jurisdiction was granted in 1875. Act of March 3, 1875, Section 1, 18 Stat. 470.

13. Commissions were written records of appointment, signed and sealed by

the appointing officer. In 1801, it was unclear whether receipt of a commission was merely a record of appointment or constituted an integral part of the appointment itself. The botched effort to nominate Ray Greene as a district judge is discussed in Edward A. Hartnett, "Recess Appointments of Article III Judges: Three Constitutional Questions," *Cardozo Law Review* 26, no. 2 (2005): 377 at n66 and relevant text. See also Hiller B. Zobel, "Those Honorable Courts—Early Days on the First First Circuit," *Federal Register Digest* 73 (1977): 511, 522.

14. Just before New Year's Day 1803, Senator Ellery was the subject of a brutal caning and physical assault by John Rutledge, a Federalist congressman from South Carolina and the son of Justice John Rutledge, who had attempted suicide when his nomination as chief justice was rejected. I guess madness ran in the family.

15. Given Marshall's insistence in *Marbury* that delivery of the commission was not required to complete the judicial appointments process (5 U.S. at 157–59), it is unclear why Marbury needed the commission in the first place.

16. John Marshall later expressed regret to his brother about his failure to deliver the commissions. See *The Papers of John Marshall*, ed. Charles F. Hobbs (Chapel Hill: University of North Carolina Press, 1990), 6:90, letter dated March 18, 1801, John Marshall to James Marshall.

17. Boisterous street demonstrations had greeted Jefferson's election on February 17, 1801. A large crowd marched through Georgetown demanding that houses be illuminated to celebrate Jefferson's victory. Marbury adamantly declined to illuminate his house.

18. Marbury's nomination on March 2, 1801, as one of twenty-three JP nominees for Washington County is recorded in the *Senate Executive Journal*, March 2, 1801, at 388, reprinted in Martin P. Claussen, ed., *Journal of the Senate* (1977), vol. 5, p. 198. Poor Marbury. They couldn't even spell his name right on the nomination papers. He's listed as William Marberry.

19. For a detailed account of Marbury's life, political background, and history of financial speculation, see David Forte, "Marbury's Travails: Federalist Politics and William Marbury's Appointment as Justice of the Peace," *Catholic University Law Review* 45 (1996): 349 (hereafter "Marbury's Travails"). In addition to fitting the mold of financial speculator (a Jefferson bête noire), Marbury had actively but unsuccessfully sought to change Maryland's electoral college voting procedure to a winner-take-all system in order to deny Jefferson any Maryland electoral votes. Because a swing of five electoral votes was involved, had Marbury succeeded, Adams would have won the election 70–68. The unsuccessful effort to alter Maryland's system is recounted in "Marbury's Travails" at 395–97. As David Forte notes at 402, ". . . Marbury must have been one of the easiest cuts for Jefferson to make." It was not the only cut aimed at Marbury. On July 9, 1801, in the wake of substantial cost overruns at the Washington Navy Yard, Jefferson's secretary of war dismissed Marbury as naval agent. "Marbury's Travails" at 385.

20. Ramsay, Hooe, and Harper had been appointed to serve in Alexandria County. Marbury was to serve in Washington County. Ramsay had been one of the six army comrades to serve as honorary pallbearers at Washington's funeral. Harper had wintered at Valley Forge and had commanded an artillery company at

Washington's funeral. When off duty, he fathered twenty-nine children. Hooe was a successful real estate speculator and former sheriff of Fairfax County.

21. *Stuart v. Laird*, 5 U.S. 299 (1803).

22. See ibid. Marshall sat as the circuit judge in *Stuart*, rejecting the constitutional arguments. He recused himself on appeal to the full Court. Marshall's lower court ruling is not officially reported, but is described in the headnotes to *Stuart v. Laird* at p. 302.

23. Presumably, that is why only three of the original four petitioners in *Marbury* presented their claims to the Court. By that time, Harper had dropped out.

24. Levi Lincoln would eventually testify that he never turned the commissions in *Marbury* over to Madison.

25. Justices Cushing and Moore were absent.

26. *United States v. Nixon*, 418 U.S. 683 (1974).

27. The Court record indicates that "on a subsequent day, and before the Court had given an opinion" Lee offered the Hazen Kimball affidavit as proof of the Marbury commission. The record does not indicate whether the untimely affidavit was accepted. 1 Cranch 137, 146. Kimball was never formally examined. 1 Cranch 153.

28. One assumes that Marshall, a stickler for fair procedure, would have provided an opportunity to challenge the untimely Kimball affidavit if the Court were inclined to rely on it. The recitation of the Kimball affidavit in *Marbury* occurs solely in the introductory material prepared by William Cranch in his capacity as court reporter, not in Marshall's opinion itself.

29. 5 U.S. 154–55.

30. 5 U.S. at 163–73.

31. Ibid., 173–81.

32. See Richard H. Fallon Jr., "Marbury and the Constitutional Mind: A Bicentennial Essay on the Wages of Doctrinal Tension," *California Law Review* 91, no. 1 (2003): 1, 52, finding it "highly doubtful" that the D.C. Circuit would have asserted authority to issue a writ of mandamus in 1803.

33. 5 U.S. at 167–68.

34. Even the historic standard-bearers for parliamentary supremacy—Great Britain and France—have adopted a form of judicial review. See Human Rights Act of 1998 (1998, c. 42), subjecting British courts to review by European Court of Human Rights, and Organic Law 2009-1523 (December 10, 2009), establishing expanded procedure for presentation of constitutional claims to the French Conseil Constitutionnel. Virtually every democracy established since the end of World War II has adopted a variant of judicial review, usually involving a specialized court with the authority to enforce the constitution against the political branches. My informal, unscientific survey reveals fifty-eight constitutional courts, although I do not warrant the efficacy of them all.

35. See *Cooper v. Aaron*, 358 U.S.1, 18 (1958), quoting *Marbury* at 5 U.S. at 177.

36. *National Federation of Independent Businesses v. Sibelius*, 132 S. Ct. 2566 (2012).

37. Antonin Scalia, "The Rule of Law as a Law of Rules," *University of Chicago Law Review* 56 (1989): 1175.

38. See generally Antonin Scalia, *A Matter of Interpretation: Federal Courts and the Law*, ed. Amy Gutman (Princeton, NJ: Princeton University Press, 1999), an essay by Antonin Scalia with commentary by Amy Gutman, Gordon S. Wood, Laurence H. Tribe, and Ronald Dworkin.

39. Nor does it provide a guide to reading religious texts. Beware of fundamentalists of any faith claiming to speak directly to god through a literal reading of religious texts composed many centuries ago. See Laurence Wood, *Theology as History and Hermeneutics: A Post-Critical Conversation with Contemporary Theology* (Lexington, KY: Emeth, 2005). As I've suggested, *infra*, literalism isn't much good in reading poetry, either.

40. Jefferson was in Paris as ambassador to France during much of the drafting of the Constitution. He commented on every stage of the proceedings, using his special relationship with Madison to learn about events and seek to influence them. Hamilton was a delegate to the Constitutional Convention, but often seemed curiously uninterested in the process.

41. Stephen Breyer, *Active Liberty: Interpreting Our Democratic Constitution* (New York: Oxford University Press, 2006).

42. *Brown v. Board of Education*, 347 U.S. 483 (1954).

43. *Prigg v. Pennsylvania*, 41 U.S. 539 (1842).

44. Article IV, section 2, clause 3 of the Constitution (the Fugitive Slave Clause) provides:

> No person held to Service or Labour in one state, under the Laws thereof, escaping into another shall, in Consequence of any Law or Regulation therein, be discharged from such Service or Labour, but shall be delivered up on Claim of the Party to whom such Service or Labour may be due.

The moral cowards didn't even have the courage to use the word *slavery*.

45. *Plessy v. Ferguson*, 163 U.S. 537 (1896).

46. *Giles v. Harris*, 189 U.S. 475 (1903).

47. See Mark Curriden and Leroy Phillips Jr., *Contempt of Court: The Turn-of-the-Century Lynching That Launched a Hundred Years of Federalism* (New York: Anchor, 2001).

48. *Santa Clara County v. S. Pac. RR Co.*, 118 U.S. 394 (1886).

49. *Smyth v. Ames*, 169 U.S. 466 (1898).

50. *Adair v. United States*, 208 U.S. 161 (1908).

51. *Hammer v. Dagenhart*, 247 U.S. 251 (1918); *Lochner v. New York*, 198 U.S. 45 (1905).

52. *Schechter Poultry Corp. v. United States*, 295 U.S. 495 (1935); *Carter v. Carter Coal Co.*, 298 U.S. 238 (1936).

53. *NLRB v. Jones & Laughlin Steel Corp.*, 301 U.S. 1 (1937).

54. *Korematsu v. United States*, 323 U.S. 214 (1944).

55. *Roe v. Wade*, 410 U.S. 113 (1973).

56. *Planned Parenthood v. Casey*, 505 U.S. 833 (1992); *Gonzales v. Carhart*, 550 U.S. 124 (2007).

57. *Regents of Univ. of California v. Bakke*, 438 U.S. 265 (1978).

58. *Schuette v. Coalition to Defend Affirmative Action*, 134 S. Ct. 1623 (2014).

59. *Sherbert v. Verner*, 374 U.S. 398 (1963).

60. *Employment Division v. Smith*, 494 U.S. 872 (1990).

61. *Lemon v. Kurtzman*, 403 U.S. 602 (1971).

62. *Zelman v. Simmons-Harris*, 536 U.S. 639 (2002).

63. *Brandenburg v. Ohio*, 395 U.S. 444 (1969).

64. *Garcetti v. Ceballos*, 543 U.S. 1186 (2005).

65. *Mapp v. Ohio*, 367 U.S. 643 (1961); *Miranda v. Arizona*, 384 U.S. 436 (1966).

66. *United States v. Leon*, 468 U.S. 897 (1984).

67. *Buckley v. Valeo*, 424 U.S. 1 (1976).

68. *Citizens United v. FEC*, 130 S. Ct. 876 (2010).

69. *District of Columbia v. Heller*, 554 U.S. 570 (2008).

70. *Heart of Atlanta Motel v. United States*, 379 U.S. 241 (1964).

71. *United States v. Morrison*, 529 U.S. 598 (2000).

72. *Cooper v. Aaron*, 358 U.S. 1 (1958); *United States v. Nixon*, 418 U.S. 683 (1974); *City of Boerne v. Flores*, 521 U.S. 507 (1997); *Boumediene v. Bush*, 533 U.S. 723 (2008).

73. *United States v. Husdon & Goodwin*, 11 U.S. (7 Cranch) 32 (1812).

74. *Garrison v. Louisiana*, 379 U.S. 64 (1964).

75. *Ex parte Merryman*, 17 F. Cas. 144 (C.C.D.Md. 1861).

76. In 1863, faced with widespread rioting over military conscription, Congress finally authorized Lincoln to suspend habeas corpus throughout the United States, in effect placing the entire nation under potential military rule.

77. *Ex parte Vallandingham*, 68 U.S. 243 (1863).

78. At least Lincoln didn't carry a grudge. In 1864, Vallandingham returned to the United States and attended the Democratic Party's National Convention in Chicago. He wrote the party's "peace plank" opposing the continuation of the Civil War.

79. *Ex parte Milligan*, 71 U.S. 2 (1866).

80. Reconstruction is the euphemism used to describe the federal government's military occupation and attempted political and social makeover of the defeated Southern states.

81. *Ex parte McCardle*, 74 U.S. 506 (1868).

82. A direct line runs from the contested Hayes v. Tilden presidential election of 1876 to the turbulent Bush v. Gore presidential election in 2000. In the wake of the congressional deal making over contested electors that changed the outcome of the 1876 presidential election, Congress enacted "safe harbor" legislation providing that state certification of a slate of winning electors could not be challenged in Congress as long as the state certification was received in Washington by a given date. It was the imminence of the safe-harbor date that caused the Supreme Court in *Bush v. Gore* to cut short the recount of Florida's popular vote, permitting the Florida secretary of state to certify electors pledged to George Bush as the winners. If the recount had continued after the expiration of the safe-harbor date, any electors Florida certified would have been subject to politically driven challenges in the House of Representatives.

83. *Debs v. United States*, 249 U.S. 211 (1919).

84. Attorney General A. Mitchell Palmer is indelibly associated in American history with the notorious post–World War I Palmer Raids, aimed at arresting and deporting leftist aliens. The raids were in response to a series of terrorist bombings, one of which damaged Palmer's home.

85. *Schenck v. United States*, 249 U.S. 47 (1919).

86. *Frohwerk v. United States*, 249 U.S. 204 (1919).

87. *Abrams v. United States*, 250 U.S. 616 (1919).

88. Recall that that's what President Lincoln did to Clement Vallandingham, only Vallandingham was deported to the Confederate States of America.

89. *Minersville School District v. Gobitis*, 310 U.S. 586 (1940).

90. *West Virginia Board of Education v. Barnette*, 319 U.S. 624 (1943).

91. Justice Jackson was the last Supreme Court justice who practiced law and served as a federal judge without having graduated from law school. He read for the bar and attended Albany Law School for a year.

92. 323 U.S. 214 (1944).

93. *Dennis v. United States*, 341 U.S. 494 ((1951).

94. *United States v. O'Brien*, 391 U.S. 367 (1968).

95. Although Justice Douglas apparently accepted the Court's free-speech analysis, he dissented on the grounds that the draft itself raised constitutional problems under the Thirteenth Amendment.

96. *Buckley v. Valeo*, 424 U.S. 1 (1976).

97. *Arizona Free Enterprise Clubs' Freedom PAC v. Bennett*, 131 S.Ct. 2806 (2011).

98. *Holder v. Humanitarian Law Project*, 561 U.S. (2010).

99. *Ex parte Endo*, 323 U.S. 283 (1944).

10. Madison, the Reluctant Poet

1. The material in this chapter is drawn from Bernard Schwartz, *The Roots of the Bill of Rights*, vol. 5 (New York: Chelsea House, 1980). I will spare you day-to-day footnoting. As James Thurber (and Casey Stengel) says, "You could look it up."

INDEX

About the Author

Burt Neuborne is the Inez Milholland Professor of Civil Liberties and the founding legal director of the Brennan Center for Justice at NYU Law School. He has served as the national legal director of the ACLU, as special counsel to the NOW Legal Defense and Education Fund, and as a member of the New York City Human Rights Commission. During his fifty years of public interest practice, Neuborne has participated in more than two hundred cases in the U.S. Supreme Court. He played Jerry Falwell's lawyer in Miloš Forman's *The People vs. Larry Flynt* and was the Court TV commentator for the trial of O.J. Simpson. Neuborne is the author of three scholarly books and more than fifty scholarly articles and has contributed to *The Nation*. He is married to Helen Redleaf Neuborne. They live in New York.

Publishing in the Public Interest

Thank you for reading this book published by The New Press. The New Press is a nonprofit, public interest publisher. New Press books and authors play a crucial role in sparking conversations about the key political and social issues of our day.

We hope you enjoyed this book and that you will stay in touch with The New Press. Here are a few ways to stay up to date with our books, events, and the issues we cover:

- Sign up at www.thenewpress.com/subscribe to receive updates on New Press authors and issues and to be notified about local events
- Like us on Facebook: www.facebook.com/newpressbooks
- Follow us on Twitter: www.twitter.com/thenewpress

Please consider buying New Press books for yourself; for friends and family; or to donate to schools, libraries, community centers, prison libraries, and other organizations involved with the issues our authors write about.

The New Press is a 501(c)(3) nonprofit organization. You can also support our work with a tax-deductible gift by visiting www.thenewpress.com/donate.